Mr. Gunn
Teachers Copy

79

Credit Geography

Eddie Broadley
Depute Headteacher, Glen Urquhart High School, Drumnadrochit, Highland Region
and
Ritchie Cunningham
Headteacher, Inverness High School, Inverness, Highland Region

PUBLISHING Ltd
Inverness

Acknowledgements

The publishers thank the following for permission to reproduce photographs or other copyright material:
Prof.D.Sugden (117); Martin Duddin (118); Eric Brown (119, 122); Alan Smith (60, 64); J.Swinton (26, 125); R.Smith (16,152); IPPF (135); New Internationalist (145,147-148, P.25(b)); R.Cunningham (20, 47, 126, 128); E.Broadley (7, 23, 30,37,P.25, 52,55, 57, 68, 69, 71, 73,76, 79,82,86, 90-93, 95, 97 101-103, 106, 123); Gemini Newscan International, London (Contents page cartoon, 1, 3-4, 19, 21, 38, 51, 114, 125, 128, P.75(t), 129 -134, 136-140, 143-144, P.85(t & b), P.186 (t & b), 150, 153-159, 161-1645, 167, P.93(t & b), P.94(t & b).

The authors and publishers would like to acknowledge the following sources which were used as a basis for figures or text: *Third World Guide* (1993-94), ITeM; *World Development Report* 1992, World Bank; N.Mayers (ed.) *Gaia Atlas of Planet management, Gaia Peace Atlas, Gaia Atlas of Future Worlds, Gaia Book of First Peoples*, Pan Books; Bob McAllister (various inspirational graphics & advice); Central Support Group Standard Grade Geography (various resource packs produced for the introduction of the new courses); Highlands & Islands Enterprise; Census Information Office (1991 Census); London's Docklands Development Corporation 1992; Northern College, Aberdeen Campus Geography & Business Studies Departments; CBI Annual Report and Trends 1993; British Coal; Zonal UK; Unilever; Corby Industrial Development Centre; Alan Doherty (various inspirational ideas over the years); Brunsden, Goudie et al, *Landshapes*, David & Charles; HMSO, Geology Reports for Scotland; *Geofile* (various issues); H.J.Critchfield, *General Climatology*, Prentice Hall; C.Warn *OS Map Skills Book*, Arnold-Wheaton; BBC Geography (*The Geography programme* (1992)); Broadley & Cunningham, *Core Themes (Physical)*, Longman/Oliver & Boyd; Broadley & Cunningham, *Core Themes (Human)*, Longman/Oliver & Boyd; Lake District Special Planning Board; BBC2, Landward (*Superquarries*, 1993); Yorkshire Dales national Park Authority; *Drumnadrochit & Local Area Plan*, Highland Regional Council, 1990; Ross-shire Tourist Area Board; British Meteorological Office, Bracknell; A.N.Strahler, *Physical Geography,* John Wiley; L.F.Musk, *Weather Systems*, Cambridge University Press; Mel Rockett, *Themes in Human Geography*, Arnold-Wheaton; N.Thomson & K.MacLean, *Landscapes and people of Western Europe*, Oxford; *The Geographical Magazine* (various issues); D.Waugh, *Europe, The World, The British Isles, An Integrated Approach*, Nelson; B.Knapp, *Systematic Geography*, Unwin-Hyman; Lines & Bolwell, *Revise GCSE Geography*, Letts; Baterman & Rowles, *Examining GCSE Geography*, Stanley Thornes; Broadley & Goring, *Studies in Geography, Books 1 & 2*, Oliver & Boyd; J.Seager (ed), *The State of the Earth Atlas*, Unwin; G.N.Minshull, *The New Europe*, Hodder & Stoughton; Seymour & Girardet, *Blueprint for a Green Planet*, Dorling Kindersley; P.Knox, *Urban Social Geography*, Longman; R.Collard, *The Physical Geography of Landscape*, Unwin-Hyman; Galbraith & Weigand, *Landforms*, Oxford; C.Clarke, *Themes in Geography (Physical, Human Environment, International Issues)*, Hodder & Stoughton; *The New Oxford School Atlas*, Oxford; The Guardian Newspaper, London; The Observer Newspaper, London; SAGT slide set "*Arctic landscapes*" 1994; A.Goudie, *Nature of the Environment*, Blackwell Scientific; BBC2 Horizon programme "*China's Child*" 1984; Oxfam and Save the Children, U.K.; Comic Relief Organisation, London; UNCTAD, 1991; ICO, 1992; ICCO, 1992; *New Scientist* (various issues); E.Broadley would also like to thank J.Smith and B.Njoku (Gemini) for their advice and help.

Cover and book design by CB Publishing Ltd, Inverness 1994.

Illustrated by *Eddie Broadley* and *Ritchie Cunningham*

C.B.Publishing Ltd,
18, Lochlann Terrace,
Culloden,
Inverness,
IV1 2PZ

ISBN 1 872985 55 6
First published 1994

Typeset in 10pt Helvetica on the Apple Macintosh; styled by E.Broadley.
Produced in Drumnadrochit, Inverness-shire, Scotland.
Printed in Stornoway, Western Isles by the Stornoway Gazette Ltd, 10 Francis Street, Stornoway PA87 2XE

Contents

It says here that....
..a pet cat in Europe eats more animal protein,
..than the average citizen of the South
Think I'll emigrate

1. POPULATION: Distribution & Density

Key Idea : Population is unevenly distributed.

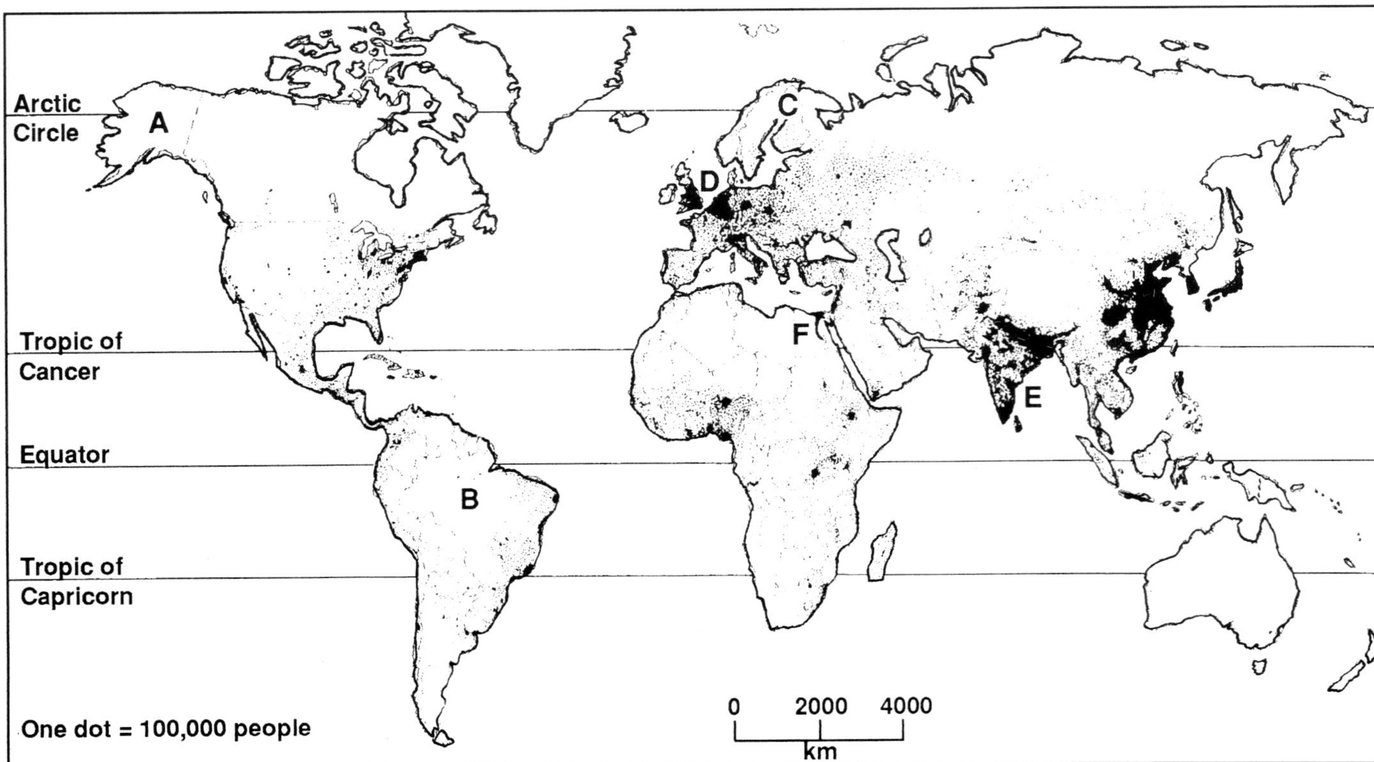

Fig.1 World Population Distribution Map

Fig.2 Scotland: Population Density Map

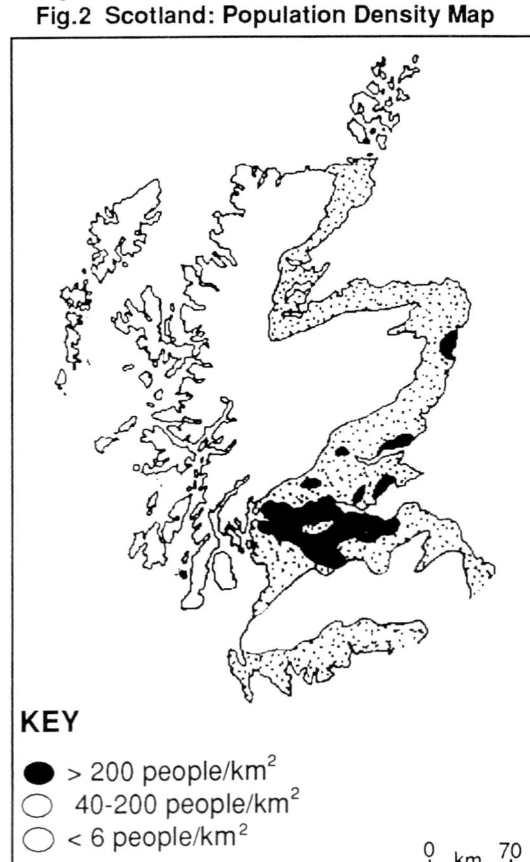

Scotland's population of 5.3 million is very unevenly spread over the whole country. Some areas of the Highlands have less than 8 people per km^2 whereas much the Central belt has more than 200 people per km^2.

People are distributed in a very uneven way across the world's surface and there are many variations in population density.

Population Distribution describes the way in which people are spread out across the Earth's surface. The world map (Fig.1) illustrates World Population distribution where each dot represents a given number of people. The map clearly shows both concentrations of people, for example in Eastern China and North East USA, and areas which are almost uninhabited, for example Siberia or Greenland.

Population Density describes the number of people living within a given area. Density is usually expressed as the number of people per square kilometre and can be shown in the form of a choropleth map such as the Population Density Map of Scotland (Fig.2). A formula used to calculate
population density is:

$$D = \frac{P}{A}$$ where **D** = Population Density, **P** = Population and **A** = Area

Areas of high population density are obviously crowded. Those of low population density are said to be sparsely populated. People live in areas easily suited to everyday life and avoid areas of difficulty. 71% of the earth's surface is water and only 29% is land - about one-fifth of the land is too cold to live in, another fifth is desert and another fifth is mountainous. The remaining two-fifths could be farmed but only a third of this is actually developed (Fig.3). This means that most of the world's population lives on only about 4% of the Earth's surface.

Fig.3 Population, Area and Cultivation

Rank	Country	Area (m. km²)	Cult. (%)	Popn. (m)	Density (per km²)	Density (per km² cult)	% incr.
	World	137.0	11	5128	37	334	+1.7
	Poor World	78.7	10	3931	49	488	+2.1
	Rich World	55.3	12	1198	22	180	+0.6
1.	China	9.6	11	1087	111	1006	+1.4
2.	India	3.3	52	817	243	468	+2.0
3.	CIS	22.4	10	286	13	127	+1.0
4.	USA	9.4	20	246	26	130	+0.7
5.	Indonesia	2.0	10	177	86	863	+1.7
6.	Brazil	8.5	9	144	17	185	+2.0
7.	Japan	0.4	13	123	328	2527	+0.5
8.	Nigeria	0.9	33	112	118	356	+2.9
9.	Bangladesh	0.1	63	110	744	1181	+2.7
10.	Pakistan	0.8	25	108	130	520	+2.9
11.	Mexico	2.0	12	84	42	346	+2.4
12.	Vietnam	0.3	19	65	188	992	+2.6
13.	Philippines	0.3	39	63	205	526	+2.8
14.	West Germany	0.2	30	61	245	817	-0.1
15.	UK	0.2	29	57	232	799	+0.2
	Italy	0.3	41	57	191	465	0.0
17.	France	0.5	34	56	102	299	+0.4
18.	Thailand	0.5	37	55	104	282	+2.1
19.	Turkey	0.8	35	53	66	188	+2.2
	Egypt	1.0	2	53	52	2592	+2.8
21.	Iran	1.6	8	52	31	382	+3.2
	Australia	7.7	6	17	2	35	+0.8

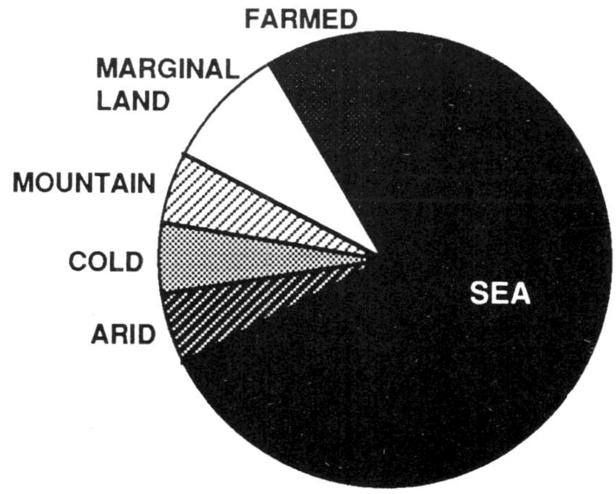

The Earth's surface : Water/Land Environment

Assignment One

1. Explain the meaning of each of the following:
Population Distribution
Population Density

2. Copy and then complete the following table.

Country	Area in 000's/km	Population in 000's	Population Density
Norway	300	3950	
France	545	5000	
Bangladesh		90,000	600
U.K.	230		239

3a Copy and complete the following table by studying Fig.1. Use an atlas to help you.

Area	Name	Area	Name
A		**D**	
B		**E**	
C		**F**	

3b Classify **A-F** above in terms of population and then explain your classification.

Study Fig.3 carefully.

4a What does the "Density per km Cultivated" column mean ?

4b What does Fig.3 indicate about Egypt ?

4c What does Fig.3 indicate about Australia ? Use an atlas to help you.

5. With the aid of Fig.4 and an atlas, explain the pattern of Population Density in China.

6. Explain why some difficult environments" are able to support pockets of dense population.

7. Quoting examples, explain why the average population density can sometimes be misleading.

Fig.4 China - Population Density

PROVINCE	People per km²
Heilongjiang	69
Jilin	120
Liaoning	245
Beijing	549
Tianjin	687
Hebei	282
Shanxi	162
Nei Monggol	16
Shandong	486
Jiangsu	590
Shanghai	1 913
Anhui	356
Zhejiang	382
Jiangxi	200
Fujian	213
Henan	446
Hubei	255
Hunan	257
Guandong	280
Guangxi	158
Shaanxi	141
Ningxia	59
Gansu	43
Qinghai	5
Xinjiang	8
Sichuan	176
Guizhou	162
Yunnan	83
Xizang	2

POPULATION

TLEMENT: *Site, Situation & Function*

Key Idea : Settlements have many common charateristics related to site, situation and function.

A **settlement** is any place where people live and work. The size of a settlement can vary from a single building (e.g. a farm) to a large and important city such as Glasgow or London (Fig.5)

The initial location of a settlement is influenced by its site. **Site** describes the land upon which the settlement sits. It is concerned with the landscape of the settlement, its local relief, water supply, slope, soils, etc (Figs. 6 and 7).

Even if the site of a settlement is a good one, the settlement is unlikely to grow into a large city unless it has a good situation.
Situation describes the location of the settlement in relation to its surroundings such as landforms, land uses, roads and other settlements.

The **function** of a settlement relates to its economic and social development and refers to its main activities. The original function of a settlement can change depending on economic or social changes within it. For example, an original defensive settlement may now have a tourist function.

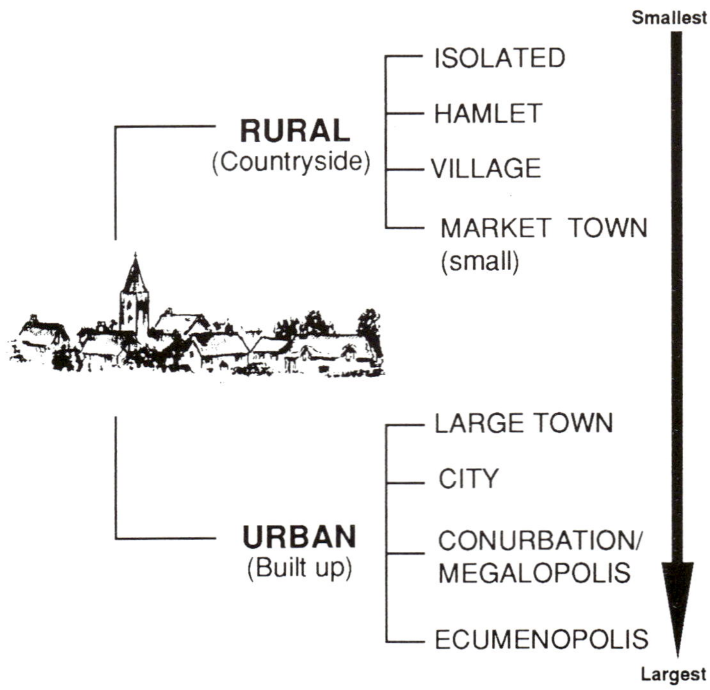

Fig. 5 An hierarchy of settlements

Fig.6 The best site ?

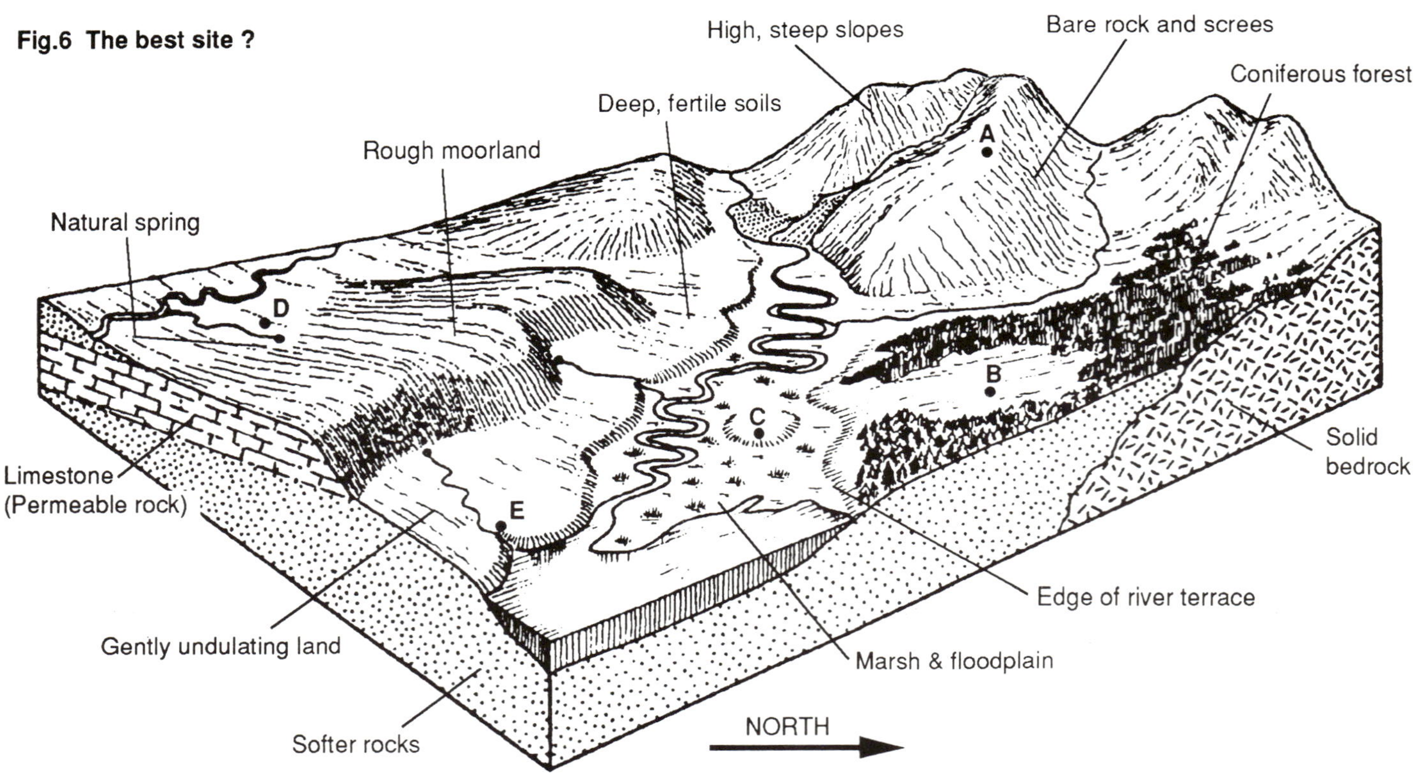

Fig.7 The site of Plockton, Wester Ross.

Rural and Urban Settlement

Study Fig.7 carefully and decide for yourself whether it shows a rural or an urban settlement. There are many ways in which to define the differences between rural and urban settlement.

Size - generally rural settlements are smaller than urban settlements.

Services - the provision of such services as secondary schools, hospitals, banks, shops and public transport are often absent or limited in rural settlements

Land use - in rural areas settlements are often widely spaced and open land separates settlements. In urban areas settlements are often in close proximity and there is a wide variety of land usewithin small areas. Open space is often in short supply

Occupations - in urban areas the working population is mainly engaged in secondary and tertiary industries (e.g. bakeries or shops & offices).In rural areas, the working population is mainly engaged in primary industries (e.g. farming).

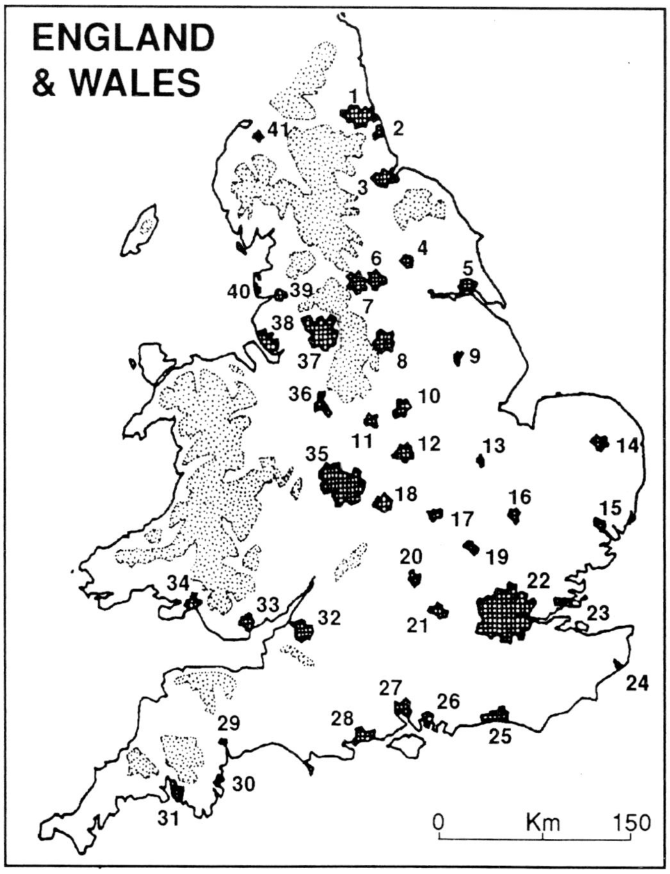

Fig.8 Major settlements in England & Wales

Assignment Two

1. Explain the differences between the **site**, **situation** and **function** of a settlement.
2. List the advantages and disadvantages of each of the sites labelled **A-E** in Fig.5
3. Rank these five sites in order for suitability of settlement. Explain your rank order.

4aStudy Fig.**7**
Draw a simple labelled sketch to illustrate the main features of the site shown

4b Why would early settlers have chosen this site ?

4c. In which ways do you think the site poses problems for modern developments ?

5. Make your own key for Fig.8 and, using an atlas, name the major settlements in England & Wales.
6. Describe the **situation** of settlements 1, 13 and 32.
7. What are main differences between rural and urban settlements ?
8. Are there any other ways in which to describe the main differences between rural and urban settlements ?
9. What is the main **function** of the settlement in which you live ?

TLEMENT: Patterns and Services

Key Idea : Settlements have many common charateristics related to site, situation and function.

Settlements display many patterns on the landscape - patterns to do with their shape and function. An O.S. map extract should be studied as you read through this section on patterns of settlement (Figs. 9 and 10).

Rural Settlement Patterns

Fig.9

Rural settlement patterns are varied in nature and although village shapes vary, it is possible to identify several main types:-

1. **Isolated** settlement - an individual farmhouse or house, often found in areas of adverse physical conditions, e.g. in the Scottish Highlands.

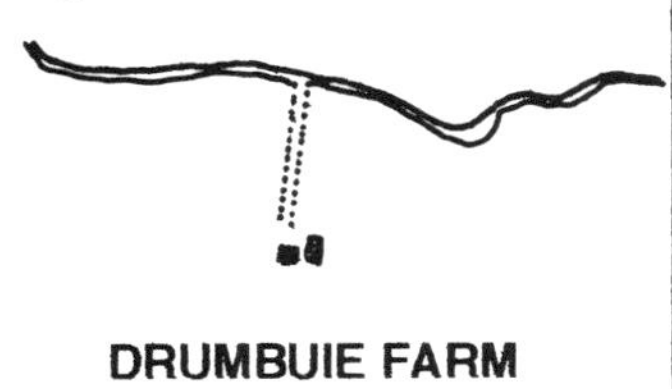

2. **Dispersed** settlement - a scattered grouping of farmsteads or buildings, often referred to as a hamlet, e.g. crofting townships in the Western Isles.

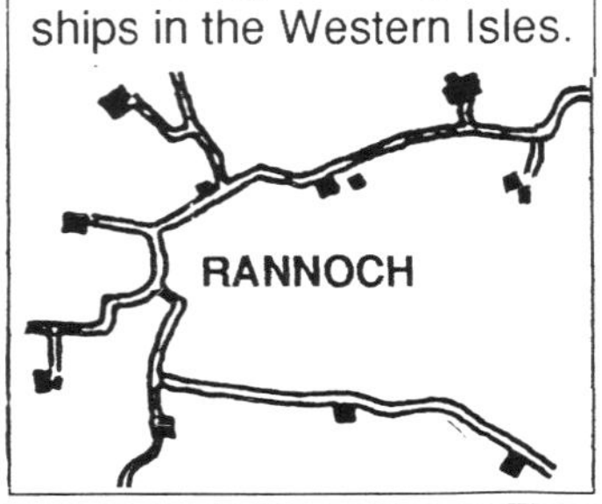

3. **Nucleated** settlement - a clustered grouping of buildings, often found at a road junction and regarded as a village, e.g. Doune, Stirlingshire.

4. **Linear** settlement - a settlement strung-out along a line of communication or confined to a valley, e.g. Kippen in Stirlingshire or Ebbw Vale, S.Wales

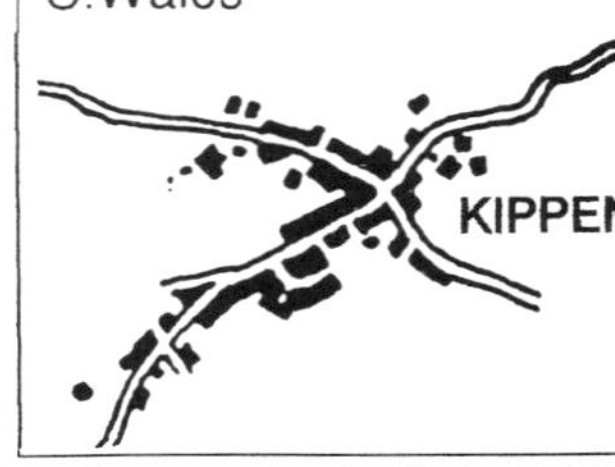

Urban Settlement Patterns

Fig.10

Urban settlements also display a variety of patterns on the landscape. The main patterns which can be identified are:-

1. Medieval Zone or Core

- Villages which expanded into towns during the Middle Ages may have an irregular pattern of narrow, closely-spaced streets in their central areas. This reflected the unplanned nature of expansion and lack of space within the common defensive walls.

THE OLD TOWN, EDINBURGH

Common features of such layouts are Market Squares, Castles or Palaces, many Churches and Town Walls, e.g. Edinburgh's Old Town

2. 19th. Century Zone

- The areas of towns which developed at the time of the Industrial expansion in the 19th. Century usually have a regular pattern of evenly spaced streets crossing each other at right angles. This is known as a grid-iron pattern. Here factories and houses were built in close proximity.

GOVANHILL

Common features of such layouts are railways, terraced housing, factories and a dense, regular road network, e.g. Govanhill, Glasgow.

3. 20th Century Zone

- During the 20th. Century, most towns expanded first of all outwards along main roads. Large areas of housing built between the 1st and 2nd World Wars, however, have a geometric street layout with crescents, semi-circular and radiating streets and cul-de-sacs (dead-end streets)

MUIRHOUSE, EDINBURGH

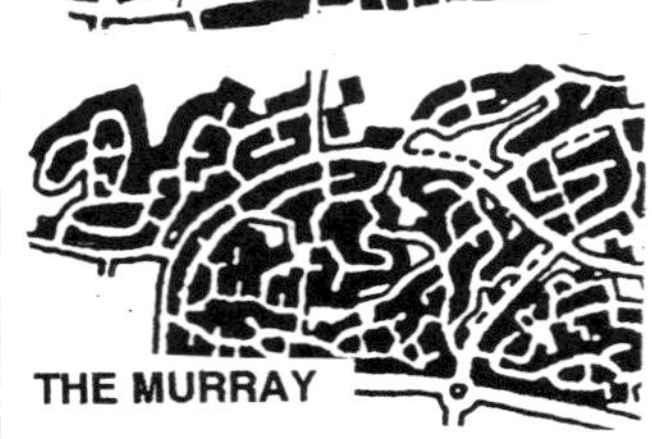

Housing areas built since the 2nd. World War tend to have less regular, gradually curving streets and numerous cul-de-sacs, e.g. The Murray, East Kilbride.

4. Industrial Zone

- Industrial zones can often be identified on O.S. maps because the built-up areas are larger than housing blocks, and the streets are not so closely or regularly spaced.
Some industrial areas, especially older ones, also have branch railway lines leading into them.

CRAIGNEUK

Large Urban-Industrial Zones are associated with Steel-making, Shipbuilding, Engineering or Chemical factories, e.g Craigneuk, Glasgow

Fig.11 Hierarchy of settlement - the relationship between size, importance & functions

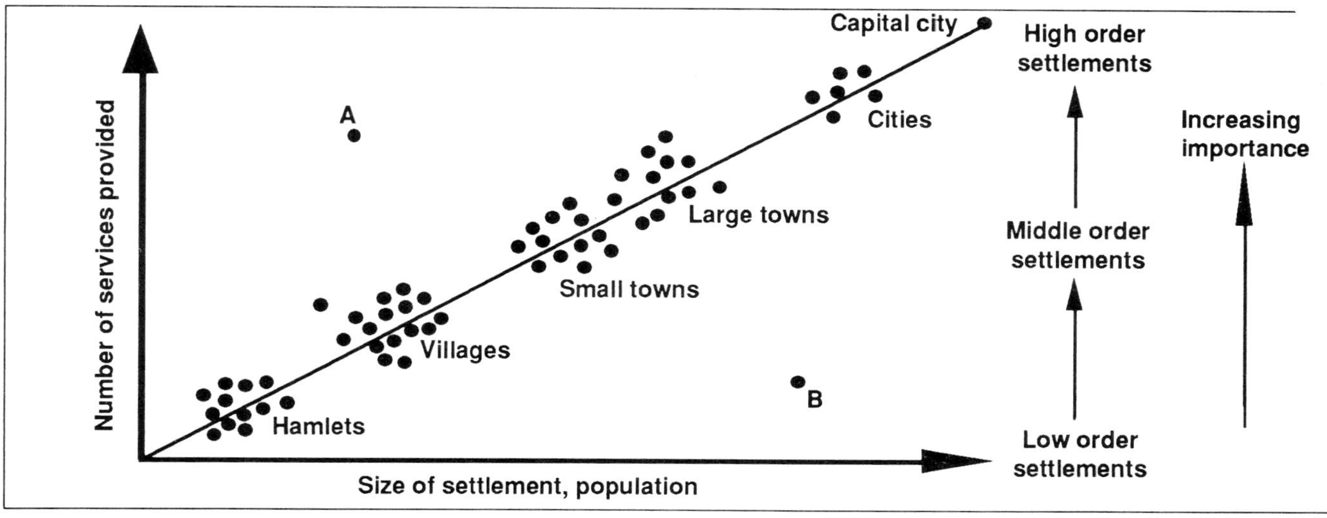

Services and settlements.

The importance of a settlement is equated with the following:-

a) The **size** of a settlement - its area and population b) The range and number of functions or **services** within a settlement c) **The sphere of influence** of a settlement.

Settlements provide services to those who live and work in them. The larger the settlement, the more services it usually provides. Fig.11 is a generalised **hierarchy** of settlements based on service provision. Important to the study of services are the terms **Threshold** - the minimum number of customers needed for a service to be profitable and **Range** of a service - the distance people are willing to travel to obtain that service. **Low order services** are those which have a small threshold and range of service. People use them frequently and they are numerous. They are found in villages, towns and cities and tend to be dispersed throughout the settlement, e.g. a newsagents. **Middle Order services** have a moderate threshold and have moderate range, in that people may be willing to travel some distance to obtain them. They are found only in towns and cities and are often located in large shopping centres and in the town centre, e.g. shoe shops. **High Order services** have very large thresholds and range of services. Normally only found in town centres and cities, they tend to be centrally located because they require large customer flows to be profitable, e.g. department stores. The **Sphere of Influence** of a settlement can be defined as the area served by it. The size of the sphere of influence depends on the size, importance and functions of the settlement and its surroundings, the transport facilities available and the level of competition from rival settlements (Fig.12)

People who live in rural settlements generally rely on towns to provide all but everyday basic services. The hamlet or village are said to be within the sphere of influence of a town because people are served by that town for middle and high order services. Towns and cities compete for the custom of people living within their surroundings (or **hinterland**). Various factors are important when people decide which larger settlement they will use, e.g.

- Distance and ease of transport
- Type and variety of services provided
- Local environment - some settlements may be more attractive or 'friendly' to shop in than others
- Personal contact or choice - relatives, easier parking or better customer service may influence people to shop in a settlement which is not necessarily closer to home.

Fig.12 Spheres of Influence

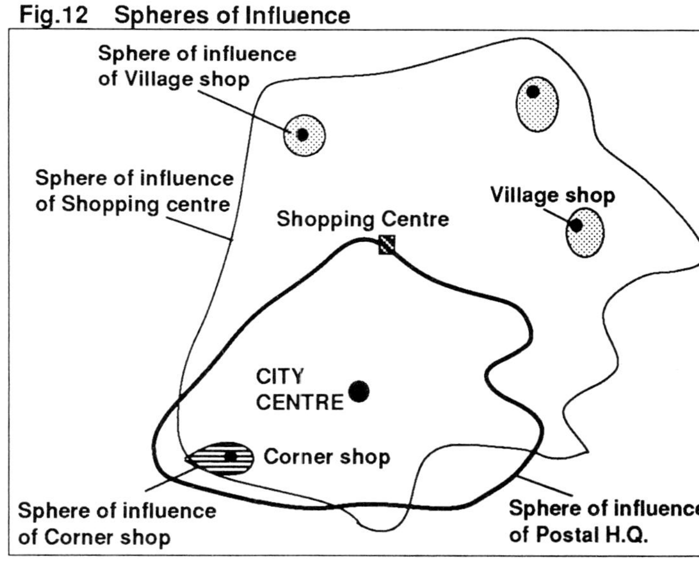

Assignment Three

1a Briefly describe the differences between a dispersed and a nucleated settlement pattern.

1b Why are some settlements linear in pattern ?

2a Explain the meaning of the following :- grid-iron pattern, cul-de-sac, irregular pattern.

2b Which urban problems may a Medieval street pattern cause a modern city ?

3a Write a definition of each of the following terms:- Service, Threshold, Range, Hinterland and Sphere of Influence.

3b Give at least 2 examples of each of the following :- Low, Middle & High order services.

4a Study Fig.11 carefully. Explain what is meant by "settlement hierarchy".

4b The function of a settlement can affect the range of services it provides. Describe the range of services provided in both a holiday resort and a commuter settlement. Explain your answer.

4c Give some examples of how the function of a settlement can affect its sphere of influence.

5 Give some possible explanations of the graph position of **A** and **B** on Fig.11.

6 Explain the differences in the size of the 4 spheres of influence shown on Fig.12.

7 In a large settlement, high order services are usually centrally located while low order services are dispersed throughout the settlement. Give examples of both.

TTLEMENT: Land use patterns

Key Idea : Urban settlements have dynamic patterns relating to their size, form and function.

There are many different **land uses** to be found in settlements and the larger the settlement, the greater the variety of land uses there are within it. Land uses - the ways in which the land is used - can include the following categories :-

Commercial - shops and offices
Industrial - factories, workshops and ports
Residential - housing areas
Recreational - parks, sports facilities, etc
Transport - roads, railways, airports, etc.
Wasteland - derelict and cleared land.

Older settlements have generally evolved - in other words they have developed and grown over time. This usually takes hundreds of years and the pattern of land use in older settlements is very often complicated. In contrast, **New Towns** are carefully planned with a clear pattern of land use more easily identifiable.

The different types of land uses listed above are often found in certain parts of a settlement. For example, Commercial land uses are usually to be found near the centre of a settlement. This land use zone is usually called the Central Business District (or **CBD**).

It is possible to distinguish patterns or zones of land use within settlements especially in larger towns and cities. These patterns reflect the development or evolution of the settlement over time. This distribution of land use can often be explained by referring to one of the following **Models of Urban Land Use**. Figures 13 - 15 are models of urban areas which show patterns of land use which may exist in larger settlements in developed countries. Each land use model contains four main zones, described below:

Figures 13 - 15 Models of Urban Land Use

Fig.13 Concentric Circle Model

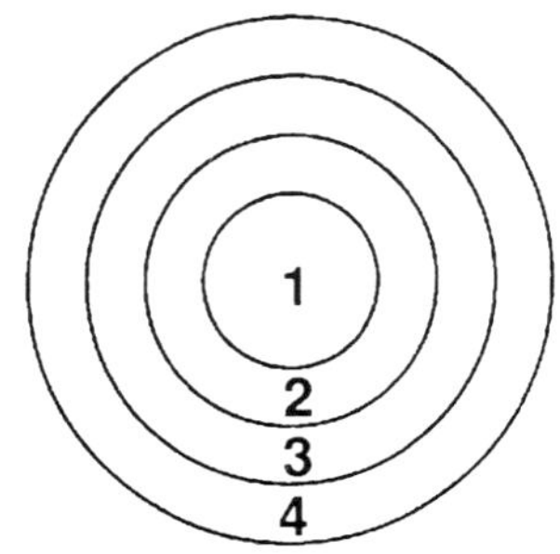

The Concentric Model of Urban Land Use is based on the theory that settlements grow outwards from their centre with age. The oldest buildings would then be nearest the centre and the most modern closest to the edge of the settlement.

Key for Figs 13 - 15

1	CBD
2	Inner City/Twilight Zone
3a	Tower Block housing
3b	Pre-1945 housing
3c	Post-1945 housing
4	Industrial zone

Fig.14 Sector Model

The Sector Model of Urban Land Use suggests that settlements are influenced by their transport routes - rivers, railways, roads - and develop in wedges or sectors of land use.

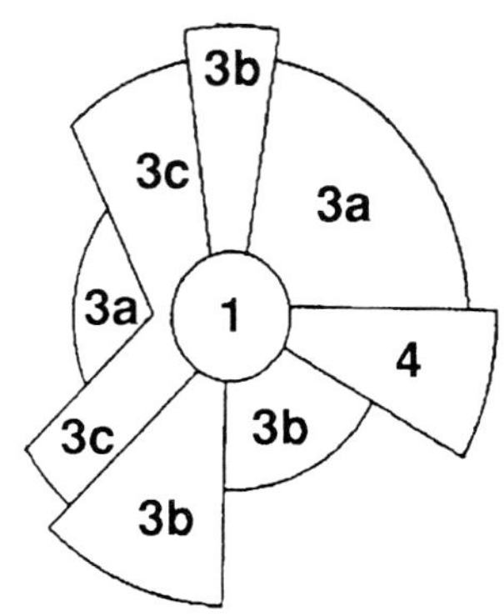

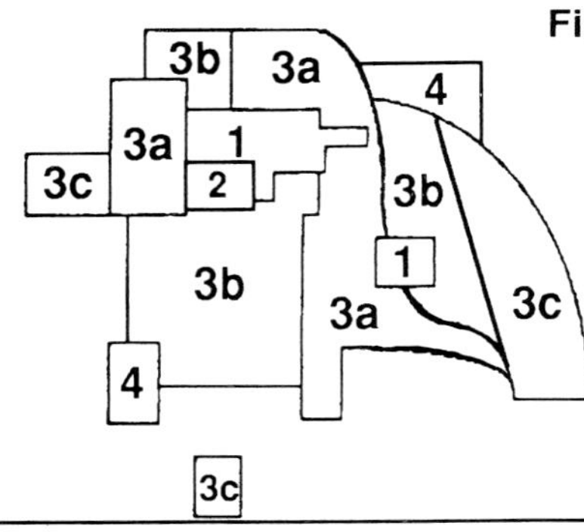

Fig.15 Multiple Nuclei Model

The Multiple Nuclei Model of Urban Land Use is based on the idea that most settlements grow from an amalgamation of smaller settlements and have more than one centre.

Central Business District
The CBD is the heart of the urban area where large department stores,offices and banks, cinemas and theatres, main transport terminals and expensive shops are found. Located here in the most accessible area of the settlement, these land uses need many customers to pay for the expensive land they use. To offset this cost, the CBD often has many high-rise blocks of offices and shops. Famous CBD areas include Princes Street (Edinburgh), Oxford Street and 'The City' (London), the Ginza (Tokyo) and Wall Street (New York).

Inner City
Located around the CBD is usually an area of tightly-packed land uses - housing and older industrial sites builtduring the last century to be within walking distance of each other. Today many of these areas are in decline and some have been extensively redeveloped. Previously known as the Twilight Zone, many of these areas have become more fashionable. Young wealthy people often move in and improve (or **Gentrify**) areas in close proximity to the CBD.

Residential areas These can be divided into different types of housing areas, for example :

a) **Pre-1945** housing areas - see Fig 10, P.5
b) **Post-1945** housing areas - see Fig 10, P.5
c) **1960s tower block** housing often in the Twilight Zone.

Residential areas may also be further classified as council- or privately-owned; inner city or suburban housing areas.

Industrial Zones Old established industries may remain near the centre but the increasing cost of land is encouraging many companies to sell this expensive land and relocate to cheaper, more accessible sites on industrial estates. These are often areas of light industry located near to good roads on the edge of the settlement.

Note: Many large settlements have more than one centre - where different centres often specialise in different functions.

Fig.16 Urban area

Assignment F

1 Explain why shops and offi... are found in the CBD of a larg... settlement.

2 Which urban land use zones are shown in Fig.16 ?
Make a very simple sketch to illustrate your answer.

3 Compare and then contrast the Models of Urban land use shown in Figs.13-15.

4 Which order do you think the settlement shown in Fig.16 is in a settlement hierarchy ?
Explain your answer.

5 Describe the ways in which you could investigate the size of the sphere of influence of the settlement shown in Fig.16.

O.S. MAP EXTRACT SECTION

Use the Stirling O.S. map extract (SE Quadrant) or another suitable map extract to help you answer the following questions

6 Use the sketch map (Fig.17) & the Stirling Map extract.
Complete your own copy of the table below:

No	Settlement	6 Fig Ref
1		
2		
3		
4		
5		
6		

7 Give map examples of each of the main categories of land use listed on page 7. Include 6 figure map references for each.

8 Copy and complete the table below using map examples. You may refer back to Fig.9, page5

Settlement pattern	Example	6 fig ref.
Isolated		
Dispersed		
Nucleated		
Linear		
Medieval		
19th.C		
Post-1945		
Industrial		

9 Which Model of Urban Land Use best fits Stirling (or large urban area) ? Justify your answer.

10 Draw a simplified Land Use Model of Stirling (or large urban area). Include a Key

Fig.17 Stirling area sketch map

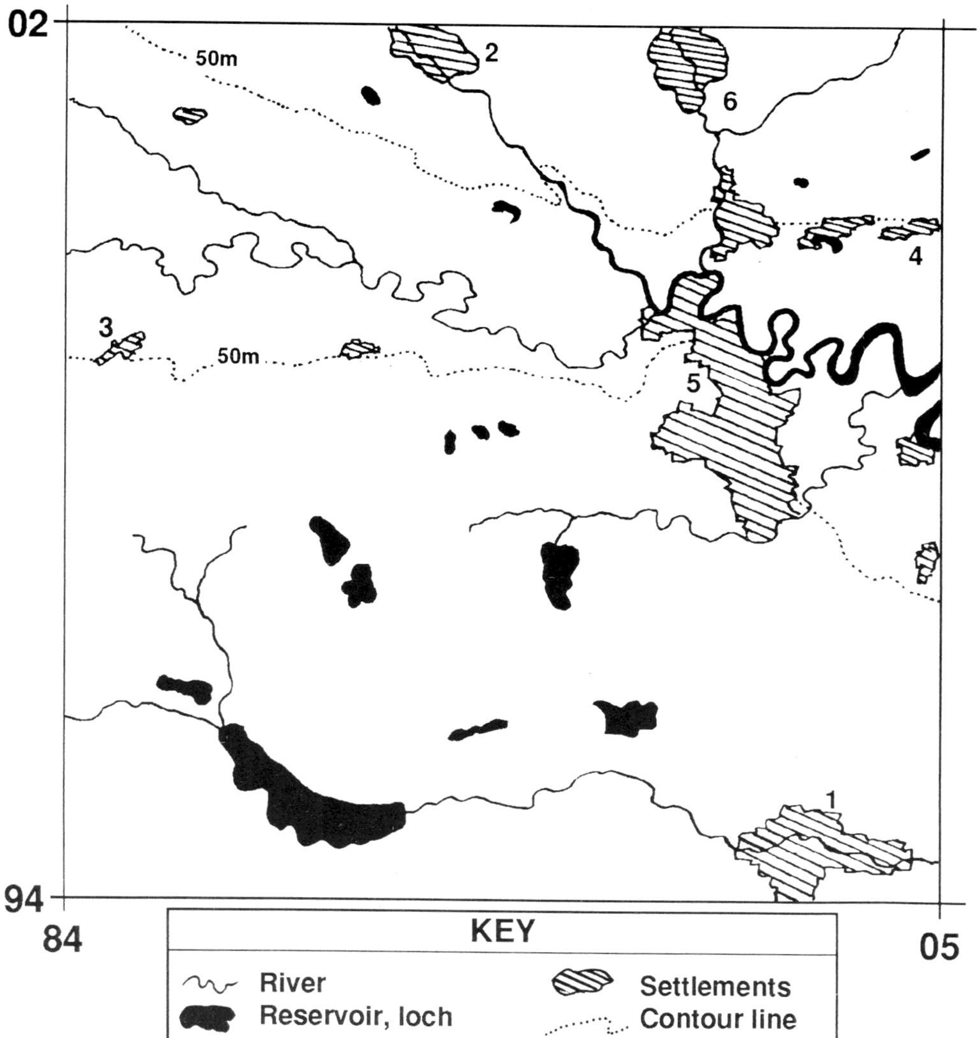

TLEMENT: *Urban change & problems*

Key Idea 8: Urban settlements have dynamic patterns relating to their size, form and function.

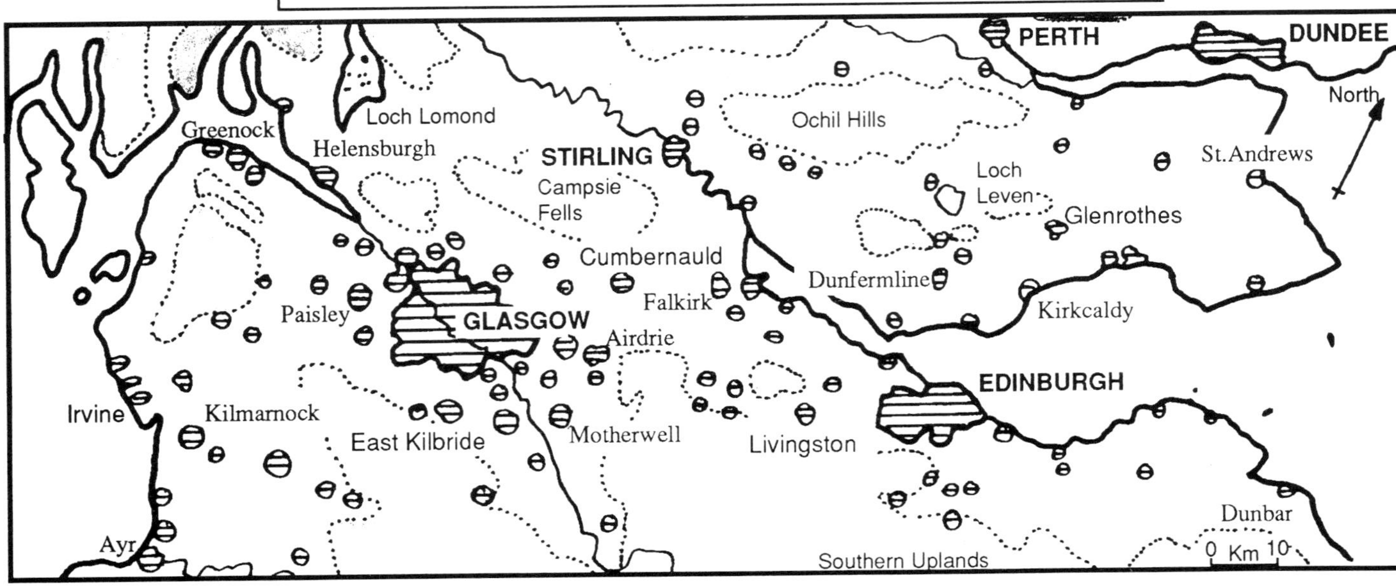

Fig.18 Central Scotland - main urban areas
Fig.19 Problems in urban areas of Scotland

As the proportion of the world's population living in urban areas continues to grow rapidly, urban areas grow larger and experience more problems. Urban decay, overcrowding, pollution, congestion and lack of basic resources (such as water supply and sanitation) are all evident problems. Urban areas in developed countries, such as Britain, however, experience different problems from those in developing countries, such as India.

Figure 18 shows the location of the main urban areas of Central Scotland all of which experience change, especially the older and larger settlements. Large settlements such as London or Glasgow have grown in size through much of the 19th. and 20th. centuries. Their rapid urban expansion has been largely due to the development of a variety of industries and ports, the expansion of business and services, growing employment and with it, increasing standards of living. This has often led to urban problems such as those illustrated in Fig.19:

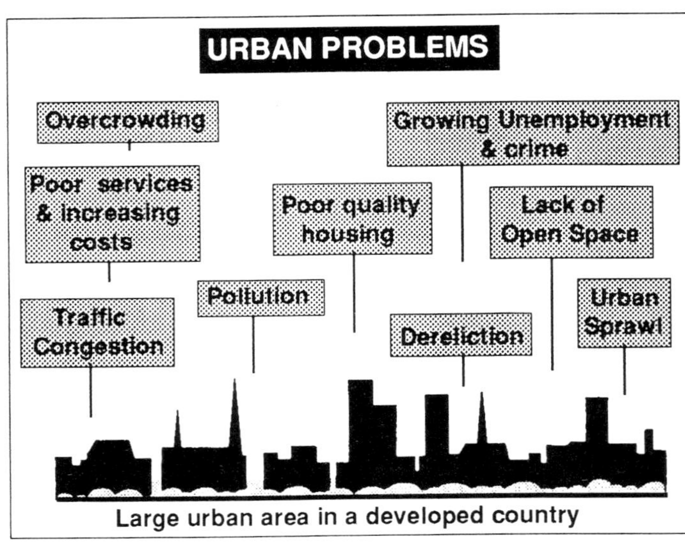

Overcrowding - in the CBD (vehicles, workers, shoppers) results in major congestion, high accident rates and pollution (litter, air and noise).

Poor quality Housing - the inner city housing in many large settlements was built in the 1890s and early 1900s in the form of tenement blocks and flats and has suffered through age and neglect. Few modern amenities (hot water, baths & toilets, private garages) and problems such as dampness or dry rot combine to create 'ghetto' areas or Twilight zones. Many of these old buildings fall into decay and become dangerous through subsidence.

Urban Sprawl and Suburban Growth - as settlements expanded, huge housing areas developed on their edge (or suburbs) often many kilometres from the inner city areas. Much suburban development was unplanned and uncontrolled. Some areas were constructed without sufficient local services or industries. The suburban development (or untidy sprawl) also increased the travel distance to work and today many of these areas have become problem urban areas.

Traffic congestion and Pollution - most large urban areas act as magnets for people as workers, shoppers and tourists. Many elaborate, expensive urban road networks have been constructed in attempts to improve traffic flow. But congestion remains a major urban problem, especially in and around the CBD of a large settlement. Industries and traffic create environmental pollution (air, noise and visual) and large settlements constantly have problems of disposal of household and human waste - polluting rivers, seas and land areas around the edge of the settlement.

Unemployment and Crime - Often major problems in large urban areas. The loss of jobs in traditional industries such as engineering, port and dock work also creates industrial dereliction. Many large settlements have large areas of waste ground (often known as 'brown earth gap sites') which look unattractive and once housed large industries employing often thousands of people. Many economic & social problems are also linked with areas of urban-industrial decline - increasing unemployment & poverty, racial tension and street crime (muggings, theft and drugtaking).

Provision of services - increasing costs of services within large settlements create problems of provision for urban authorities.

Lack of Open Space - in many large settlements open land is scarce, especially near the centre. 'Built-up areas' often have a drab appearance.

The problems of urban growth in developed countries, such as Britain, have been tackled in a variety of ways with varying degrees of success:

Urban Decay and Renewal - areas suffering urban decay have the following negative characteristics - structural deterioration of buildings, high density housing (tenements, flats) and unsanitary conditions including dampness and vermin infestation. However, many inner city areas also have positive characteristics - the convenience of close proximity to shops, entertainments and workplaces, especially those in and around the CBD, strong local community spirit, cheap houses, cheap rents and local rates. Governments since the 1950s have been attempting to solve the urban problems of such areas by combinations of the following strategies:-

Comprehensive Redevelopment Schemes - concerned with the demolition of whole areas of housing and old industry. Low density modern housing with parking and safe play areas was planned to replace the old poor quality housing. Purpose built modern industrial estates were constructed to try to attract a wide variety of industries. Areas such as the Gorbals in Glasgow or Leith in Edinburgh became C.R.A.s in the 1960s & 1970s. But there were problems. In many areas tower blocks (high rise flats) were built (fig.20). These were found to be unsuitable for the elderly and young families and suffered major dampness and design problems. Whole communities were destroyed in the CRA scheme process and many areas failed to attract a wide and sufficient industrial base from which to recreate high employment rates among the local population. Where local consultation and the traditional terraced or flatted housing designs were preferred, CRA schemes were more successful such as in the G.E.A.R. (Glasgow's Eastern Areas Renewal scheme) area. In such areas, consideration was concentrated upon the human aspects of redevelopment and not solely on the built environment.

Housing Estates - huge areas of countryside usually on the edge of the city, were bought over and devoted to the construction of modern tenements. Glasgow built such 'schemes' at Easterhouse, Castlemilk, Drumchapel and Pollock. Edinburgh built Muirhouse and Craigmillar. Thousands of people from inner city areas of urban decay were moved out up to 13 km from their traditional homes and family networks, into modern estates which often had very few local services, few shops or bus services and little employment. The housing retained a high density and was often of poor construction. These large estates, housing sometimes in excess of 60,000 people, had a lack of community spirit and a high unemployment rate. Today many areas have fallen into disrepair and have become the major problem areas in themselves. Many areas have become unoccupied and vandalised. Private housing developers have bought over some areas such as parts of Pilton, Edinburgh in an attempt to improve them.

New Towns - five Scottish new towns have been built in Central Scotland, some distance from existing large cities in an attempt to create a completely modern, planned urban environment in pleasant surroundings with the attraction of new jobs in ultra-modern industries (eg. electronics, food processing, telecom, etc) East Kilbride, Cumbernauld, Irvine, Glenrothes and Livingston (fig.18) have common characteristics as new towns - modern CBDs usually as shopping malls, neighbourhood residential areas with localised services linked to the CBD by good roads, industrial estates located away from residential areas usually on the urban fringe, high amenity housing and greenspace for various recreational purposes.

Renovation schemes - CRA schemes were very expensive and not guaranteed success. Where inner city areas had structurally sound old housing, renovation proved a much better solution to urban decay. Renovation schemes included re-roofing buildings, installing central heating, modern WC facilities, baths and double-glazing. Car parking areas and safe children's play areas were also included. Housing density was reduced by knocking two small flats into one. The local community was largely retained and any overspill population housed in New Towns or overspill towns such as Airdrie or Bathgate.

Fig.20 A Tower block residential area

Fig. 21 Some solutions to urban problems

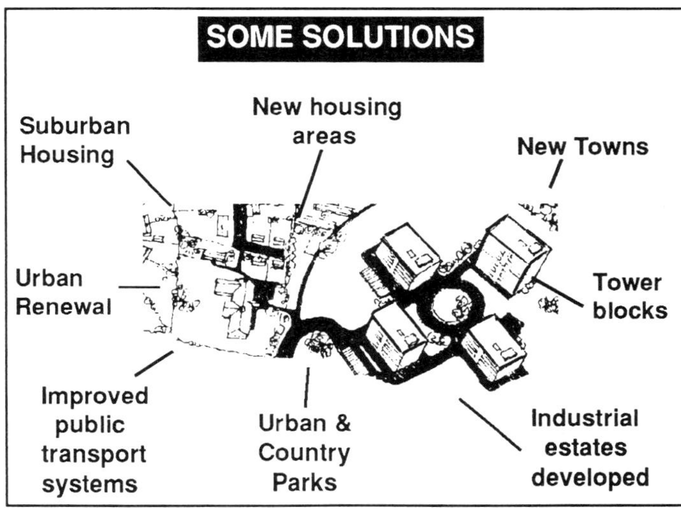

Assignment Four

1a Complete your own copy of Fig.18 by naming all the settlements & uplands shown.

1b Investigate then put into **Rank Order** of size of population the top ten settlements in Central Scotland.

1c Describe the situation of Stirling, Irvine and Glasgow.

2 Make brief explanatory notes for each of the urban problems listed in Fig.19.

3 Study Fig.20 above. Give detailed reasons for each of the following:-

i) The need for tower blocks in the 1960s

ii) Their main problems.

4 For each of the solutions attempted, give both advantages and disadvantages in terms of :

i) The **Social** aspects (on family, friends, travel)

ii) The **Economic** aspects (jobs, wealth, services)

iii) The **Environmental** aspects (appearance, etc)

5 Which of the above solutions to the problem of poor quality inner city housing do you think would best suit

i) A old widow living alone ii) A young family of four ? Justify your answer.

6. SETTLEMENT: Urban growth or sprawl ?

Key Idea 8: Urban settlements have dynamic patterns relating to their size, form and function.

The original settlement of Inverness was built on a high knoll (or cnoc in Gaelic) overlooking the narrows of the River Ness- on which still stands Inverness Castle (11th.Century). Today the settlement has grown and spread out over the land surrounding the original settlement (Fig.23). Inverness, often referred to as the capital of the Highlands, occupies an excellent situation at a point where the Moray and Beauly Firths narrow sufficiently to allow their crossing by main road over the Kessock Bridge. The settlement enjoys good road and rail links in all directions and has its own airport at nearby Dalcross.

Inverness is the main market, administrative and shopping town for the North and West, a major communications centre and an important tourist destination. Inverness houses important financial and commercial functions as well as a major industrial estate providing both services and employment for the region.

The sphere of influence of Inverness (Fig.21) encompasses most of the Highlands and Islands which have a combined total population in excess of 250,000 people. The importance of Inverness is also reflected in the steady growth of its population (Fig.22). Improvements to its communications - the upgrading of the railway, airport and main A9 road in the 1980's together with the siting of the Highlands & Islands Enterprise Headquarters and the awarding of E.C. Objective One status for the area have combined to give Inverness the reputation of an expanding, upmarket and important settlement. Urban expansion has become a major feature of the area in recent times.

Fig.21 Inverness - situation & sphere of Influence

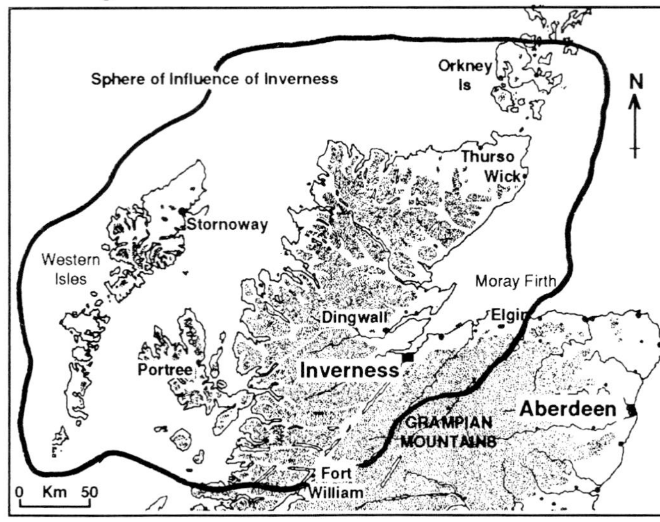

Fig.22 Inverness Population Data (1841-1991)

1841	9,100	1921	20,940
1851	9,970	1931	22,580
1861	9,520	1941	No census (war)
1871	14,510	1951	28,100
1881	17,385	1961	29,770
1891	19,300	1971	34,660
1901	21,240	1981	36,470
1911	22,220	1991	41,766

Inverness, however, has expanded to the point where almost all the available flat land for development has been utilised. Whilst the site of the settlement served urban expansion in the 1970's and 1980's well, Inverness is now on the brink of what some local experts consider to be an urban sprawl.
Planners and developers face difficult decisions as to the best way forward for the expansion of Inverness.

Fig. 23 Inverness - the Highland capital

Fig.24

Inverness Transect

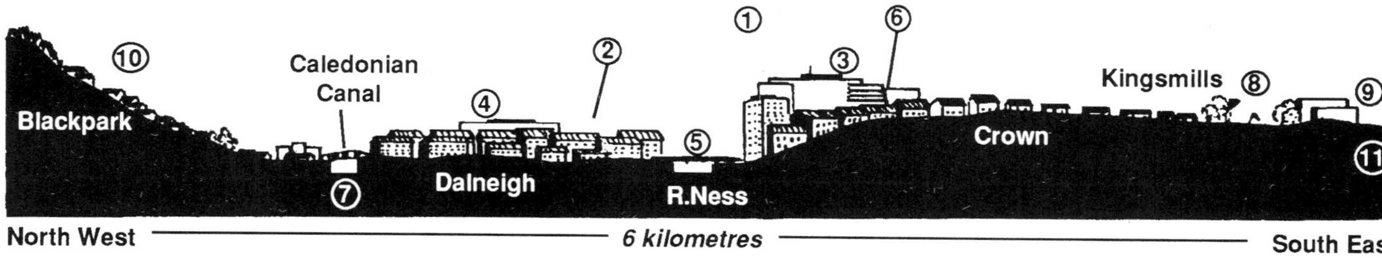

Some points to consider in the urban expansion or urban sprawl debate of Inverness are listed below:-

Inverness is the ideal location to tourthe Highlands from. Improved communications have helped the growth of tourism. There has been a big boost to the hotel and conference trade in the area. There has also been a large influx of people in search of work and high quality of life in the 1970's to 1990's to the area around Inverness. A new shopping centre - the Eastgate (1983) - attracts 72% of all visitors to the town who travel by car. Extensions to the centre are planned for the 1990's. Improvements to the communications network have also attracted modern industries to Inverness.

There are new light engineering and micro-technological industries. Better communications to Inverness have led to traffic congestion problems especially on the two main bridges over the River Ness. Traffic jams, noise and air pollution are a problem in and around the town centre. The main road west towards suburbs and Beauly has to cross the Caledonian Canal swing bridge. This is a major area for road congestion especially at peak travel times.

Golf courses and parks are now surrounded by large housing estates as the town expands into countryside mainly to the south and west. Space for new developments , eg. Out of Town shopping centres, leisure parks and new housing is now found mainly to the East of the town (Fig.25) Good road links with the main A9 route are being constructed to encourage developments in these areas. Housing areas are now to be found on the steep slopes surrounding the town, especially to the West. Inverness is running out of flat land for building. A new southern distributor road is planned as a bypass linking the A9 with the main roads to the West and South.

Fig.25 Inverness development

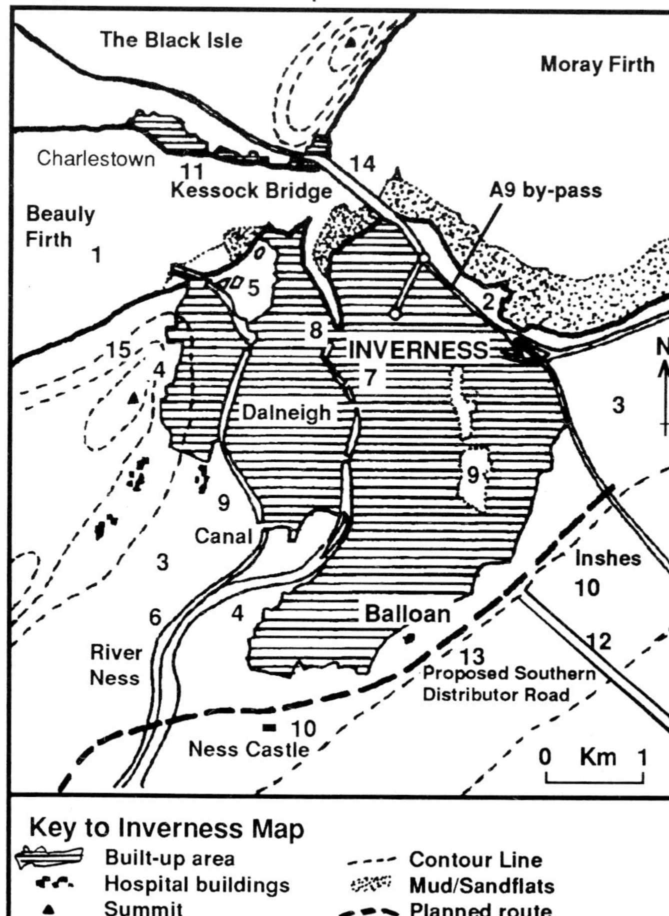

1 Inverness cannot expand Northwards because of Beauly & Moray Firths.
New Southern distributor road, planned to link the A9 and the Loch Ness route (A82) cuts through the Green Belt.
The Kessock Bridge (1982) encourages commuting to Inverness from the Black Isle.
Sloping and undulating north facing areas suitable for developmentbut lie in poor aspect especially in winter months.
Main physical obstacles to development include the steep western slopes, the River Ness and the Caledonian Canal.
Low lying industrial land is unattractive to house builders.
Large quarry prevents southern development.
Newly reclaimed land along coast earmarked for recrestion.
Fertile farmland surrounds Inverness. Expensive to buy for housing areas.
Little open space in and around the town centre.
Bottlenecks at canal and river bridges cause major congestion as Inverness expands.
The few existing open spaces are utilised for golf courses & parks.
Ness castle, Inshes and Balloan areas are ripe for development as housing areas but lack communications with the town centre and the A9 road.
The Black Isle settlements of North Kessock & Charlestown have little room for expansion on their narrow coastal plain.
12 General Wade's Military Road area is a prime development site but conservationists oppose development in this area.

Assignment Five

1 Using an annotated diagram or sketch map, describe the site and situation of Inverness.
2 Draw a line graph to illustrate the growth of the population of Inverness.
3 Justify the statement that Inverness can be considered to be a **growth pole** (a major centre of economic and social growth)
4 The Kessock Bridge was completed in 1982. What have been the likely impacts of this bridge on the following:- i. North Kessock ? ii. Inverness Town Centre ?
5 Complete a key to the Inverness Transect (Fig.24) matching numbers 1-11 with extracts from the text on this page. Study Fig.25 carefully.
6 Rewrite the Key to Fig.25 matching numbers 1-14 with the statements made in the key.
7 Using the information provided on pages 11-12, write an essay on the growth of Inverness entitled "Urban Growth or Sprawl". Include details of the advantages and disadvantages of urban growth for the town. Does Inverness suffer from urban sprawl ? Give reasons for your answer.

7. EXAM STYLE QUESTIONS

Site, Situation, Function, Services, Land use.

Ordnance Survey Mapwork

These questions can be answered by referring to any of the following map extracts:

a. Banff and Macduff 1:25 000 Extract No 830/0148-9
b. Great Yarmouth 1 : 50 000 Extract No 866/134
c. Lincoln 1 : 50 000 Extract No 828/121
d. Stirling 1 : 50 000 Extract No 732/57-58

1 For any of the following pairs of settlements state which settlement is the more important service centre. Give **two** reasons for your answer supported by map evidence.
a) Banff (GR 6844) and Macduff (GR 7064)
b) Belton (GR 4803) and Reedham (GR 4202)
c) Bracebridge Heath (GR 9867) and Branston (GR 0267)
d) Fallin (GR 8391) and Alva (GR 8897)

2 Ordnance Survey maps are of limited use when studying service centres. List **three** other types of evidence which might be used to compare service centres.

3 In what ways has the site of the following settlements influenced their growth and functions.
a) Macduff (GR 7064)
b) Great Yarmouth (GR 5207)
c) Lincoln (GR 9771)
d) Stirling (GR 7993)

4 In what ways has the situation of the following settlements influenced their growth and functions.
and what evidence is there that the functions of the settlements have changed with time?
a) Banff (GR 6864)
b) Belton (GR 4803)
c) Lincoln (GR 9771)
d) Dunblane (GR 7801)

5 For the following pairs of grid references state which of the two areas is likely to be an area of newer housing. Support your answer with map evidence.
a) 686645 or 685638
b) 5207 or 5209
c) 9772 or 9873
d) 7992 or 8091

6 Which urban growth model best reflects the growth of the following settlements?
Give map evidence to support your answer.
a) Banff (GR 6864)
b) Great Yarmouth (GR 5207)
c) Lincoln (GR 9771)
d) Stirling (GR 7993)

7 With the aid of the annotated diagrams below explain the form and land use pattern of a New Town and a Market Town.

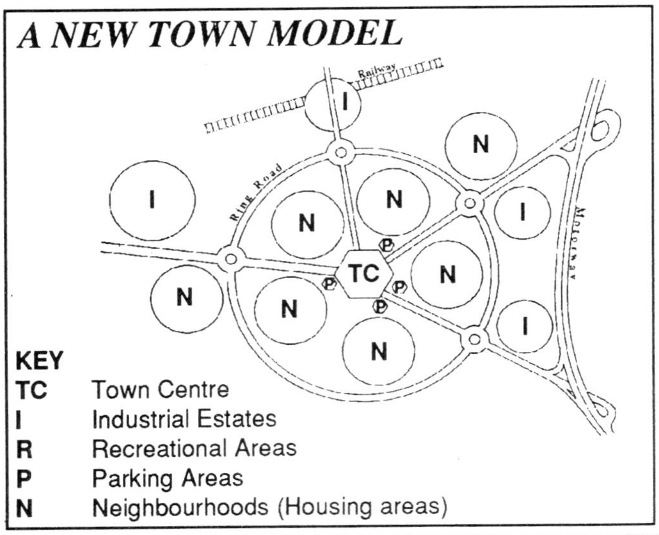

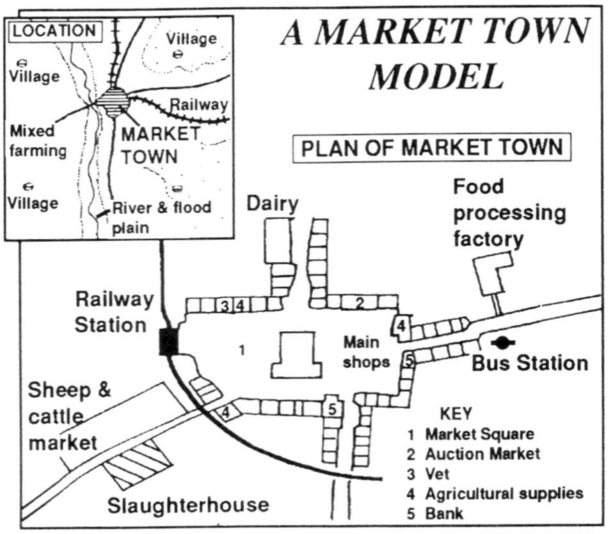

Settlement

SETTLEMENT : Urban Renewal

Examine the diagrams and information below

Original Docklands Area

THREE POSSIBLE DEVELOPMENT SCHEMES

1. All industry and housing removed

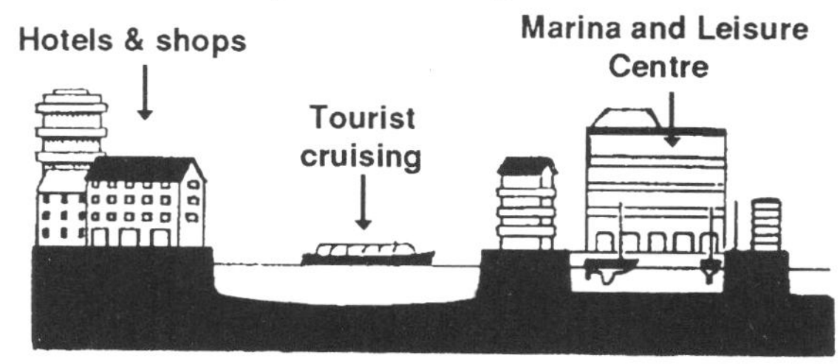

2. Some small factories, offices & luxury housing

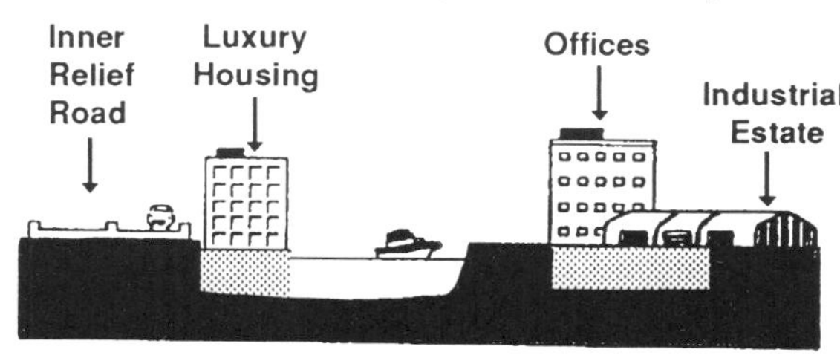

3. All waterways filled in. Most industry removed. New and renovated housing.

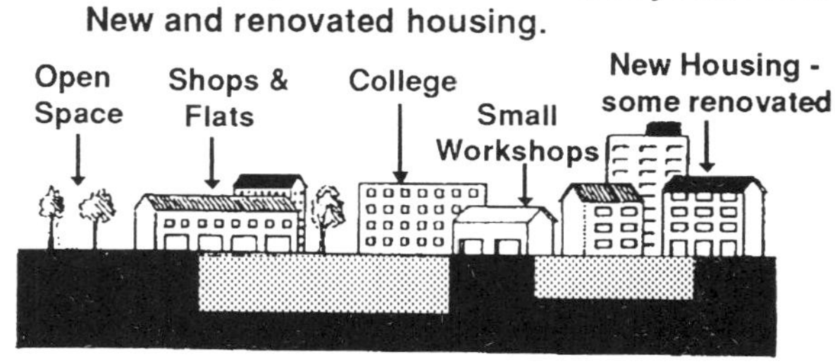

1a What economic, social and environmental effects do major industrial closures have on the areas around them?

1b Illustrate your answer with examples you have studied.

2a Examine the three possible redevelopment schemes, for a dockland area. Identify the advantages and disadvantages of each scheme.

2b Identify groups of people who might oppose or promote each of the three development schemes.

2c Give the point of view of one named group opposing any of the three schemes.

2d Explain why urban renewal has been necessary in many dockland areas of British cities.

3 Describe **four** urban problems found in contemporary Britain and explain some of the solutions which attempt to solve them.

4 Explain the changes in land uses from city centre to suburbs quoting examples from a major settlement you have studied.

5 For a major city you have studied describe the range of functions and activities which are to be found in its **Central Business District** (CBD).

LAND USE TRANSECT THROUGH A CITY

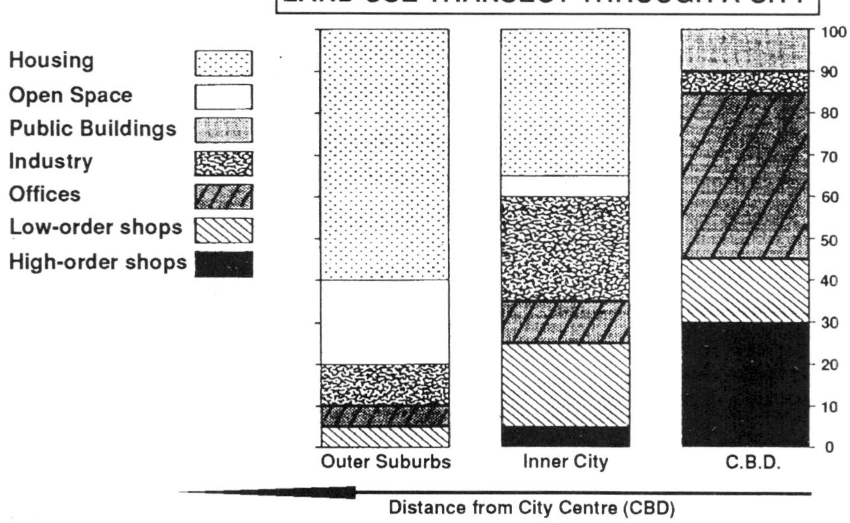

8. INDUSTRY: Classification of Industry

Fig.26 An industrial area

Key Idea : The viability of industry is affected by a variety of factors

Industry covers any activity which is performed for profit. **Industrial areas** can vary from the traditional industrial scene shown in Fig.26 to a single farmstead or cottage in which work for commercial gain is undertaken.
Industries can be viewed as **systems** (Fig.27) where various Inputs, processes and outputs are matched to markets which determine profit or loss and therefore the success of the industry.

Inputs include resources (raw materials, energy, etc), capital (Invested money), labour (workers), technology (equipment, machinery, computers, etc), communications (roads, phone lines, etc) and environment (land, climate, space, etc).

Processes can include manufacturing (making steel, flour or petrochemicals, etc), assembling (putting together various components into, eg. cars, computers, televisions, etc), designing, writing, communicating, etc. Processes depend on the nature of the industry and can vary within any one industry.

Outputs can include a wide variety of products and services, eg. wheat, propane gas, bread, ships, educated people, computer software, information, etc. Changing **markets** (where products or services are sold) and competition from other businesses often mean decisions must be taken to change or update the products or services in order to keep the business in profit.

Many industrial experts believe that the only constant in business is change and that adapting to industrial change (even anticipating change) is the key to maintaining profits and industrial growth.

Fig.27 The Industrial System

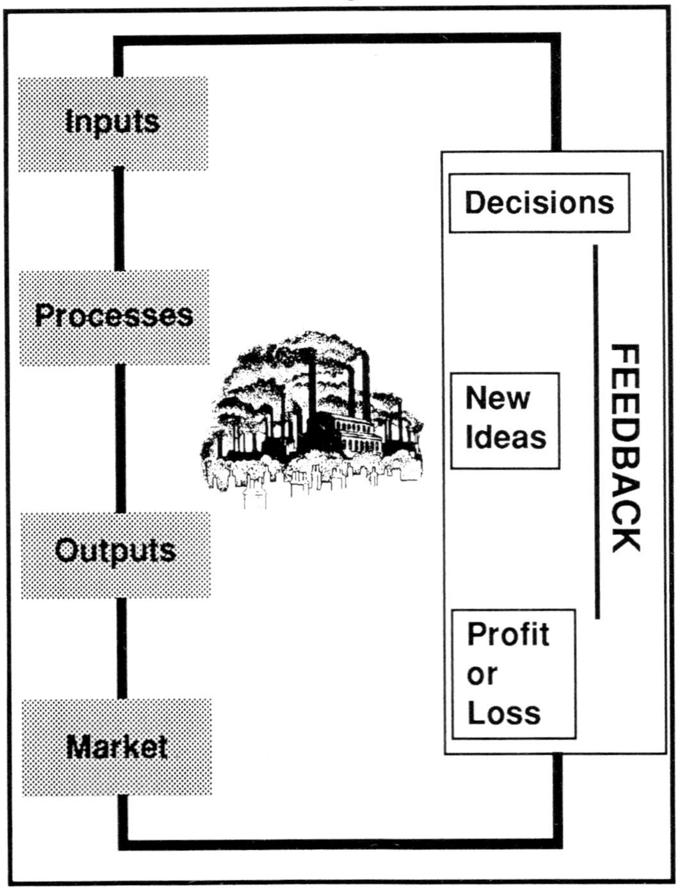

Industry is often divided into **5** main classifications or categories depending on their function (the job that they do). Industrial surveys also use a Division type classification for research purposes (Fig.29).

Fig.28 Selected main industries as systems

Industry	Inputs	Processes	Outputs	Market	Feedback
Coal Mining	Energy, Labour, Machinery	Mining Quarrying	Coals of different types	Power Stations Industries, Households	Profits Quality of coal Cheap imports
Steel making		Iron smelting Furnacing Rolling			Profits, Quality of Steel Foreign imports
Nuclear Power Stations	Uranium rods Water (Cooling) Large buildings		Electricity, Waste, Hot water		
Doctor		Interviewing Communication Diagnosing Operating			Quality of Care, New medicines & treatments
Computer System Software Production	Hardware system Skill		Software Programs Documents	Industries Households Schools	

1 **Primary Industry** - *extractive* industries which produce raw materials, such as farming, mining, fishing, etc.

2 **Secondary Industry** -*manufacturing* industries (where raw materials are processed into finished products, such as steel-making, biscuit factory, brewing, etc) and *assembling* industries (where components are put together with skill to produce a finished product, such as car and computer assembly, etc).

3 **Secondary Industry** - *power producing* industries such as thermal power industries where fuel from oil or coal is used to generate electricity for domestic or light industrial purposes.

4 **Tertiary Industry** - *service* industries which involve no finished product but provide personal services to the community, such as teaching or the police force.

5 **Quaternary Industry** - *information* and *office*-based industries such as finance, insurance and computer software services.

Secondary (Manufacturing) Industry is often referred to as **Light** or **Heavy** industry.
Light industries produce lightweight goods (such as electronic components). Heavy industries produce large, usually heavyweight products (such as ships, girders, boilers, etc)

Assignment Six

1 Study Fig.26.
Which classification(s) of industry are shown here ?

2 Write definitions of each of the following :-
Industry, Industrial system, Inputs, Processes, Outputs, Market, Feedback.

3 Copy and complete your own version of Fig.28 (Industries as systems).

4 For each of the 5 main classes (or categories) of industry give :-
i. a definition
ii. at least 2 examples of your own.

5 Study Fig.29.
i. Match each Division (0-9) with one of the 5 main classes of industry. Illustrate your answer in a table.
ii. Using the Industrial Classification shown, investigate the main types of industry in your local area. The Yellow Pages Directory is a useful source of information.
iii. Write an illustrated report on industries in your local area (eg. include bar graphs showing each division, give reasons for types of industries, etc).

Fig.29

AN INDUSTRIAL CLASSIFICATION

Division 0 *AGRICULTURE, FORESTRY & FISHING*
Agriculture & Horticulture, Agricultural Machinery, Forestry, Fishing, Fish-Farming, Fish Processing

Division 1 *ENERGY & WATER SUPPLY INDUSTRIES*
Extraction of Oil, Oil Processing, Nuclear Fuels, Production & Distribution of Electricity, Gas and Other forms of Energy, Water Supply Industry

Division 2 *EXTRACTION OF MINERALS & FUELS, MANUFACTURE OF METALS, MINERAL PRODUCTS AND CHEMICALS* Extraction of Minerals, Extraction of Stone, Clay, Sand & Gravel, Concrete, Cement & Plaster, Glass, Ceramic Goods, Chemical Industries, Paints, Inks, Soaps, Detergents, Perfumes, Cosmetics

Division 3 *METAL GOODS, ENGINEERING & VEHICLE*
Metal Goods, Bolts, Nuts, Springs, Chains, Mech.Engineering, Machine Tools, Textiles, Electronic Data & machinery, Telecomm. Equip. Radio, Electronic Components, Motor Vehicles, Shipbuilding, Instrument Eng.

Division 4 *OTHER MANUFACTURING INDUSTRIES*
Slaughterhouses, Animal Products, Milk, Fish Processing, Grain Milling, Bread & Flour, Ice-cream, Cocoa & Chocolate, Wines, Beers, Spirits, Brewing Textiles, Leathers, Footwear, Furnishings, Sawmilling, Paper & Printing, Rubber & Plastics, Jewellery, Coins, Toys, Games, Sports Goods, Others

Division 5 *CONSTRUCTION* Building, Civil Eng., Demolition

Division 6 *DISTRIBUTION, HOTELS & CATERING; REPAIRS* Scrap Metals, Distribution of Raw Materials, Fuels, Timber, Building Materials, Machinery, Vehicle components, Food, Drink, Tobacco, Repair of Consumer Goods, Vehicles, Machinery

Division 7 *TRANSPORT & COMMUNICATION*
Railways, Road passenger Transport, Road haulage, Sea & Air Transport, Postal Services, Telecommunications, Supporting services

Division 8 *BUSINESS, PROFESSIONAL & TECHNICAL SERVICES* Banking, Finance, Insurance Architects, Surveyors, Training, Office supplies, Computer Services, Property, Marketing, Graphic Design

Division 9 *OTHER SERVICES* Public Admin, Police, Fire, Health Education, Tourist Offices, Radio & TV Stations, Libraries, Laundries

USTRY: Changing locational factors

Key Idea : The viability of industry is affected by a variety of factors

Fig.30

The industry shown in Fig.30 has a coastal location close to a good road network with plenty of flat land nearby with room for expansion should the industry require it. All industries attempt to select an ideal location in order to minimise their costs and maximise their profit potential (the money they make).

Industrial location is dependent on a number of factors which vary over time in response to new developments in products and services, changing markets and improvements to communications, etc.

Capital - is the money available for investment in the industry, to set up and run new industries.

Raw Materials - many industries locate as close as possible to supplies of raw materials which they use most, eg.. a cement works is usually located in close proximity to a limestone quarry. This location saves money on transport costs, especially where the raw material is heavy and bulky to transport.

Communications - good communication and transport links are essential factors influencing the location of industry. The movements of people, goods and ideas along natural and artificial routeways, utilising roads, railways, air and sea routes and various telecommunication links play a vital part in the successful operation of many industries.

Site - the actual land the industry is built upon is also an important consideration. Ideally it should be cheap, flat with adequate room for expansion and close to good communication links.

Markets - places where goods and services are sold. Many industries supply goods and services for sale in large urban areas. By locating near to or within a large city, a large market is provided and transport costs reduced.

Labour and Skills - every industry needs people (their technical and organisational skills) as workers. The larger the required labour force, the more likely that location is close to a large urban area.

Power - all industries require power of some sort. Industries which require large amounts of power, e.g. aluminium smelting or petro-chemical refining may locate close to a power station or even build their own. Industries which can locate almost anywhere there is a power supply are known as *footloose industries*.

Government Policy - governments usually try to encourage industries to locate in less developed areas - where unemployment is high - using a selection of incentives such as grants, pre-built factories, training schemes, etc.

Fig.31 Factors influencing location of industry

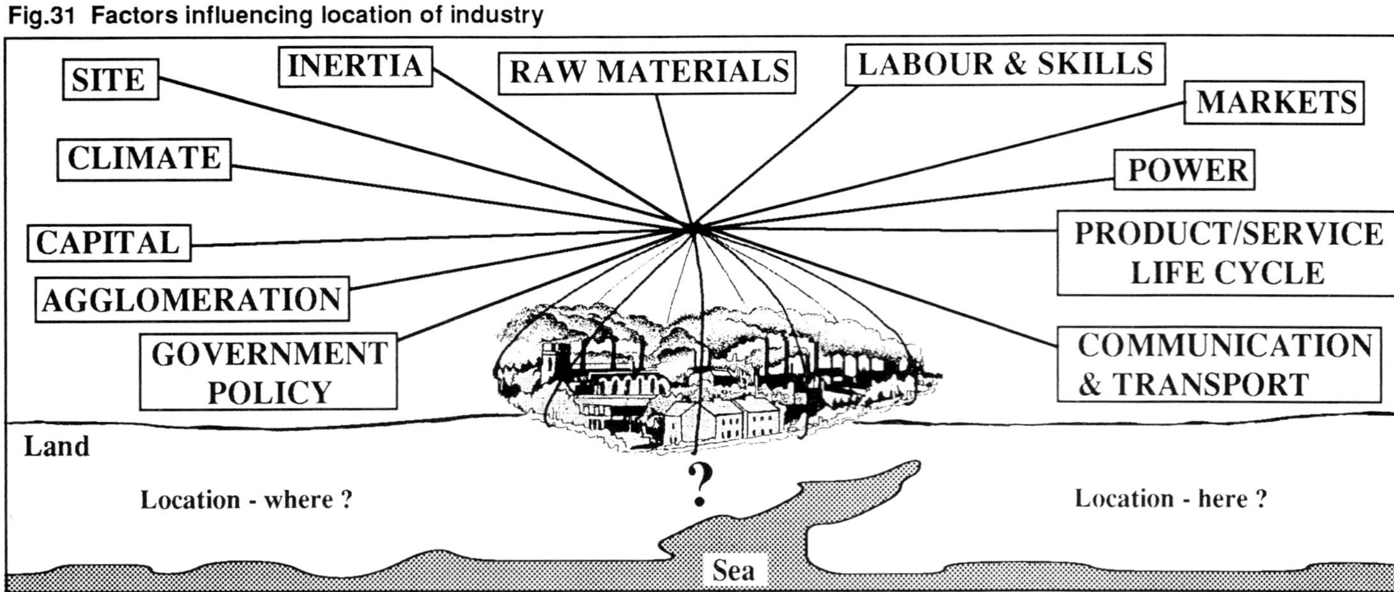

Fig.32 An industrial landscape

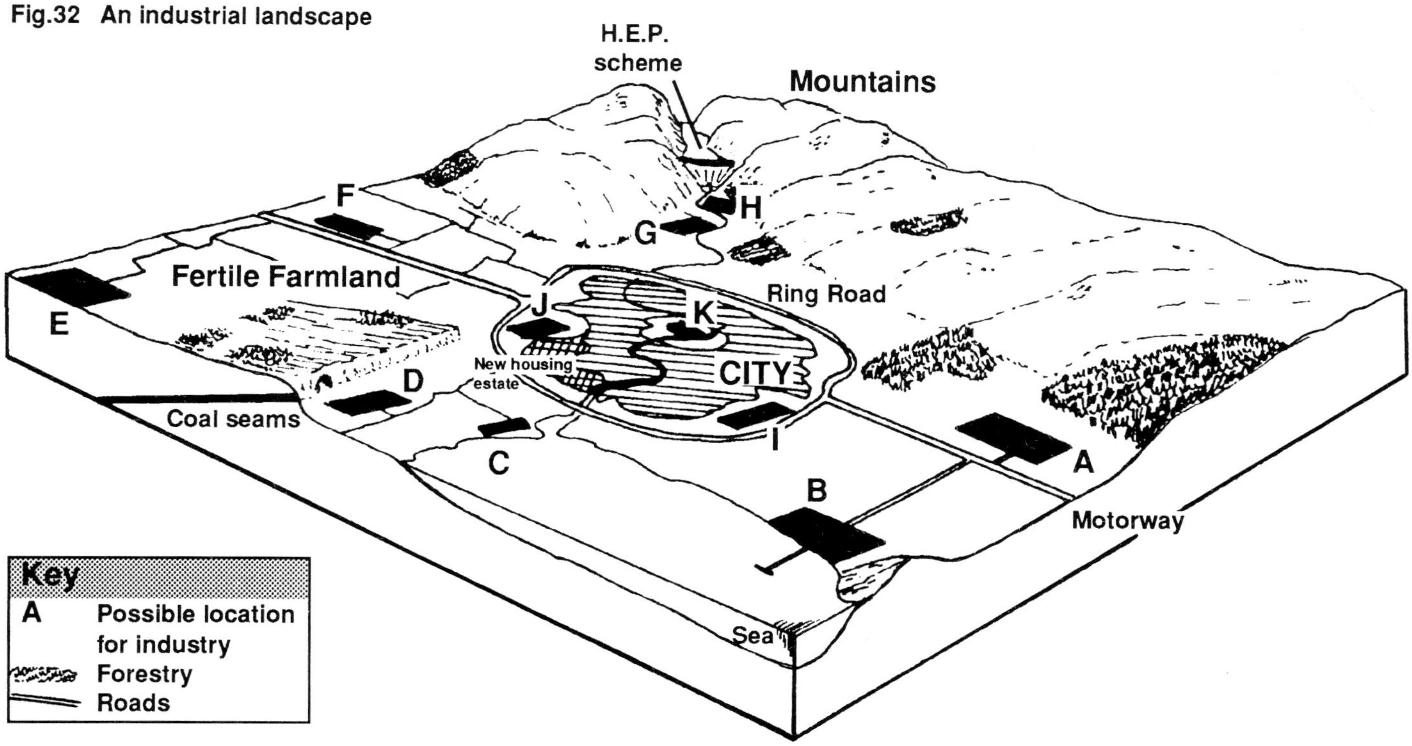

Climate - some climates are too extreme for certain industries to locate in. Other *environmental* considerations which influence the location of industry include the laws on polluting of land and water within certain areas, and the amount of greenery in the surrounding area. For example modern electronics industries require dust-free, greenfield areas in which to manufacture silicon products.

Inertia - because it is always extremely expensive for industries to relocate elsewhere, many old industries have tended to stay in the locality where they were first established. This is called industrial inertia.

Agglomeration - some industries attract others to locate beside them. Such a collection of industries is known as an agglomeration.

Product or Service Life Cycle - a product or service usually goes through various stages in its life-cycle (Infancy-Youth-Maturity-Old Age) which can influence its location.

Industries can also be classified according to their particular type of location (Fig.32). Some locations are better suited to some industries than others, e.g.Site **A** is a *greenfield site*. Site **B** is a *tidewater site*.Both have pleasant locations with cheap flat land available. Large industries may be attracted to locate in these areas even although they lie some way from the city and will attract fewer visiting customers. Site **K** is a city centre location where land is very expensive and transport of products difficult due to congestion. However site K has access to many thousands of city centre workers, shoppers and visitors.

The factors influencing the location of industry (Fig.31) are not all of equal importance. They may vary in different places and at different times. But wherever industry is located it requires a good **infrastructure** - buildings, power & water and good communications networks.

Assignment Seven

1 Make a simple fieldsketch of Fig.30. Annotate your sketch to show the following: type of location, main features of the industrial location shown, likely type of industry.

2 Write a definition of each of the following terms: industrial location, infrastructure, inertia, agglomeration.

3 Using Fig.31, classify each of the factors influencing industrial location as either **Physical** or **Human** factors.

4 For both Physical and Human factors influencing the location of industry, complete a table with the headings:

Factor	Notes on importance	Examples

5 Factors which cause an industry to move out of an area are known as **PUSH** factors. Those which attract an industry into a new area are known as **PULL** factors. Copy these definitions out and list at least 3 of each type of factor.

6 Match each of the following industries to a suitable location on Fig.32 (**A** to **K**). Give reasons for your selection of location for each industry:-
Oil refinery, Superstore/Hypermarket, Creamery/Dairy, Magazine Distribution Warehouse, Pulp & Paper Mill, Nuclear Power Station, Coal Mine, Computer Assembly plant, Insurance Offices, Bottled Water Plant, Petrol Station & Repairs Shop.

7 Why do location factors change and what problems does this cause for industries and communities ?

INDUSTRY: Industrial Change

Key Idea : Economic change has social and environmental consequences.

As the nature and type of industry in Britain developed *from* the subsistence agriculture (farming for survival) of the pre-1800s *to* the tertiary and quaternary industries of the 1990s, change has had a major effect on industrial location.

Fig.33 illustrates the major **traditional industrial areas** within the U.K. The older, heavy industries located within many of these areas for physical reasons - close to supplies of raw materials, sources of energy and close to good rail or water transport. Industries such as steel-making, engineering and textiles were concentrated within areas such as London, South Wales, Lancashire and Central Scotland where the population density was high and there were large markets nearby. Due to changes in demand for products, out of date or uneconomic mining or manufacturing processes, changing markets or foreign competition, many older, traditional industries have closed down.

Some industries have **relocated** because their source of raw materials or markets have changed.
Others have undergone major **rehabilitation** such as factory renovation, modernisation of machinery or the installation of modern telecommunications. Industrial changes (Fig.36) have brought about **economic** (unemployment, decline of local services), **social** (increasing divorce, crime rates) and **environmental** (derelict or gap sites) consequences.

Modern industries are located in a variety of areas (Fig.34) for a range of different reasons. Footloose industries such as electronics, aerospace, computing, media and telecommunications are located in urban areas, some to attempt to combat the aftereffects of traditional industrial decline, others to take advantage of the high density of population or skilled labour force available, for example, in London or Scotland's New Towns. Other modern industries are not tied to any particular location and can locate in greenfield areas such as the Scottish Highlands or Cornwall since their products are low bulk/high value and use modern telecommunications to contact their markets.

Industrial change also affects the *Structure of Industry* (Fig.35). The tertiary sector is now the most important employer and where traditional industry is in decline, unemployment increases.

Fig.33 Traditional industrial areas in the U.K.

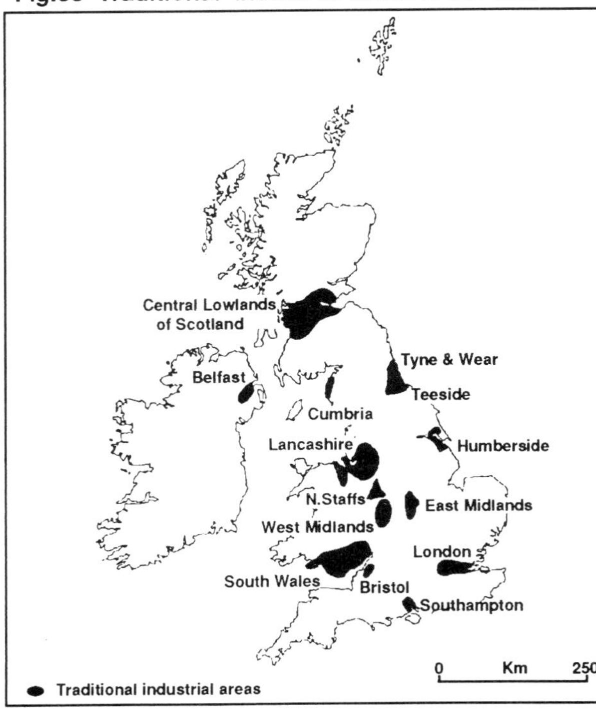

Fig.34 New industrial areas in the U.K.

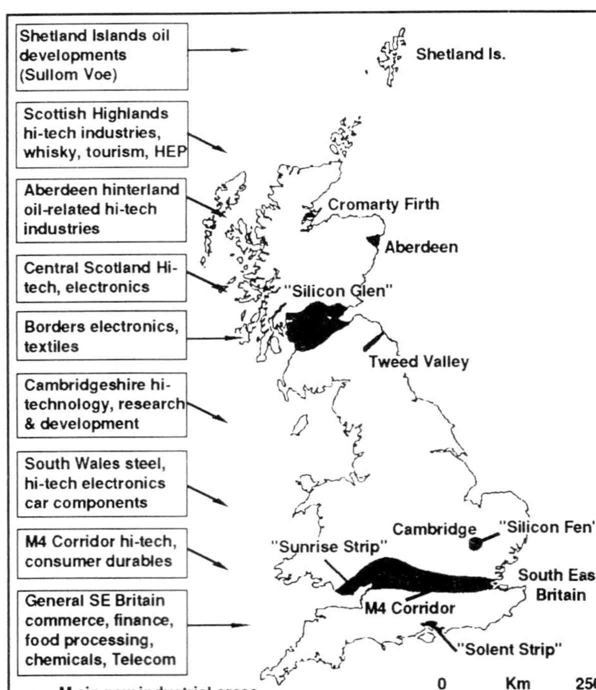

Fig.35 Employment in the U.K. 1945 - 1992

Year	Primary Extractive	Secondary Manufacturing	Tertiary Services	Quaternary Info Technology	Unemployed
1945	8	52	34	1	5
1965	6	42	46	2	4
1985	3	27	48	7	15
1992	2	25	52	10	11

Fig.36 Industrial Change of varying types

INDUSTRIAL CHANGE

The location of and importance of different industries changes over time for a variety of reas

Agricultural Phase	→	Industrial Revolution	→	Industrialisation Major industrial development	→	Late Industrial	→	Post Industrial Phase
		C.18th.		Late C.18th. to mid C.20th.		1970s - 1980s		1990s - C.21st.

Mainly subsistence farming with manual labour. Simple technology used. Population living mainly in rural areas.

Development of new "Industrial" processes, eg. steam engines & metal processing, etc.

Major investment in industrial processes, complex technology and communications, eg. rail, road, air, telecommunications, etc. Population shift to urban areas, leisure time and tourism major employers.

Decline of older and development of modern industries. Resulting economic & social problems

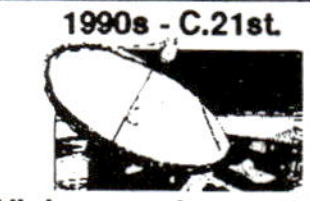

High unemployment, hi-tech industries, Footloose industrial location, environmental issues.

PRIMARY INDUSTRY

Major changes have affected a variety of Primary Industries in recent years, for example,

Agriculture: Amalgamation of small farm units into large units, increased use of technology (laser-levelling, etc) subsidies from Governments (National & E.C.), expansion of urban and industrial areas into farmland, changes in demand for farm products cause changes in the location of industry.

Mining & Quarrying: As reserves of natural resources such as coal, oil, gas, sand & gravel, etc become exhausted or uneconomic to obtain, mines and quarries close down. The development of modern mining techniques, use of giant technology (massive excavators, pipelines), accurate satellite surveying of mineral reserves and competition from foreign sources of raw materials all cause changes in the location of industry.

Fishing: Over-fishing in certain areas such as the North Sea has led to the seasonal tying up of fishing boats and introduction of fish quotas all of which affect both the location and future of the industry.

SECONDARY INDUSTRY

Sunset Industries: older, traditional, heavy industries such as shipbuilding, engineering, factories, etc have gone into decline as a result of changes in demand for their products, foreign competition, out-of-date processes and the relative expense of their products, poor locations too far from markets, lack of space to expand, etc. Half a century ago major cities such as Sheffield or Glasgow had a narrow industrial base as they were dependent on many heavy industries for employment & wealth creation. Sunset industries are sometimes known as smokestack industries, often located around city centres and in dockland areas (Fig.33). Many settlements have suffered the economic, social and environmental consequences of industrial decline, of such industries.

Sunrise Industries: modern, light, footloose industries such as electronics, biotechnology, computer assembly, etc. These "hi-tech" industries are expanding in greenfield areas with good infrastructure and clean environments. Sunrise industries produce lightweight, low bulk/high value products such as semi-conductors and often require highly skilled workforces. Occasionally they are located in areas of traditional industrial decline to alleviate problems associated with unempolyment. New Towns such as Livingston and the M4 Corridor linking London with Bristol, are the focus of sunrise industrial development (see Fig. 34).

TERITARY INDUSTRY

As a country's economy develops, the proportion of the workforce employed in service industries increases to become, as in the case of the United Kingdom, the most important sector of industry (Fig.35).

There are several types of service industry each mainly located within urban areas, for example

Professional services - expert services supplied by doctors, solicitors, etc.

Community or social services - for the community as a whole such as Police, Fire, Hospital, Education, Social Work. *ndustrial Linkage services* - support services for industries, e.g. computer repairs or stationery supplies for large companies. Other linkages exist, e.g. between a manufacturing industry (shoe making) and the shops which sell the product (shoe shops). *Consumer services* - serve the public goods or advice.

QUATERNARY INDUSTRY

The development of new information industries such as the provision of information technology, multi-media, satellite and telecommunications, software writing, etc. These are good examples of the Post-Industrial (Manufacturing) Phase of a country's industrial development.

Quaternary industries are not tied to a particular location and can locate almost anywhere. Large scale quaternary industries are often located in large urban centres taking advantage of excellent communication networks and inter-company contacts for information capture or distribution. Small quaternary industries such as software or data anlysis companies are often located in attractive environments with good communications, e.g "telecottages".

Assignment Eight

1 Study Fig.35 carefully.
   a. Construct pie-charts for both 1945 and 1992.
   b. Describe the differences shown by the pie-charts.
   c. Give reasons for these differences.

2 Write a definition for each of the following terms:
   Heavy Industry, Footloose Industry, Sunrise & Sunset Industries, Greenfield areas

3 Identify the main types of Industrial Change discussed and illustrated on pages 19 & 20.

4 Compare the areas of traditional industries with those of modern industry in the United Kingdom.

5 Copy and complete a larger version of the following table using Fig.36 to help you.

Industrial Phase	Main types of location	Location Factors	Examples
Agriculture			
Ind Revolution			
Industrialisation			
Late Industrial			
Post-Industrial			

6 An industrial area such as Consett depended upon its Steelworks for most of its local employment. What problems does a narrow empolyment base create for a town like Consett ?

7 What have been the consequences of increasing tertiary & quaternary industries in the U.K. ?

11. INDUSTRY: *Industrial decline*

Key Idea : Economic change has social and environmental consequences.

Fig.37

Fig.37 represents a major industrial change. Castlebridge Colliery is Scotland's most modern deep mine. The complex at its height can produce over 1 million tonnes of coal per year, none of which ever reaches the surface. The mine is linked by a 4 kilometre underground conveyor system along which all coal produced is transported to nearby Longannet Power Station.

This picture of successful hi-tech mining, however, also masks massive changes in the coal mining industry of the United Kingdom. In 1955 the U.K. had over 850 active collieries. In the 1990s the U.K. has less than 70 active collieries with recent plans to close almost 50% of those remaining (fig.38) causing acrimony and unrest in the traditional mining areas such as South Yorkshire.

Modernisation of mining techniques has improved coal production but resulted in a decline in the number of workers required. The development of giant excavators and haulage equipment has also led to the expansion in more economical Open Cast (or surface) coal mining. Cheaper foreign coals and competition from other forms of energy production (eg. nuclear power stations) have also contributed to the decline in deep coal mining. Increasing environmental concern over the burning of **fossil fuels** increasing greenhouse gases (Carbon Dioxide), and acid rain (Sulphur Dioxide) is a major worldwide issue.

The decline of coal mining has had major economic, social and environmental consequences in traditional mining communities, especially those with a narrow industrial base (**monotechnic**, one industry settlements).

In many of these communities, large scale redundancies, increasing poverty, diminishing local services, lack of industrial development and industrial dereliction often lead to depopulation as younger skilled people and their families migrate in search of work in other areas.

Fig.38 Coal mining in the U.K. 1990s

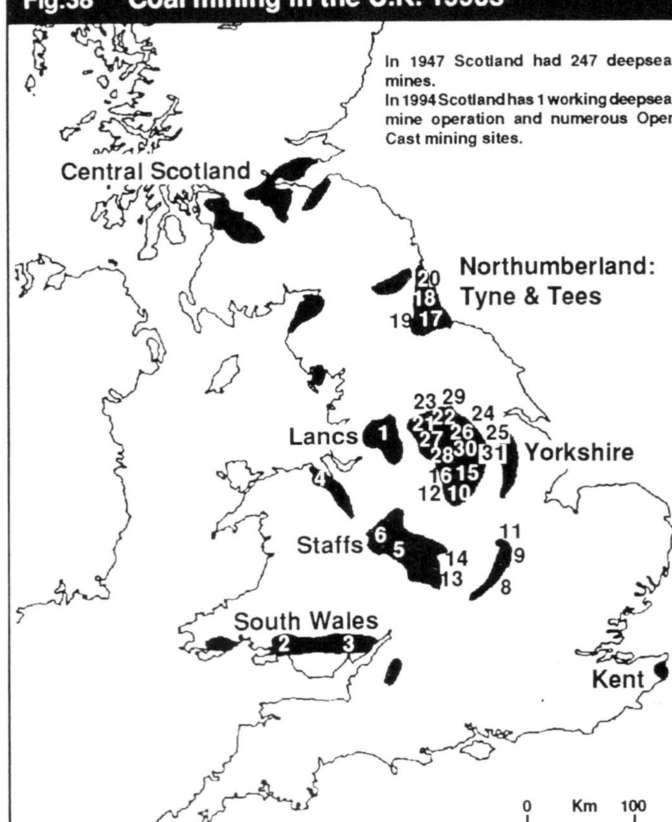

Key to Coalfields Map

Coal mines under threat of closure

1 Parkside	10 Rufford	19 Wearmouth	28 Prince of
2 Betws	11 Shirebrook	20 Sharlston	29 Wales
3 Taff Merthyr	12 Cotgrave	21 Rossington	30 Kiveton
4 Point of Ayr	13 Calverton	22 Bentley	Park
5 Trentham	14 Bolsover	23 Hatfield	31 Maltby
6 Silverdale	15 Markham	24 Markham Main	
7 Bevercotes	16 Easington	25 Frickley	
8 Bilsthorpe	17 Seaham	26 Grimethorpe	
9 Clipstone	18 Westoe	27 Houghton Main	

The steel industry can also be described as an industry in crisis after massive industrial change over the last 50 years. The location of the steel industry both in the U.K. and across Europe, was determined largely by physical factors - local supplies of raw materials (coking coals, limestone and iron-ore), easily obtainable supplies of fresh water and easy transport routes (usually by water). Major steel centres (Fig.39) such as Central Scotland (based around Ravenscraig, Motherwell), South Wales (Port Talbot & Llanwern), the Ruhr (Germany), the Franco-Belgian (Saar) coalfield and Lorraine produced large amounts of steel both for export and local use in engineering, construction and consumer durable industries. By 1979 European steel production peaked at over 155 million tonnes employing over 750,000 workers. New works had been constructed through directed Government aid-schemes at coastal sites such as Taranto and Fos as demand increased.

During the world recessions of the1980s, demand for steel fell (Fig.40). Many European steelworks operated at a loss. There was large-scale overmanning and other increasing costs due to inflation and the exhaustion of European iron-ore reserves. Competition for worldwide and European steel markets from Japan, USA and Korea together with the expansion of steelmaking facilities in many developing countries also contributed to the decline of the steel industry in Europe. There were also inertia-related problems. Many existing steelworks were inland and traditional working practices were inefficient by comparison with Asian steelworks. For example, 1 tonne of European steel in 1984 took 8.0 hours to produce compared with 5.5 hours in a Japanese steelworks. The development of alternative materials such as plastics and fibreglass also gained a share in the once traditional market for steel (e.g. in vehicles production).

The effect of major changes in steelmaking has also led to very serious economic, social and environmental consequences in traditional inland steel centres, such as Ravenscraig (Fig.41).

With declining coal and steel production many experts suggest that there is an accompanying **'domino effect'** on local and national industry which is often unforseen.

Fig.39 European Steel centres

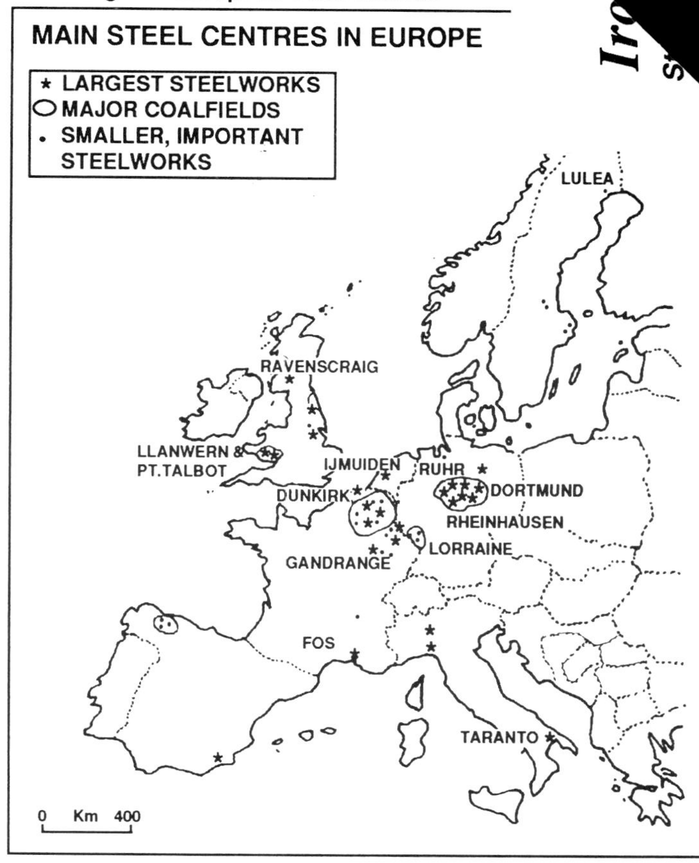

Fig.40 Factors influencing steel decline

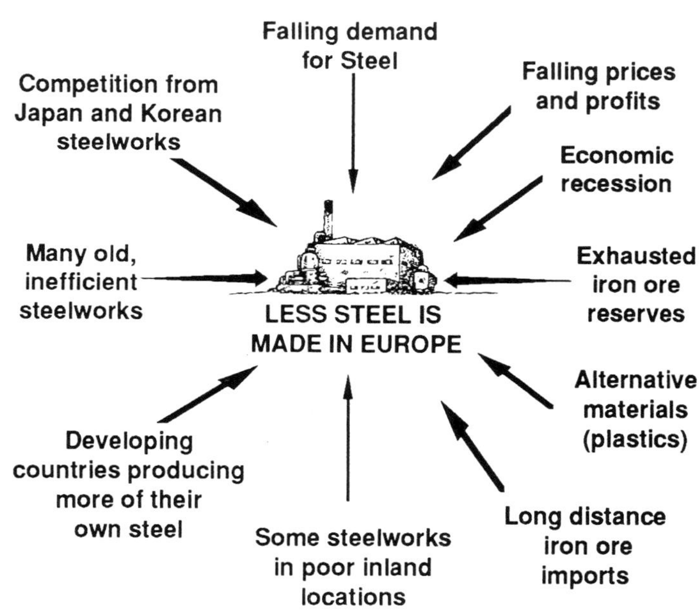

Fig.41 Ravenscraig Steelmaking in decline

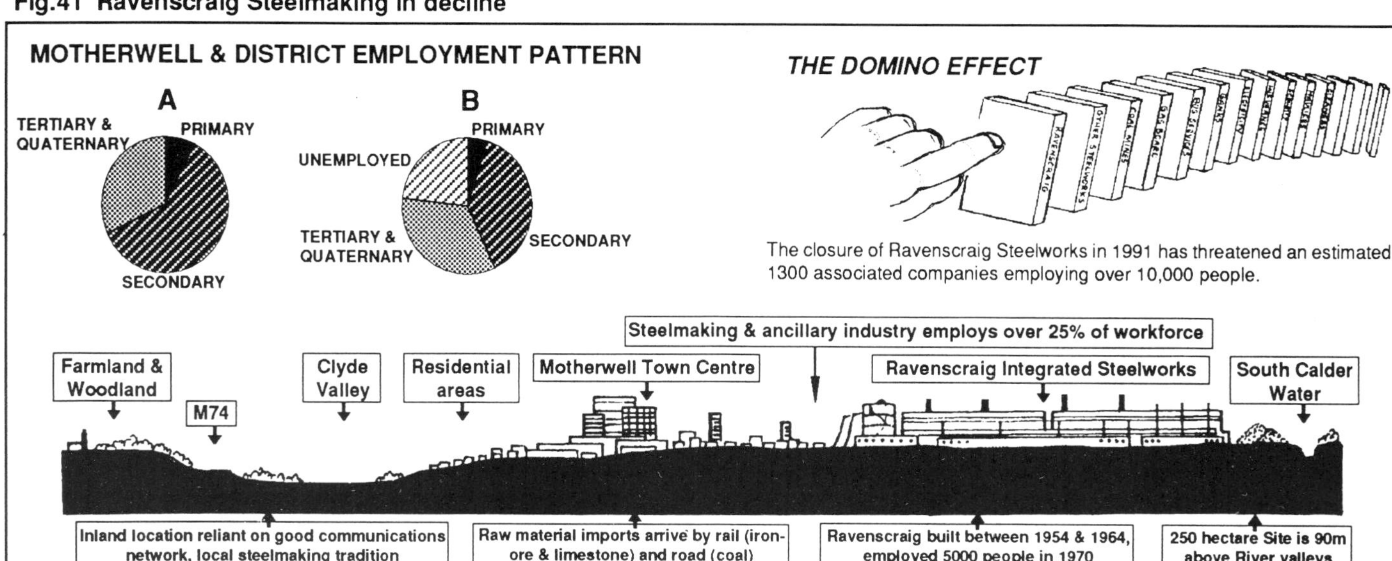

Iron & Steel in Scotland

Figs.42 to 46 Central Scotland through the ages

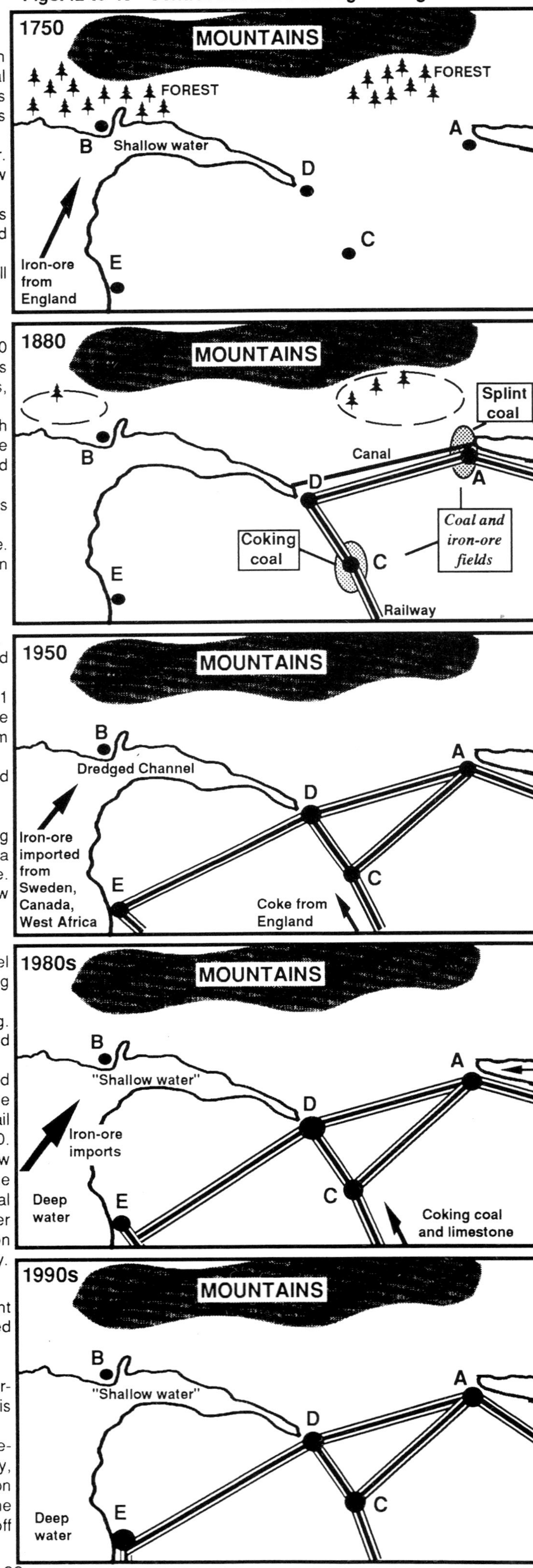

Stage 1: 1750 Central Scotland

Conditions affecting the location of the iron industry in 1750 are:-

RAW MATERIALS: Charcoal made from wood was used to smelt iron in small furnaces. 5 tonnes of wood were needed to produce enough charcoal to smelt 1 tonne of iron. Low grade iron-ore was obtained from local sources (bogs, small mines) but high grade iron-ore was obtained in larger quantities from England.

TRANSPORT: In 1750 there were no canals or railways. Roads were poor. Ships could carry many tonnes and heavy goods traffic was limited to a few large rivers.

LABOUR: Each furnace employed 30 people - mostly skilled. Scotland was short of skilled furnace workers so others were brought from Ireland and England.

MARKETS: The largest market on the map was at **D**, but demand was small in comparison with English markets.

Stage 2: 1850 Central Scotland

In addition to the furnace at B others were also built at A and D between 1750 and 1830. These however were using coke made from coal to smelt iron. This technique, first used by Abraham Derby in Coalbrookdale, West Midlands, has been slow to spread through England to Scotland...

RAW MATERIALS: 4 tonnes of coal were now needed to make enough coke to produce 1 tonne of iron. Iron-ore and coal were often found in the same mines in central Scotland. Splint coal was cheap and plentiful but could only be used to smelt iron using "Neilson's Hot Blast" process (1928).

TRANSPORT: Sea transport was still the cheapest but canals and railways had improved and cheapened inland transport enormously.

LABOUR: Works were much larger and employed several hundred people.

MARKETS: Engineering especially at D now provided a large market in Scotland.

Stage 3: 1950 Central Scotland

Ironworks were built at A in 1850 and expanded but not into steelmaking. A steelworks was constructed at C in 1870, expanded and was modernised in the C20th.

RAW MATERIALS: By 1950 only 1 tonne of coke was needed to make 1 tonne of iron. It was now cheaper to import foreign ores than to mine the remaining reserves of Scottish low grade ores. Most coking coal came from England.

TRANSPORT: large quantities of ore were moved by ship, coal and limestone came by rail and canals were no longer in use.

LABOUR: Thousands of skilled workers were required in 1950.

INDUSTRIAL INERTIA: Huge investments had been made in existing works, developing transport, training and social facilities, etc. There is a reluctance to move to a new site (inertia) due to the large investments made.

GOVERNMENT POLICY: The Government is prepared to subsidise new industrial developments in areas of high unemployment (eg. A, C & D).

Stage 4: 1980s Central Scotland

A large integrated steelworks was built at C between 1956-63. Light steel strip was used for motor vehicles and consumer durables (fridges, sewing machines, etc). Over 90% of steel was exported to England.

RAW MATERIALS: All iron-ore used was imported from distant sources (eg. Brazil, Australia). Much scrap metal was used and fresh water was needed in large amounts.

TRANSPORT: Giant super-ore carriers are used but their large size limited the number of ports that could be used. The estuary at D could not be deepened to accommodate ships larger than 30,000 tonnes. Inland rail transport is cheap. **LABOUR & INDUSTRIAL INERTIA:** as for 1950.

GOVERNMENT POLICY: In 1967 the steel industry was Nationalised. New integrated steelworks were built in England and South Wales (1970s). The Thatcher Government (1979 onwards) had a new approach to industrial policy - little financial support & privatisation of the steel industry. Other dispirit influences on the location of the steel industry included trade union power, rising unemployment, conservation and the European Community.

Stage 5: late 1990s

The large integrated steelworks at C has now been closed with a subsequent loss of over 10,000 jobs in steel and ancillary industries. The planned development of a coastal steelworks at E has been 'mothballed'.

RAW MATERIALS & TRANSPORT: as for 1980s above.

LABOUR: High unemployment in the traditional steelmaking and engineering areas of Central Scotland. A large pool of highly skilled workers is available.

GOVERNMENT POLICY: The British government is maintaining a free-market policy for steelmaking and as part of the European Steel Community, must acknowledge steel production quotas laid down. Foreign competition (mainly from EC and Asian countries) produces very cheap steel for the British market. Nationalists in Scotland pressurise the Government to sell-off the existing steelplant at C.

Factories & workshops close down. Workers face redundancies.

Loss or work. The local unemployment rate increases.

Less atmospheric pollution from closed industrial sites

Local shops & services are affected by decreasing local income. Some close down.

Local authority income reduced as former workforce and industries lose earnings.

Higher divorce, alcoholism and suicide rates may be found in areas where large scale redundancies occur.

Depopulation may occur as unemployed workers move in search of work in other areas.

Older industrial areas become "run-down."

Local "markets" supplying businesses & consumers contracts.

Local transport services & systems are affected by lack of custom.

The local area receives less income.

The domino effect - 'when one industry falls, it knocks down others' - may affect other industries or nearby communities.

Dereliction of industrial sites occurs. Wasteground and waste tips are not reclaimed or landscaped.

Separated families as workers may move to other areas for long-distance work to return at weekends, holidays etc.

Fig.47 A traditional, older industrial landscape.
Fig.48 Cartoon.

"It just seemed to to give up the will to live !"

Industrial decline brings many consequences (fig.42). The **economic** consequences of decline in major industries are not only great on a local scale but have serious implications for the country as a whole. The decline of heavy industries such as steelmaking in the UK has meant fewer export earnings and a greater dependence on imported 'heavy' products.

The **social** consequences associated include redundancies, depopulation of younger adults in search of work, high rates of unemployment,and increasing divorce, alcoholism and suicide rates in depressed areas.

The **environmental** consequences can be varied. Waste tips and waste ground and industrial dereliction are common features of the aftermath of industrial decline. Amongst a few positive environmental effects are a reduction in atmospheric pollution and the re-introduction of species once lost due to industrial development, eg. plants, flowers and animals.

Assignment Nine

1 What are the main reasons for the decline of the U.K. coal industry ?

2 Compare the different coal landscapes shown in Figures 37 and 42.

Study Page 22 carefully.

3 For each Stage in the **Iron & Steel Game**, select the best location for an iron or iron & steel works from locations **A-D**. Copy and complete the table below to calculate your total score. Your teacher will supply you with the correct answers for each stage of the game once you have completed Stages 1 to 5.

Stage	Your Choice	Score Achieved	Maximum Score
1			100
2			200
3			300
4			400
5			500
	TOTAL		1500

TOTALS
Over 1200 - very profitable
Over 750 - profitable
Over 250 - borderline of bankruptcy
Under 250 - you are fired !

4 Describe the changes in steelmaking in Europe

5 Which factors have led to the decline in European steelmaking since the early 1980s ?

Study Fig.41 carefully.

6 Which of pie-charts A and B is most likely to represent Motherwell's employment pattern in 1989 and 1997 ? Explain your answer fully.

7 Write a definition of each of the following terms : domino-effect, industrial dereliction, monotechnic

8 What message is the cartoonist attempting to send in Fig.48 ? Explain your answer.

9 Using Fig.47 and further ideas of your own, classify the consequences of industrial decline into those which are economic, social or environmental.

10 For a monotechnic industrial area, use the Spiral of Decline opposite to describe fully the consequences of industrial decline.

11 What do you think should be done to alleviate the consequences in areas suffering industrial decline ?

12. INDUSTRY: Industrial growth

Key Idea : Economic change has social and environmental consequences.

Industries respond to changing circumstances and conditions in a variety of ways and at different rates. Economic progress is interlinked with industrial development of all types. There is therefore an **'industrial cycle'** through which industries develop and expand, respond to changes in society (eg. changes in demand and supply, national or global recession, etc) and grow or decline depending on how they respond to change.

Responses to change can include both **Industrial decline** (section11) - where many traditional industries close down or suffer cut-backs - and **Industrial growth** and expansion as a result of:-

a) **Modern or High Technology** developments including micro-electronics, nano-technology (tiny technology).
b) **Diversification** of existing industry into other fields.
c) **Rehabilitation** of existing plant and processes or of entire industrial areas, where modernisation has occurred
d) **Aid to Industry** schemes.

High Technology Industry

ZONAL UK Ltd

Originally located in Redhill, near Gatwick Airport, SE England, Zonal UK Ltd (fig.49) opened their new factory on the Invergordon Industrial Estate in 1987 for several main reasons. Transport congestion and high land values together with increasingly high wage settlements combined to force the company to seek expansion in a different location within the UK. The availability of a ready-made factory with room for expansion at Invergordon and the high amenity value of the surrounding area together with the Enterprise Zone status of the area made the location an attractive one (fig.51)

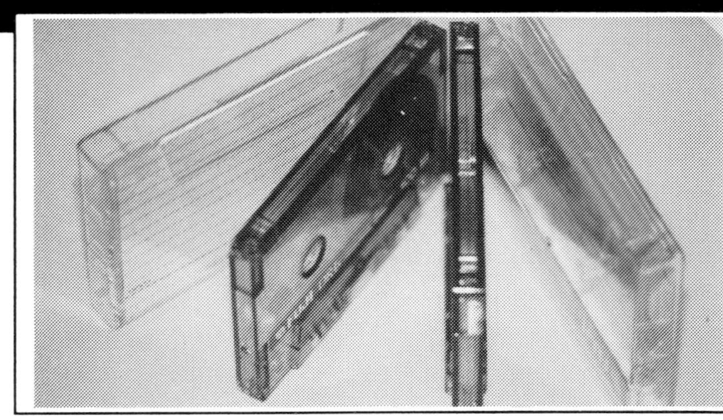

Fig.49 Zonal UK products

Zonal use hi-technology to produce a variety of products including audio tapes for the Hollywood Film Industry, the BBC and other European broadcasting companies. Over 1.5 million metres of audio tape is produced daily by a workforce of over 72 people. The company are investing in hi-tech production facilities in order to produce blank CD (Compact Discs), and boxes for CDs and audio tapes. Imports of iron-oxides, needed in the production of tape products, are currently supplied from Germany. With nearby Inverness Airport, improving road links and the latest satellite telecommunication links, the distribution of products and interchange of information between Invergordon and the Redhill plant cause no problems. The UKs largest tape manufacturer, Zonal are expanding their business on a worldwide scale and are opening an new plant in 1994 in India to supply the growing Indian and South-East Asian tape & CD market.

Hi-tech or sunrise industries often employ fewer people than the industries they have replaced such as engineering or textile manufacturing. A highly skilled, inventive and mobile workforce is seen as essential to many footloose hi-tech industries and access to raw materials is viewed as less important than a modern infrastructure and the high amenity of the industrial location. Many Highland or Lake District locations can accommodate such industries, bringing alternatives to the tourist-related and seasonal employment patterns of such areas. The main locations for hi-tech industries in the UK are indicated on fig.34 (page 19) and include Silicon Glen (Central Scotland), Silicon Fen (Cambridgeshire), the M4 Corridor, the Aberdeen area (mainly oil-related technology industries) and parts of the Scottish Borders.

Diversification of Industry

Many large companies diversify - supply a variety of products and services - as a means of both protecting their investments and generating greater profits. Diversification is often carried out through the take-over of other smaller companies. As a large company is formed through various take-overs and mergers, diversification may also lead to the company gaining a **Multinational** or **Transnational** status (trading across many countries often on a global scale).

Unilever is the world's ninth largest company and the world's largest food processing and household goods company. Unilever owns over 70 companies and trades in over 80 countries. In the 1980's and 1990's the company has expanded and diversified its business operations to include international divisions which include:

UNILEVER

FROZEN FOODS	DETERGENTS & WASHING POWDERS	EDIBLE FATS & DAIRY	SOFT DRINKS BEERS, WINES & SPIRITS	TEA COFFEE	HOTELS & CAFES	MAGAZINES ADVERTISING	TIINNED FOODS

Unilever brand name products include Lux, PG Tips, Pears, Flora, Shield, Stork, Surf etc. Companies which diversify and have a wide range of products and markets are less likely to suffer as a result of economic change.

Industrial Rehabilitation

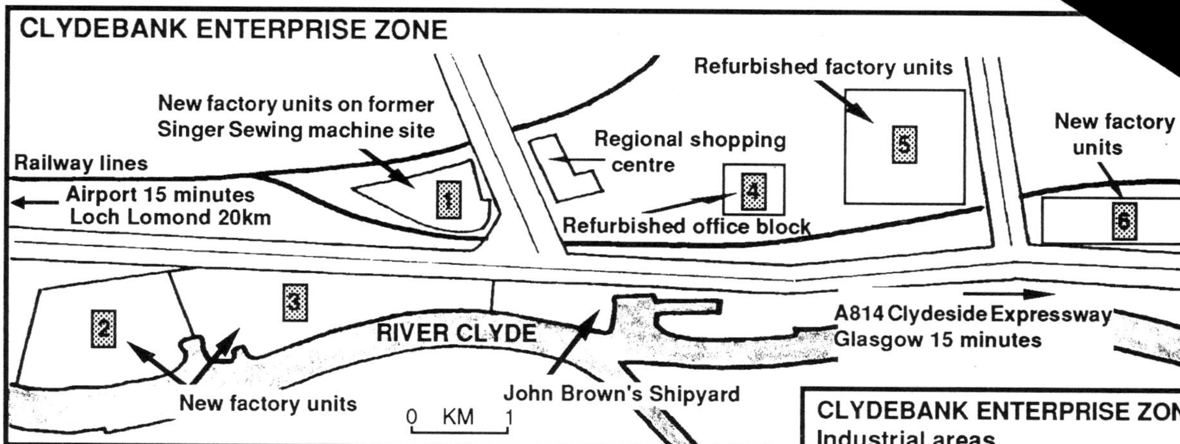

Fig.50 Clydebank Enterprise Zone

CLYDEBANK ENTERPRISE ZONE Industrial areas
1 Clydebank Business Park
2 Clydebank Industrial Estate
3 Riverside Industrial Estate
4 Whitecrook
5 New Albion Industrial Estate
6 Yoker Industrial Estate

Former areas of traditional, heavy industry such as Clydebank near Glasgow have suffered the consequences of industrial decline but with national and local government assistance have begun a long term process of industrial **rehabilitation**. In 1981 the Government established Scotland's first Enterprise Zone in Clydebank in an attempt to alleviate high unemployment, physical and economic decay by creating conditions for industrial growth through the rehabilitation of the area.

The Clydebank Enterprise Zone (fig.50) is generally recognised as a successful example of industrial revival. Many of the original industrial sites such as the Singer Sewing machine site have been demolished and modern industrial estates have been created in their place. Advance and purpose built factory units have been constructed and major improvements to the infrastructure of the area have been made. Financial incentives such as rent-free factories, removal grants, tax relief on new technology, etc. have also been introduced to attract new industry to the area. Between 1981 and 1993, the EZ status of the area has helped introduce over 400 new businesses and reduce the local unemployment rate.

CLYDEBANK ENTERPRISE ZONE Facts & figures

1980 Major crisis - high unemployment area becomes Scotland's first E.Z.

1993 Over 400 companies set up employing over 4000 people

Unemployment rates

	1981			1991		
	M	F	Tot	M	F	Tot
Clydebank	16.7	12.5	21.0	14.7	9.1	18.3
Scotland	14.3	9.9	12.2	16.9	9.0	17.2
U.K.	11.6	7.7	9.6	12.2	7.0	9.5

Aid to Industry

Fig.51

Assisted Areas in the UK 1993

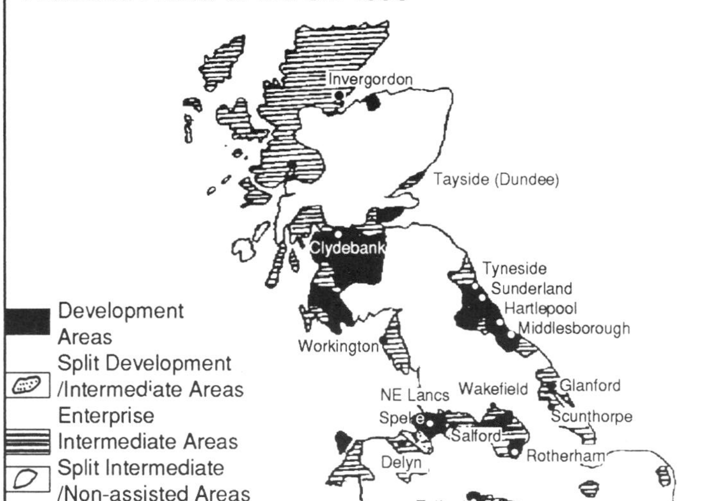

Since 1945 British governments have attempted to assist areas of industrial decline by using incentives such as grants, free factories, improving communications, Job Creation and Enterprise Zones, etc. To qualify for government assistance in 1993, new industries must locate within the areas designated above.

Assignment Ten

1 Explain what is meant by "*Industrial cycle*".

2 Fully explain the meaning of each of the following: Hi-Tech/sunrise industry, Diversification, Transnational, Rehabilitation, Enterprise Zone.

3 Many of the most modern industries can be described as *footloose* and are often located on industrial estates (which are located either on the outskirts of urban areas or in brown-earth gap-sites).
   a. Describe a footloose industry you have studied.
   b. Give at least 3 reasons for the location of industrial estates
      i. On the outskirts of urban areas
      ii. In rehabilitation areas.
   c. Prepare a detailed design for an industrial estate incorporating planned infrastructure and indicate the types of industries likely to occupy the estate.

4 Study Fig.50 carefully.
   a. Describe the main changes which have occurred in the Clydebank EZ since 1981.
   b. Suggest reasons for the main changes in employment rates illustrated in Fig.50.
   c. Compose an advert to be placed in a national newspaper to show the advantages of locating a new industry in the Clydebank Enterprise Zone.

5 Prepare an answer to the following question, "What are the advantages and disadvantages for locating industry in both rehabilitated industrial areas and modern industrial estates ?"

1 STYLE QUESTIONS

AL CHANGE

.he North of England have experienced a marked decline in traditional "heavy" industry. social, economic and environmental implications of the decline of traditional industries.

2 Lo. .e sketch diagram below. Do you think that site **X** is a suitable location for an electronics factory or a paper factory ? Support your answer with reasoned arguement.

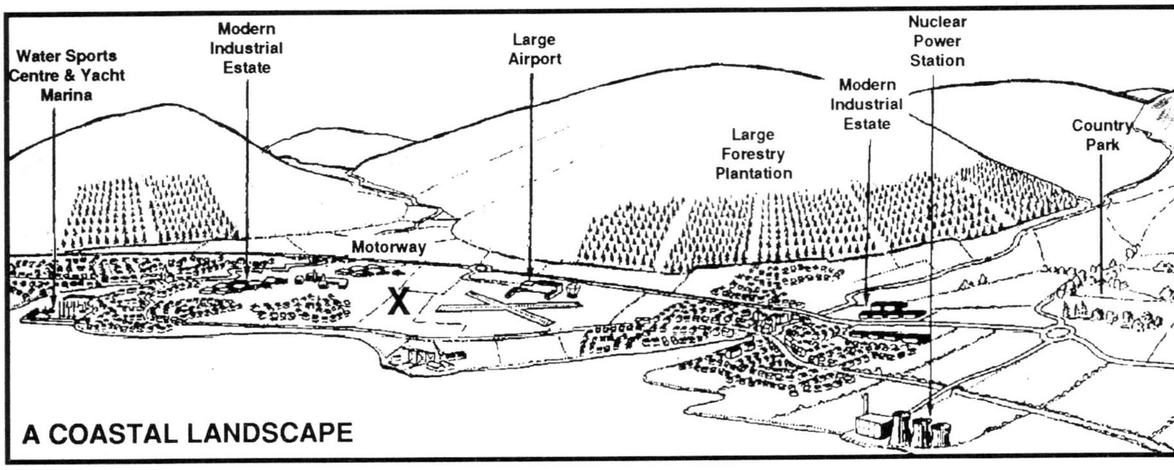

3 The iron and steel industry has changed location in the UK since the 1700's. Explain the factors which account for the concentration of the steel industry, in the 1990's, into only a few sites.

4 Describe and explain the changes in the industrial landscapes shown below.

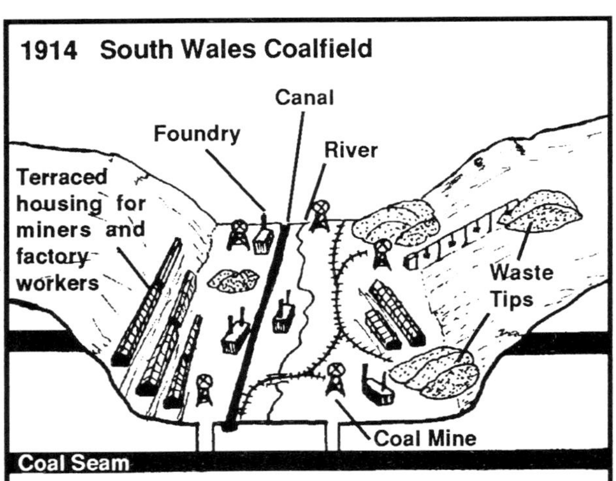

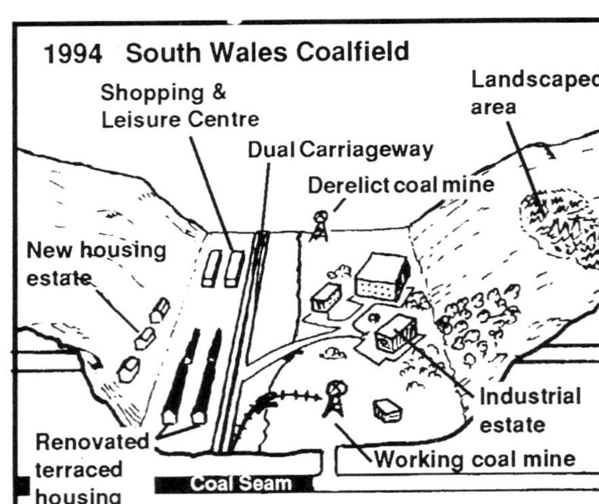

5 For an industrial area you have studied, describe the attempts to bring about redevelopment and comment on their success or failure.

6 Examine the advertisement below for **Corby**.

i. What advantages are there for businesses setting up in Corby?
ii. What advantages do you think Corby has over other Development areas shown on the map?

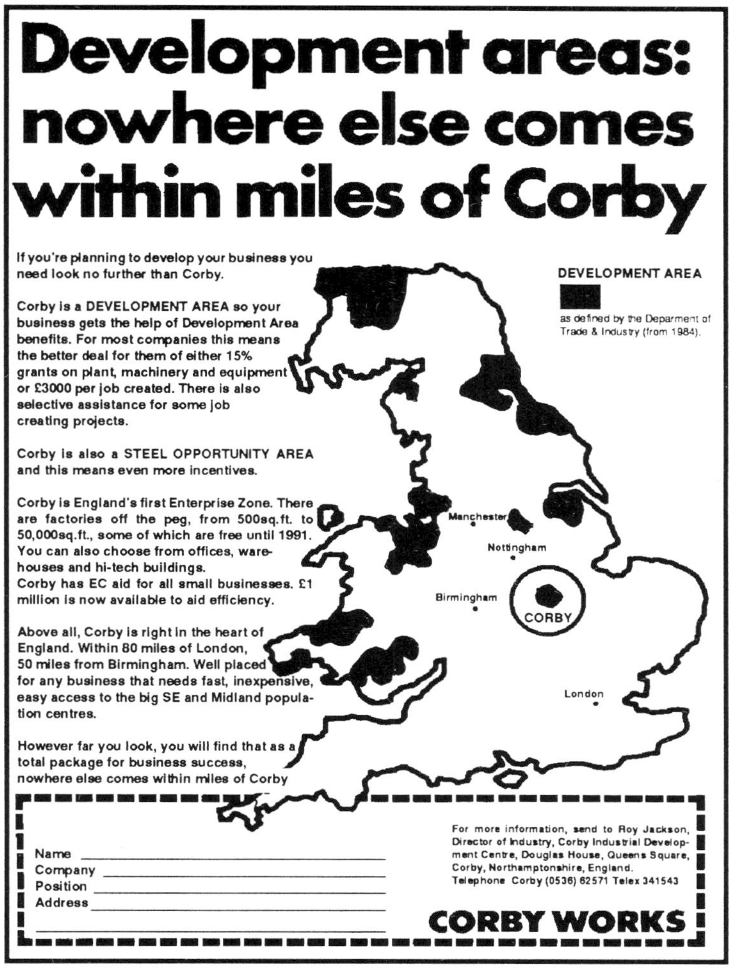

Ordnance Survey Mapwork Questions

These questions can be answered by referring to any of the following map extracts:

a. **Motherwell** 1:25 000 Extract No 763/NS65/75
b. **Sunderland** 1 : 50 000 Extract No 863/88
c. **Middlesborough** 1 : 50 000 Extract No 827/93
d. **Liverpool** 1 : 50 000 Extract No 744/108

7 Quoting map evidence, indicate any negative **environmental consequences** of the old industrial landscapes shown on the maps.

8 For any of the following industrial locations, describe the advantages of the **site**, using map evidence.
Motherwell (GR 7756)
Sunderland (GR 3458)
Middlesborough (GR 5722)
Liverpool (GR 3798) and/or (GR 4484)

9 For any of the industries in question **2** explain the advantages of the **location** for the particular industry.

10 **Modern industrial estates** are located at the following grid references.
Motherwell (GR 7658)
Sunderland (GR 3256)
Middlesbrough (GR 4620)
Liverpool (GR 4398)

What factors have influenced the location of the industrial estate?

11 Using map evidence, explain why a large number of industries are located in the area of the map extract.

12 Many industrial areas in British cities are no longer suitable for present day factories. Indicate some alternative uses of old industrial areas, referring to named examples you have studied.

13 A **hi-tech computer factory** is proposed for the following grid reference, discuss the advantages and disadvantages of the area for such a development.
Motherwell (GR 733553)
Sunderland (GR 3357)
Middlesborough (GR 4714)
Liverpool (GR 3600)

14. PHYSICAL LANDSCAPES: *Variety*

Key Idea: Physical landscapes are the product of natural processes and are always changing.

Fig.52 Bealach na Ba, Applecross

Fig.53 Selected physical features of the British Isles

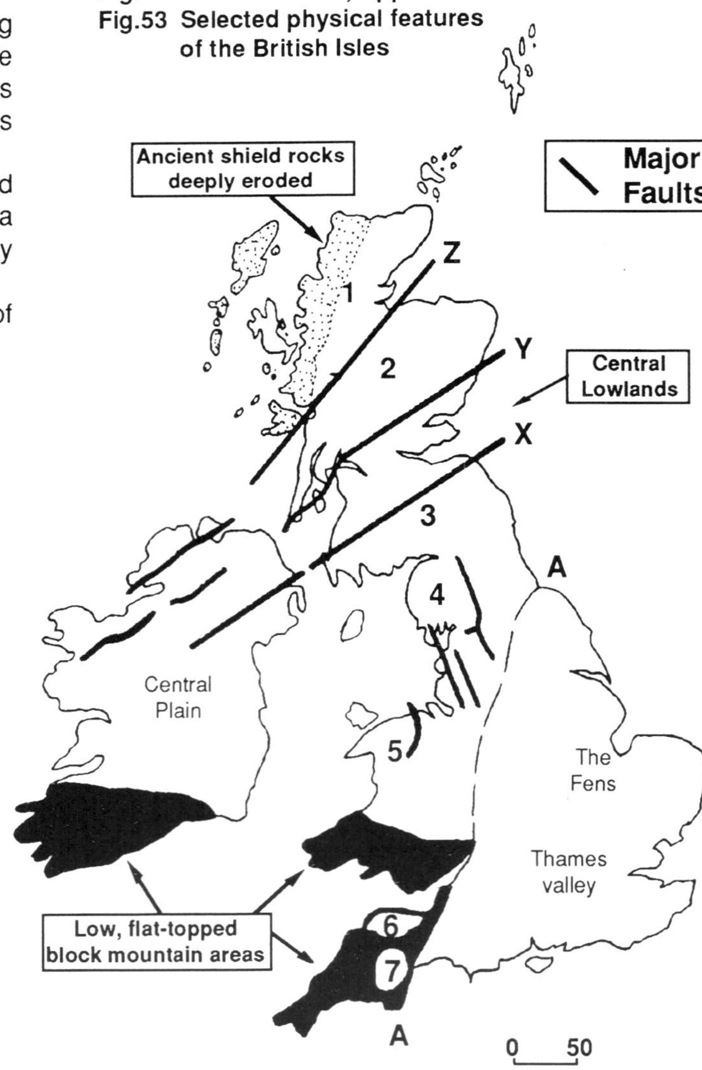

Physical landscapes are a mixture of landforms of varying ages, origins and types. For example, a glaciated landscape could consist of a series of steep-sided, U-shaped valleys separated by a series of arete ridges eroded by ice thousands of years ago.

The photo above (fig.52) shows part of the varied and beautiful landscape of the British Isles - the Bealach na Ba (the Pass of the Cattle) in the Applecross peninsula, deeply eroded by glaciers over millions of years.

Landscapes evolve through the influence of a variety of factors, including:

Internal forces - operating within the earth's crust:
Plate tectonics, the movement of the giant plates of the earth's crust can result in earth movements so powerful as to create major fault zones (see Fig.53), massive fold mountain ranges (such as the Alps), great rift valleys (such as the Central Lowlands of Scotland and the Rhine Valley) (Fig.54) and volcanic eruptions such as those found in the Mediterranean Sea and in Iceland.

External forces - operating on the earth's surface:
These forces include weathering, mass movement, erosion, transportation and deposition as well as the influence of people.

Physical landscapes result, therefore, from the balance between internal and external forces - as soon as the internal forces build up the land, external forces combine to wear it down. This balance is known as **Isostacy**.

The varied physical landscapes of parts of the earth's crust such as those of Europe (fig.54) are the result of what is known as **isostatic balance**.

Fig.54 Europe - structure, relief and drainage

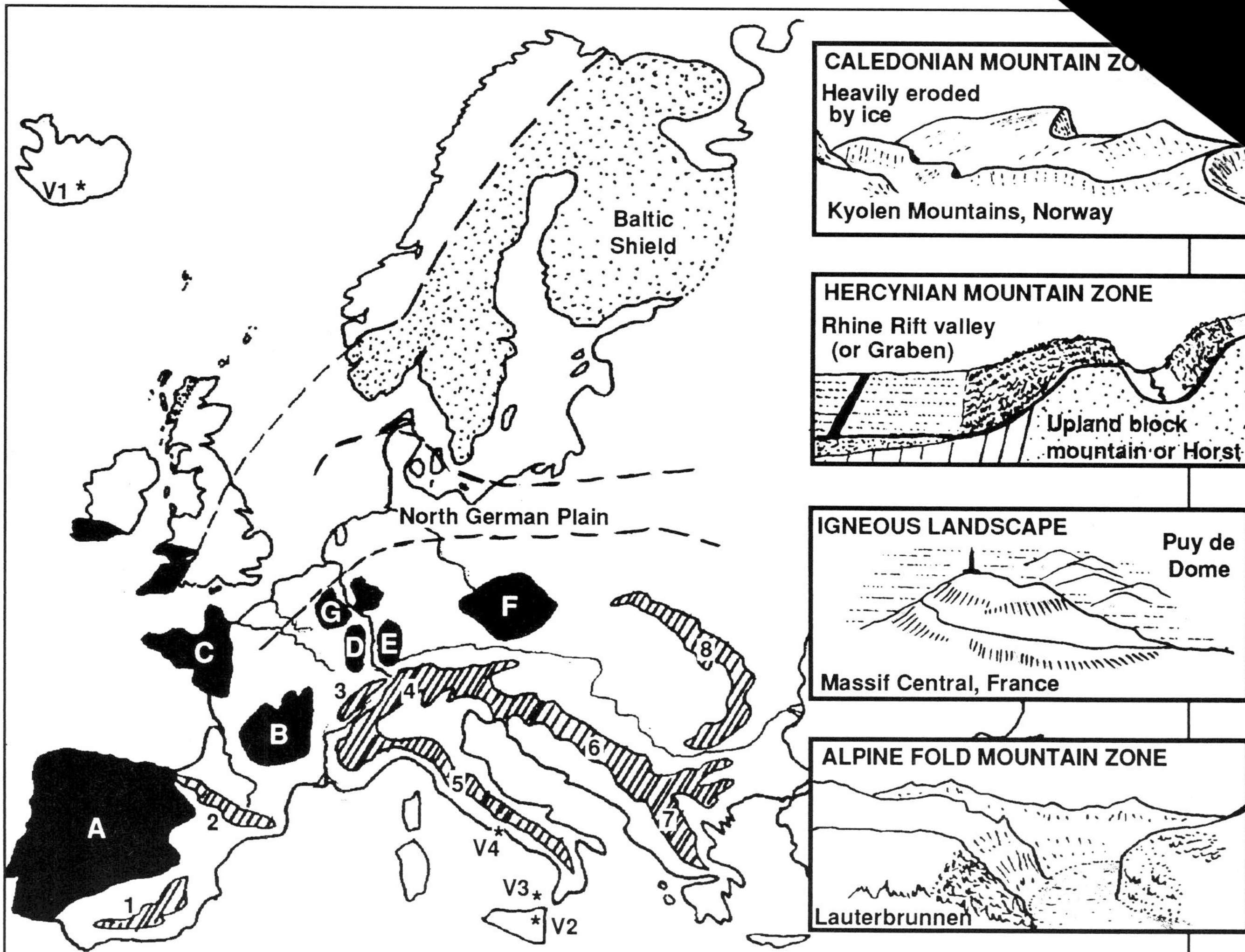

EXPLANATORY KEY TO EUROPE MAP

- **The Baltic Shield** - the oldest part of Europe - a low undulating plain of old, hard metamorphic rocks.
- **The Caledonian Mountain Zone** - the remains of an old mountain chain dating back to 400 million years ago. Now a series of worn down plateaux.
- **The Hercynian Upland Zone** - another mountain building period occured about 280 million years ago. Hercynian Upland areas are a series of low, flat-topped uplands often with steep sides, and faulted or rift valleys.
- **The Alpine Mountain Zone** - Europe's highest mountain scenery formed between 85 and 30 million years ago. Many high areas, eg. the Alps are still being glaciated.
- **The North German Plain** -a sedimentary lowland consisting of an undulating plain of a variety of deposits stretching from the North Sea to Eastern Poland.
- * **Volcanoes**, eg. Mt.Etna, form spectacular mountain scenery along plate boundaries to the North and South of the continent.

Assignment Eleven

1a What is meant by the term physical landscape ?
1b What is a landform ?

2 Make your own copy of fig.53 - the British Isles. Use an atlas to help you complete the following map exercise. Write your answers on the map:
i. Name major fault lines **X, Y** and **Z**.
ii. Name mountain & upland areas **1** to **7**.
iii. Line **A-A** is often used to divide Britain into two zones of physical landscape. What do you think these zones are ?

3 Design a simple system diagram to explain the term isostatic balance.

4 Make your own copy of fig.54
i. Name the Hercynian Uplands **A** to **G**.
ii. Name Alpine mountain areas **1** to **8**.
iii. Name Volcanoes **1** to **4**.
iv. Mark on the map the names of the main rivers Danube, Rhine, Rhone, Seine sea areas Mediterranean, Baltic, North Sea, Bay of Biscay, North Atlantic, Norwegian Sea.

5 Europe has five main physical zones: the Baltic Shield, the Caledonian Mountains, the Hercynian Uplands, the Alpine Mountains and the North German Plain.
Write a brief description of each.

6 What are the main differences and similarities between
i. the Caledonian and Alpine Mountain zones
ii. the Central Lowlands of Scotland and the Rhine Valley ?

CAL LANDSCAPES: Processes

al landscapes are the product of natural processes and are always changing.

Fig.55 Great Langdale, Lake District

Landscape processes

0 — Time — Present day

Landscape **Creating** processes
Crustal movements, mountain building, earthquakes
Tens of millions of years

Landscape **readjustments**
Ice Ages, development of deserts
1-2 million years

Landscape **modifications**
by glaciers, rivers, seas, wind
Thousands of years

Landscape **shaping** processes
weathering, mass movements, human activity
Hundreds of years

Physical landscapes are shaped by a number of **processes** which act on the landscape and cause it to change.

In the photograph above (fig.55) the landscape of the Great Langdale valley consists of a varied geology -different rock types including basalts and tuffs (ash layers) interspersed with granites (fig.56) originally formed over 500 million years ago. Crustal movements, resulting earthquakes, intense glaciation and recent human activity have combined to shape the landscape shown.

It is important to understand that the story of the shaping of any landscape is a never-ending one. The processes operating to shape a landscape include weathering, mass movement, erosion, transportation and deposition and depend on each other.

Weathering - is the small-scale breakdown of rock by physical, chemical and biological processes which produce rock debris known as **regolith** (fig.57).

Mass Movement - the movement of debris or regolith downhill is known as mass movement or **wasting** and occurs at a variety of speeds producing different effects (see fig.58)

Erosion - the removal of rock, soil and minerals carried out by **agents of erosion** which include ice (glaciers), water (rivers, seas), wind, people & animals. Erosion may be classified as Physical or Chemical (fig.59)

Transportation - all agents of erosion carry or transport eroded materials to other areas(fig.59)

Deposition - materials being transported will eventually be dropped or deposited as the agent of erosion loses energy.

All these processes act on a landscape over varying periods of time and at different rates depending on the resistance of the rocks being acted upon. This variation is known as **differential erosion**.

Fig.56 Main Rock Types

ROCKS AND SCENERY

Landscapes and landforms are influenced by the type and structure of rock. The Highlands of Scotland are mainly composed of granite, schist and gneiss - they are harder than the sedimentary rocks which make up most of the Lowlands. Many hills in the Central Lowlands of Scotland (eg. Ochils, Pentlands) are composed of lavas and are harder and more resistant than surrounding rocks. Older rocks tend to be harder than young sedimentary rocks which tend to be soft and easily eroded.

IGNEOUS ROCKS — derived from "Ignis" (Latin) - meaning fire

An **Igneous** rock is made up of material which was once molten. Igneous rocks can be classified into two main types:

Extrusive rocks - lavas & ashes which cool on the surface developing smaller crystal structures. Hard and resistant rocks which include Basalts, Andesites, Obsidian, Pumice and Tuffs (ash).

Intrusive rocks - molten magmas which cool below the surface and develop large-medium crystals. Very hard and resistant rocks which include Granites, Dolerites, Pegmatites, Porphry (giant crystals).

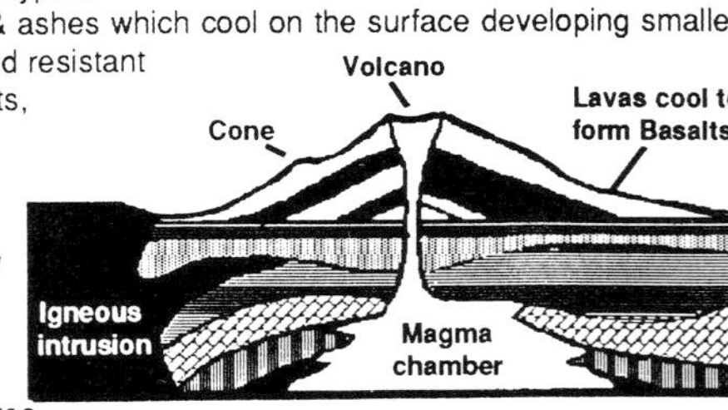

SEDIMENTARY ROCKS — derived from sediment - loose materials

Sedimentary rocks are formed from tiny particles (sediments) which are carried by rivers and are eventually deposited in lakes, seas and oceans. Examples of sedimentary rocks include Limestones(including Chalks), Sandstone, Shales, Coals & Rock Salts.

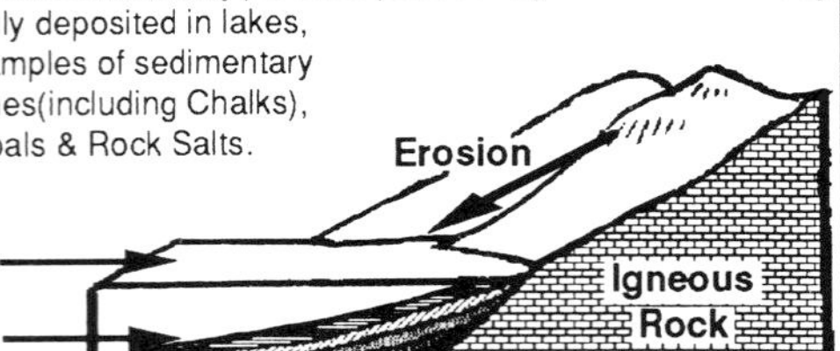

METAMORPHIC ROCKS — meaning change

A **Metamorphic** rock is an existing rock - an igneous, sedimentary or other metamorphic rock - which has been changed either by heat or pressure or both. Often very hard and known as recrystalline, metamorphic rocks include Marble, Quartzite, Schist and Gneiss.

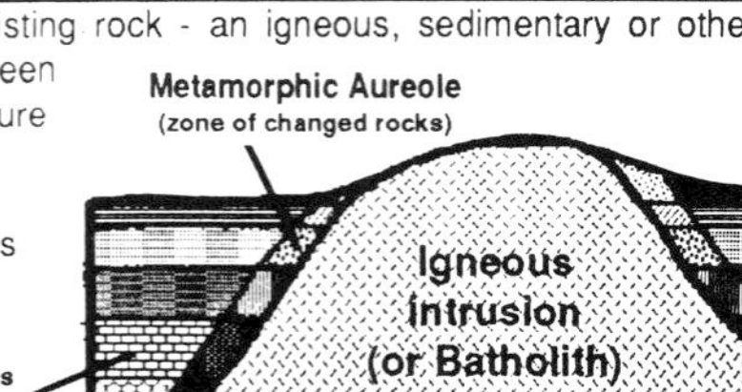

Fig.57 Weathering processes

WEATHERING PROCESSES

PHYSICAL WEATHERING

occurs where physical forces cause rocks to break up into smaller pieces.

FROST-SHATTERING

occurs in high, cold wet areas

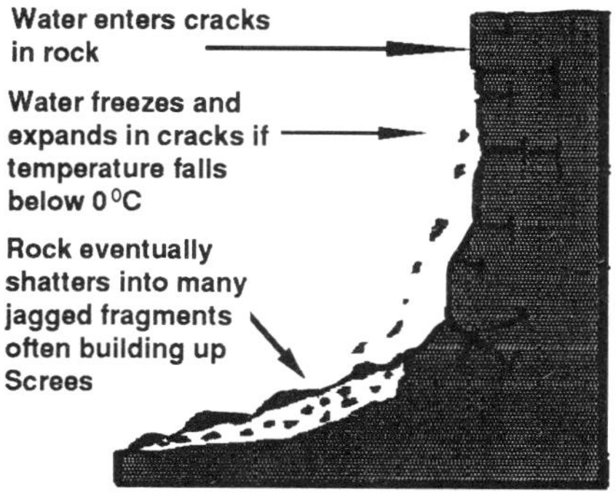

ONION WEATHERING

occurs in areas of high temperatures

CHEMICAL WE

occurs when there is a che

between water or a weak acid

Rainwater is a weak Carbonic acid which dissolves Calcium Carbonate($CaCO_3$)

Limestones consist of $CaCO_3$) and are dissolved slowly to form Limestone Pavements of clints & grykes(photo)

If a soil cover exists this process of chemical weathering is more effective

MASS MOVEMENT

is the name given to the movement of weathered material downhill and includes:

ROCKFALL

Broken rock falling downslope usually very suddenly and quickly. The material collects at the foot of the slope and is known as a talus (eg. a scree slope).

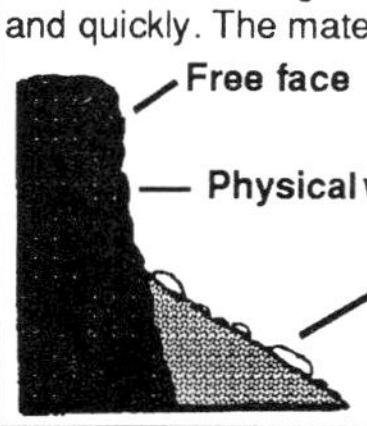

LANDSLIDE

Rapid movements of soil or rock on less steep slopes. Slides usually occur after heavy rain or snowmelt.

MUDFLOW

A flow of saturated materials downslope usually after torrential rainfall and in areas of sparse vegetation. They are deeper than slides and resemble the flow of a stream.

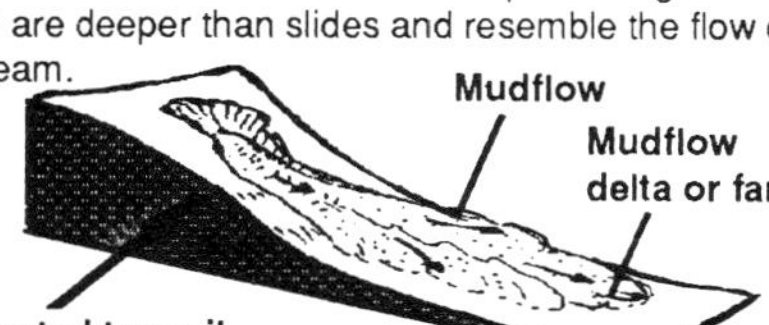

SOIL CREEP

A very slow process in which saturated soil expands at right angles to the slope. As the soil dries out it contracts in a vertical direction - the result is a creeping, downward movement.

Where soil cover or vegetation is removed the rate of creep is greatly increased.

Fig.58 Mass Movement

THE CYCLE OF EROSION

the processes which combine to shape the landscape

The **Cycle of Erosion** is the combination of the processes which operate on any landscape and takes place in 5 stages:

WEATHERING processes small scale decay of rock surfaces

MASS MOVEMENT movement downslope of weathered materials or regolith

EROSION processes - the removal of rock, soil and minerals by agents of erosion

TRANSPORTATION processes - the carrying of eroded materials to other areas, usually downhill

DEPOSITION processes - the dumping of eroded materials in river valleys, lake beds, on sea-floors, etc

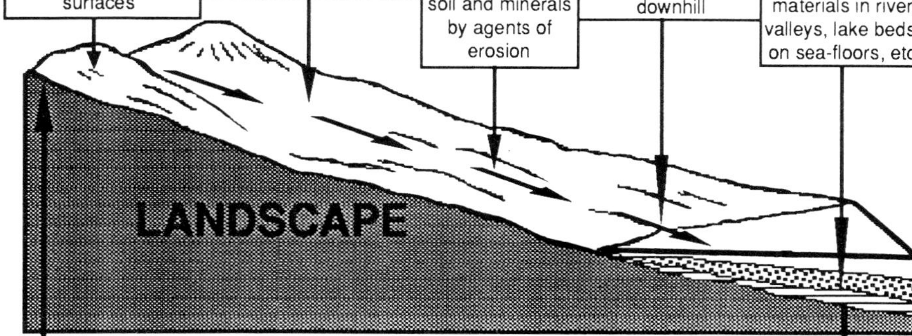

All physical landscapes have been formed by either erosion processes or deposition processes or a combination of both. The Cycle of Erosion above shows that physical landscapes are always changing. Humans often interfere with the cycle of erosion through actions which can speed up or slow down the processes involved.

Fig.59 The Cycle of Erosion

Assignment Twelve

1 Make your own study notes to help you revise the main Rock Types using the information provided in section 15.

2 Explain the link between rock type and scenery.

3 Write full definitions (with illustrations) for each of the following terms: Weathering, Mass Movement, Regolith, Talus, Scree, Erosion, Transportation, Deposition.

4 Name the weathering processes responsible for the following:
   i. Pot holes in roads in winter
   ii. Wearing away of statues in city centres
   iii. CO_2 in rainwater dissolving $CaCO_3$
   iv. Piles of sharp-edged rocks at the base of a high mountain in cold areas
   v. Rocks heard to crack with a noise like a pistol shot in a desert area

5 Research and then give examples of biological types of weathering.

6 Arrange the main types of Mass Movement in terms of
   i. Speed ii. Scale

7a Make your own copy of the Cycle of Erosion.

7b Give examples of the ways in which humans interfere with the processes involved.

ATED LANDSCAPES: *Erosion*

landscapes are the product of natural processes and are always changing.

Fig.60 The Mer de Glace, near Chamonix, France

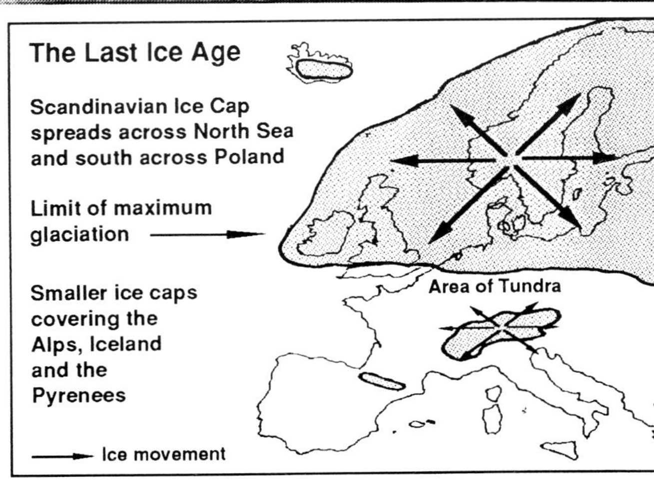

Fig.61 European 20,000 years ago

The climate of much of Europe, including the British Isles, over the last 2.5 million years has been cold enough to support the spread of ice sheets. Experts believe that there is evidence of as many as 20 different glaciations. The last major (**Pleistocene**) Ice Age ended about 10,000 years ago - although there are areas in the Alps where glaciers still exist (Figs 60-61). The ice advanced in sheets from mountainous areas such as Scandinavia and the Alps in colder periods known as **glacials**. As the climate warmed, the ice retreated in periods known as **interglacials**. The bad news is that it is thought that we are living through a short interglacial period and that the ice will return in about 3,000 years time !

Massive quantities of snow and ice built up at the beginning of each cold period. For millions of years, heavy snowfalls accumulated to impressive depths across large tracts of Northern Europe. Geologists believe that the scenery of much of the British Isles would have resembled that of present day Greenland: huge areas of ice covering all but the highest mountain tops. The majority of Northern Europe lay under hundreds of metres of ice. Even mountains such as Ben Nevis and Cairn Gorm lay buried by over 300 metres of ice just 15,000 years ago.

Underneath the ice, the landscape was slowly being shaped by the tremendous weight and erosive power of ice. Existing river valleys were gouged and deepened leaving U-shaped valleys after the ice retreated (Fig.62).

Fig.62 Ice erosion processes

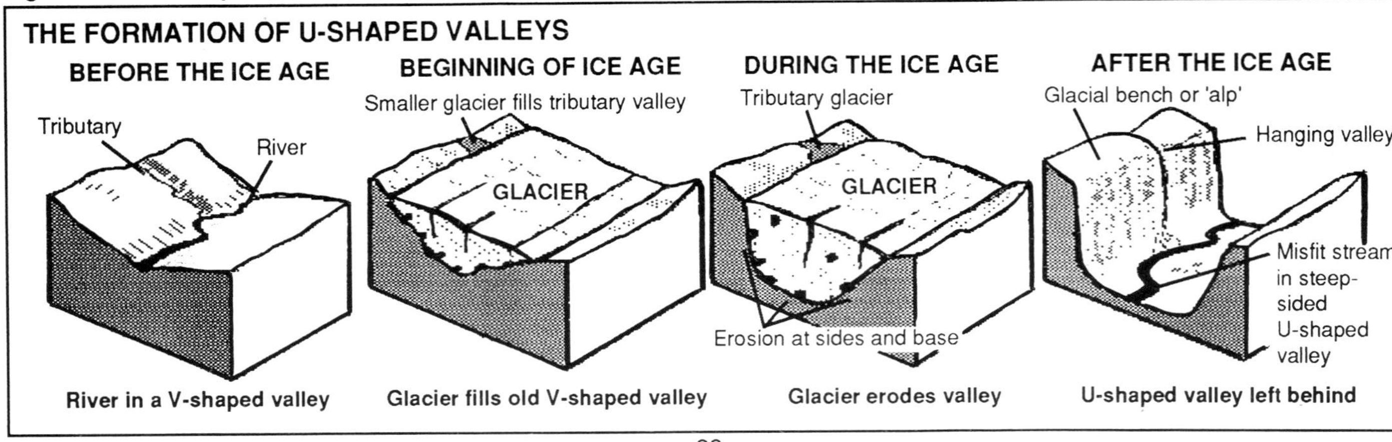

Fig.63 Mountain glaciers

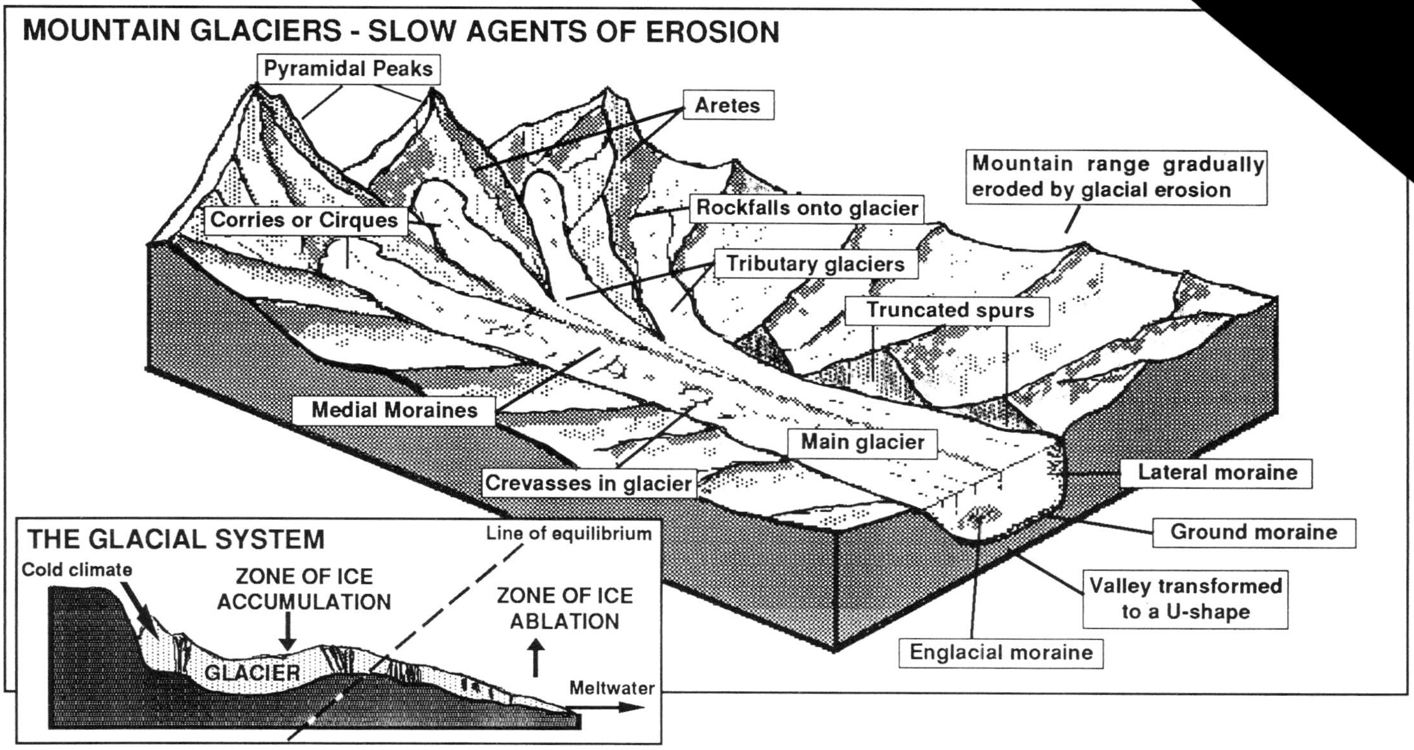

Glaciers, ice sheets confined to valleys, behave as a **system** (Fig.63). **Inputs** to the glacier include snow (falling as precipitation or from avalanches above), rocks falling onto its surface and rock fragments frozen into its base. **Processes** include transportation as the glacier carries rock fragments, water and ice downhill. Erosion processes include **plucking** (underlying rock becomes frozen into the base of the glacier and is torn away as the glacier moves downhill), and **abrasion** (rock embedded in the ice grinds away at solid bedrock). As a result, the glacier may leave scratches or **striations** in bedrock beneath it. Frost-shattering above the glacier supplies rock fragments to the glacial system. **Outputs** from the system include water (as either meltwater or as water vapour, rock debris and ice trapped in hollows.

Where inputs exceed outputs, **accumulation** occurs and the glacier advances. **Ablation** occurs where there is an increase in temperature and the glacier (retreats) melts. As melting occurs, massive amounts of meltwater become a major agent of erosion, shaping the landscape. As a result of the glacial system, distinctive landforms are produced and spectacular scenery created (Figs.64-65).Mountain ranges are lowered. Glacial troughs are left behind, showing the scars of glacial erosion in the form of truncated spurs and corries. Moraines (debris excavated and transported by ice) are deposited on valley floors.
Landscapes produced by ice are complicated since landforms created by one advance of ice may be wiped away by the next one.

Fig.64 After the ice has gone - the Lauterbrunnen Valley

UNTAIN LANDSCAPE

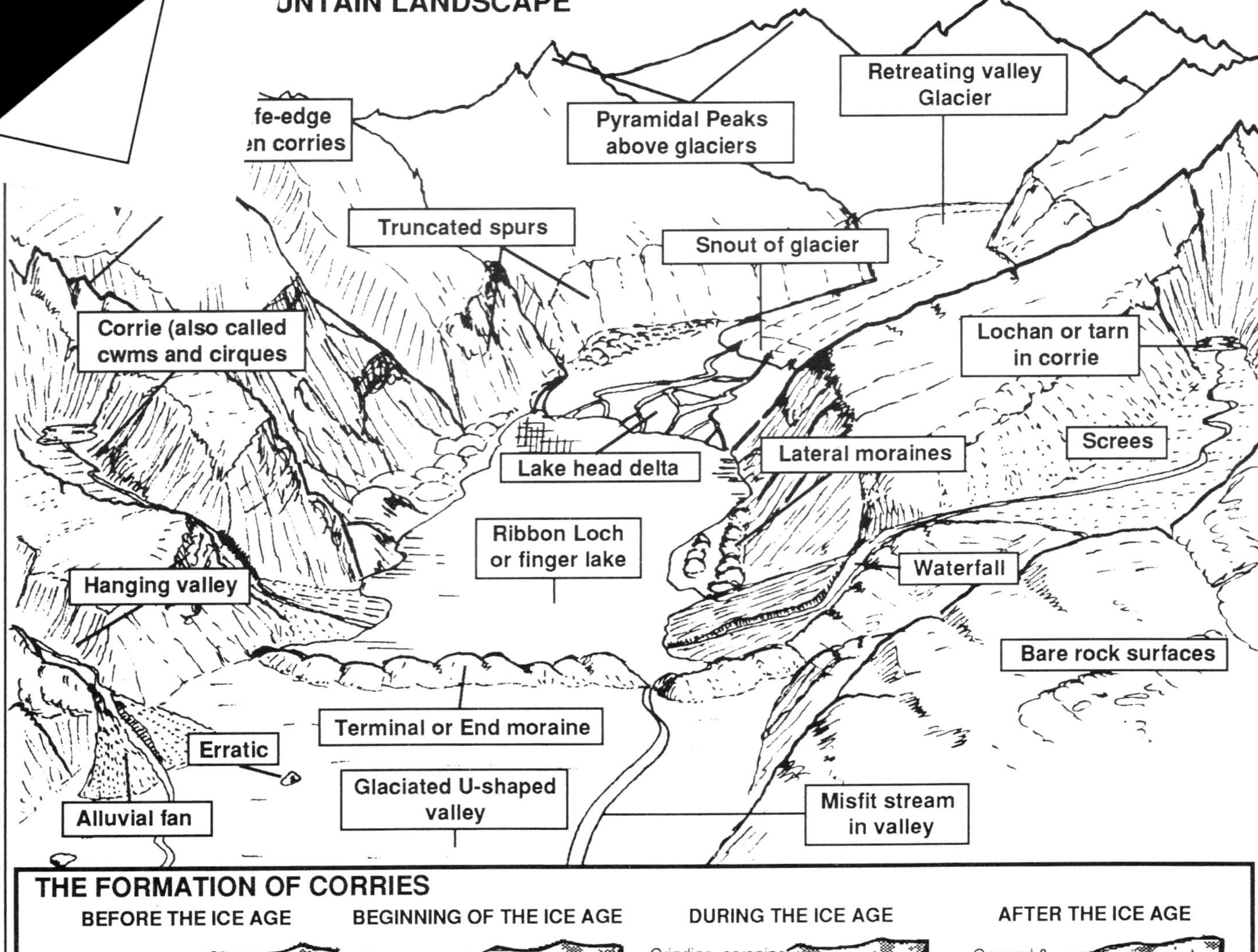

THE FORMATION OF CORRIES

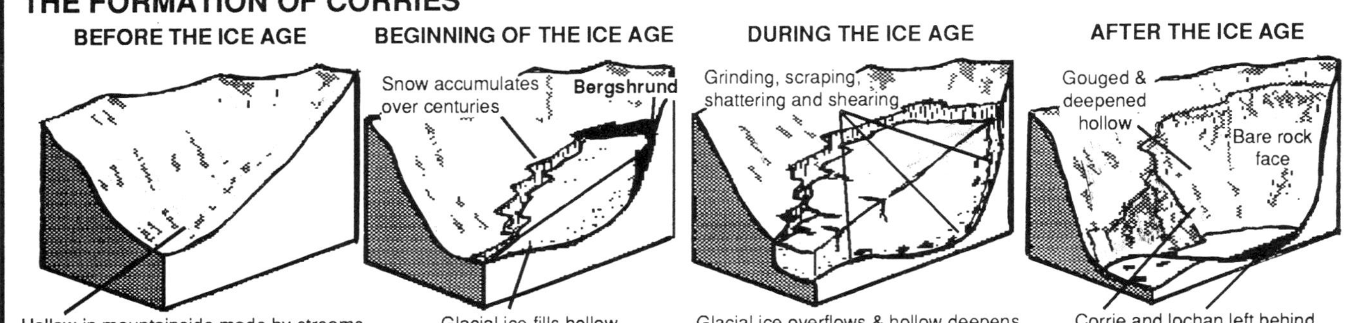

Fig.66

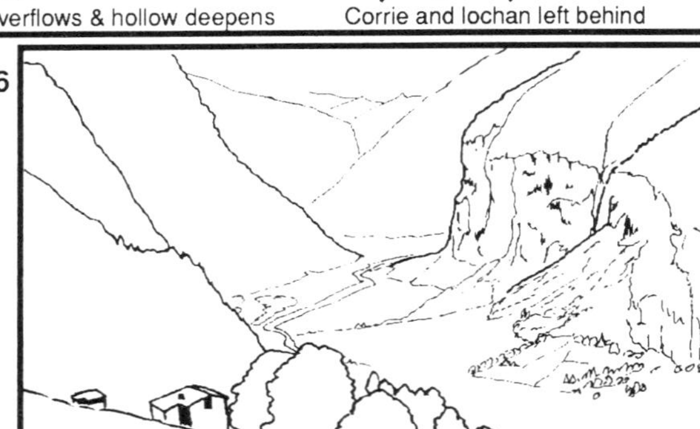

Assignment Thirteen

1 Using an atlas, name two glaciated upland areas found in:
Switzerland, Scandinavia, The British Isles.

2 Write full definitions for each of the following terms: Pleistocene, glacial, interglacial, ice sheet, glacier, ice ablation, ice accumulation, moraine.

3 Design your own diagram to help you explain the glacial system.

4 Which factors influence the rate of glaciation of an area ?

5 Draw a labelled diagram of a valley glacier.

6 Describe in your own words the processes by which glaciers act as agents of erosion.

6 Label a larger copy of Fig.66 - the Lauterbrunnen Valley to show evidence of glaciation (use fig 64 to help you).

7 Describe the glaciated mountain landscape shown in Fig.65.

8 Describe the likely distribution of tourists and tourist-related developments in the area shown in Fig.65.

9 Explain using simple diagrams the formation of **two** of the following glacial landforms:
U-shaped valleys, Corries, Aretes, Truncated spurs.

17. GLACIATED LANDSCAPES: Deposition

Key Idea: Physical landscapes are the product of natural processes and are always changing.

Glaciers are able to transport huge quantities of materials (rock debris). The debris can be carried in three ways:-

Subglacial debris - moved along the floor of the valley either by ice (as ground moraine) or by meltwater streams **under** the glacier.

Englacial debris - carried **within the glacier** itself.

Supraglacial debris - carried **on the surface** of the glacier.

The collective name for all the materials (boulders, sands, gravels, clays, etc) deposited by glaciers is **drift**. These deposits can be classified into:-

Ground moraine (or **till**) including unsorted materials directly deposited by ice.

Fluvioglacial materials (or **outwash**) - including sorted materials deposited by meltwater streams.
Fluvioglacial deposits also include materials originally deposited by the ice and later picked up and redeposited by meltwater. Materials deposited by water are **sorted into layers** as deposition occurs - the heaviest debris being deposited first (at the bottom) and the lightest debris deposited last (at the top).

Landscapes produced by glacial deposition are very complex. Melting ice deposits moraine mainly at the ends and edges of retreating glaciers (fig.67). The later advances of ice (remember there have been as many as 20 Ice Ages affecting the British Isles) steamroller and bulldoze the earlier glacial deposits, reshape and redeposit them in new areas.
Glacial deposition takes place in two main ways:-

a. Debris carried in and on the ice is dumped on the surface of the land as the ice melts. The debris is unsorted with all sizes of rocks, stones and fine fragments mixed up and left on the surface. This material is known as ground moraine (or till) and it often contains evidence to indicate the main direction of ice flow. Elongated boulders are often left with their long-axes pointing in the ice movement direction.

b. As the ice melts, outflowing streams of meltwater flowing from the snout of the glacier carry away rock debris. The streams deposit this material, mainly sands and gravels, across the floor of U-shaped valleys. This fluvioglacial material is sorted - arranged in layers - as it is deposited.

Landforms characteristic of glacial deposition can therefore be classified as either those deposited by ice (glacial) or those deposited by meltwater (fluvioglacial) (Fig.70).

Fig.67 Deposition by ice

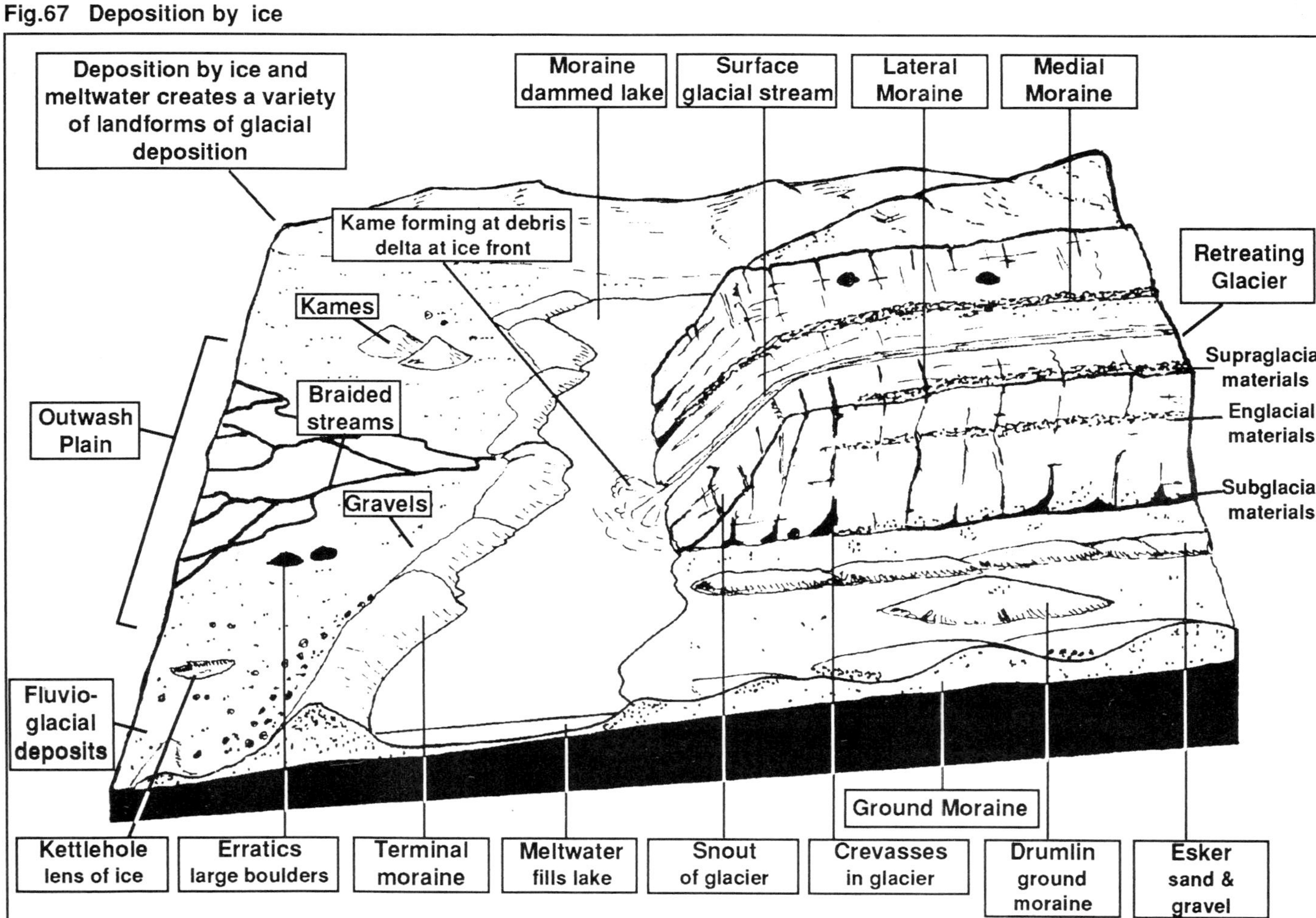

Features of glacial deposition include:-

Erratics are boulders transported by glaciers, often for many kilometres (fig.68). Boulders can be carried either inside the ice or on the glacier surface. Very often the erratic is of a different rock type to that of the area in which it is deposited.

Moraines, unsorted materials deposited by melting glaciers are of three main types:

Terminal or end moraine is often a high, narrow mound extending across a valley floor. The terminal moraine is deposited at right-angles to the direction of ice movement and mark the furthest extent of the advance of the ice.

Lateral moraine is debris dumped along the sides of a glaciated valley in the form of an embankment or hummocky ridges.

Medial moraine is usually found in the centre of a glaciated valley as hummocky ridge. Medial moraines are formed as a result of the merging of two lateral moraines where two glaciers meet.

Drumlins are smooth, elongated mounds of ground moraine or till which has been deposited by the ice but shaped while the ice was still moving (fig.69). The long axis of a drumlin lies parallel to the direction of ice movement.

Drumlins occur in groups or swarms and may be over 50 metres in height .

Features of Fluvioglacial deposition include:

Outwash plains are composed of gravels, sands and clays. These materials are deposited by meltwater streams during summer or when the glacier melts. Often up to 70 metres deep, outwash may be deposited on top of ground moraine following the retreat of a glacier (fig.71).

Fig.68 Slate boulder deposited on top of limestone

Fig.69 Forested drumlin in glacial lowland

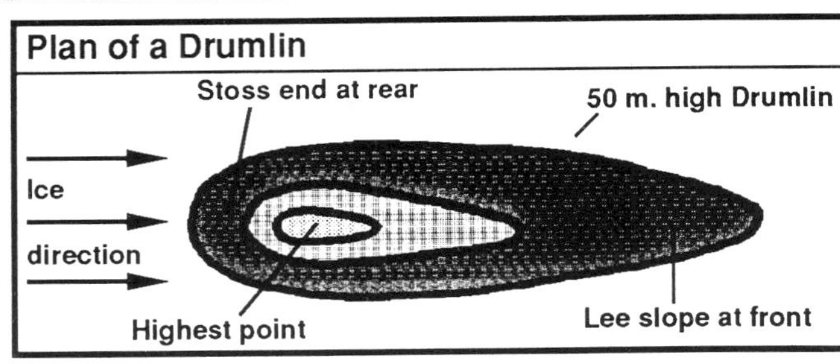

Fig.70 Depositional features and formation.

Deposition Feature	Description	Formation of Feature
Boulder clay or Till or Ground Moraine	Unsorted materials distributed across a valley. Stones often at an angle with long axes indicating ice direction.	Mainly unsorted subglacial materials deposited by melting glaciers.
Terminal moraine	A narrow ridge of unsorted materials extending across a valley.	Mounds of boulders deposited at the maximum advance of the ice.
Medial moraine	Mounds of material carried in the centre of a glacier.	Formed by the joining of two lateral moraines.
Lateral moraine	Unsorted materials found along the sides of glaciers and glaciated valleys.	Materials found along the sides of a glacier or a valley as a result of frost-shattering above.
Erratic	Rocks which are not normally found in the area in they are deposited.	Rocks transported by glaciers from their source to an area of different rock.
Drumlins	Streamlined, elongated mounds of unsorted materials with a steep end facing up the valley.	Till is deposited and shaped by still moving ice.
Esker	Long, narrow sinuous ridges of unsorted materials crossing valley floors.	Material deposited by a subglacial stream.
Kame	Mounds of sorted materials deposited by meltwater across a valley or a delta in lakes at the edge of the ice	Material deposited where meltwater streams are in contact with ice.
Kettle-holes	Small shallow lakes containing sorted materials.	Dead ice surrounded by sand and gravel melts and forms a small lake.
Outwash Plain	Sorted deposits of sands, gravels and clays spread over a valley floor.	Meltwater streams deposit materials across a wide and low lying valley floor.
Moraine-dammed Lake	Shallow lake formed where a moraine dams a river.	Terminal moraine blocks the natural course of a river in a U-shaped valley.
Fluvioglacial deposits	Sorted materials or outwash (sands, gravels, clays).	Sands and gravels deposited by meltwater
Meltwater Channel	Shallow valley - often a dry valley today.	Valley carved by the erosive power of meltwater as a glacier retreats.

Fig.71

Eskers are low, narrow, sinuous ridges composed of sorted coarse sands and gravels. Eskers are thought to be the deposited courses of subglacial streams.
Kames are undulating mounds of sorted debris, sands and gravels washed into crevasses in stagnant ice. As the ice melts the debris is deposited on the ground. Kames may also be formed by the build up of deltas in lakes at the ice front (Fig.67).
Kettleholes form where a block of ice is detached from a glacier as it retreats. The kettlehole may be partly buried by fluvioglacial deposits left by meltwater streams. When the ice block melts it leaves an enclosed hollow which often fills with water to form a kettlehole lake.
Kames and kettleholes are often found in the same depositional areas and give rise to the phrase 'kame and kettle' topography.
Braided streams form where channels of meltwater become clogged by coarse deposits, encouraging the stream to braid or divide in smaller streams.
Meltwater streams can be very powerful depending on the season or the rate of ice decay. Many meltwater streams are powerful enough to erode their own valleys. In some upland areas such as the Bathgate Hills in West Lothian, Scotland, streams from retreating glaciers not only carved their own channels (known as **meltwater channels**) but were powerful enough to flow uphill and over obstacles to their path.
On a wider scale, Europe's most fertile deposit is wind blown **loess**. The loess results from strong winds blowing at the end of the last Ice Age, picking up fine particles from glacial and fluvioglacial deposits. Large areas of northern France, Germany and Poland are blanketed with up to 20 metres depth of loess forming some of Europe's most fertile agricultural areas.

In summary, glacial erosion and deposition can affect both upland and lowland areas, creating landscapes of varying use to people in the glaciated areas of the British Isles and Europe.

Assignment Fourteen

1 In which ways are landforms produced by glacial deposition ?

2 Make your own simple copy of Fig.67 and add labels to each of the features of glacial deposition.

3 Study Fig.68.
   a. Which deposition feature is shown here ?
   b. Explain why it could not be the remains of a layer of rock eroded above the limestone below.

4 Study Fig.69. Explain how the landform has formed.

5 What are the differences between englacial, supraglacial and subglacial materials ?

6 Write full definitions of each of the following:-
   Esker, lateral moraine, outwash, kettleholes, Loess.

7 Label a larger copy of the sketch below (based on Fig.71) to describe the differences between the types of deposit shown.

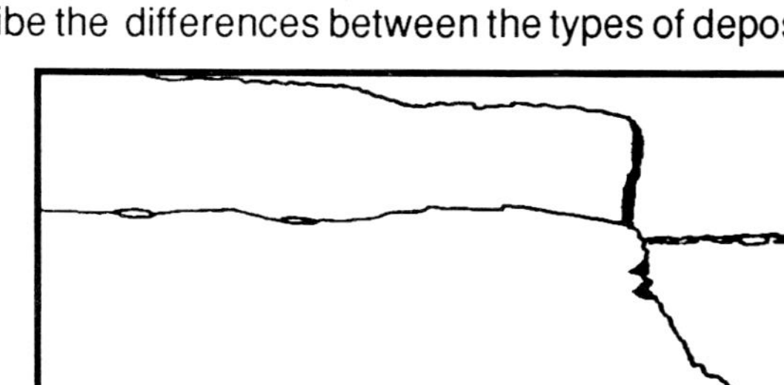

8 Classify the features of glacial deposition listed in Figs.67 & 70 as either:
   Stratified (sorted) or
   Unstratified (unsorted) or
   Water features.

9 Make a list of glaciated landforms useful to people.

18. RIVER LANDSCAPES: Water Movement

Key Idea: Physical landscapes are the product of natural processes and are always changing.

Fig.72 The Hydrological Cycle

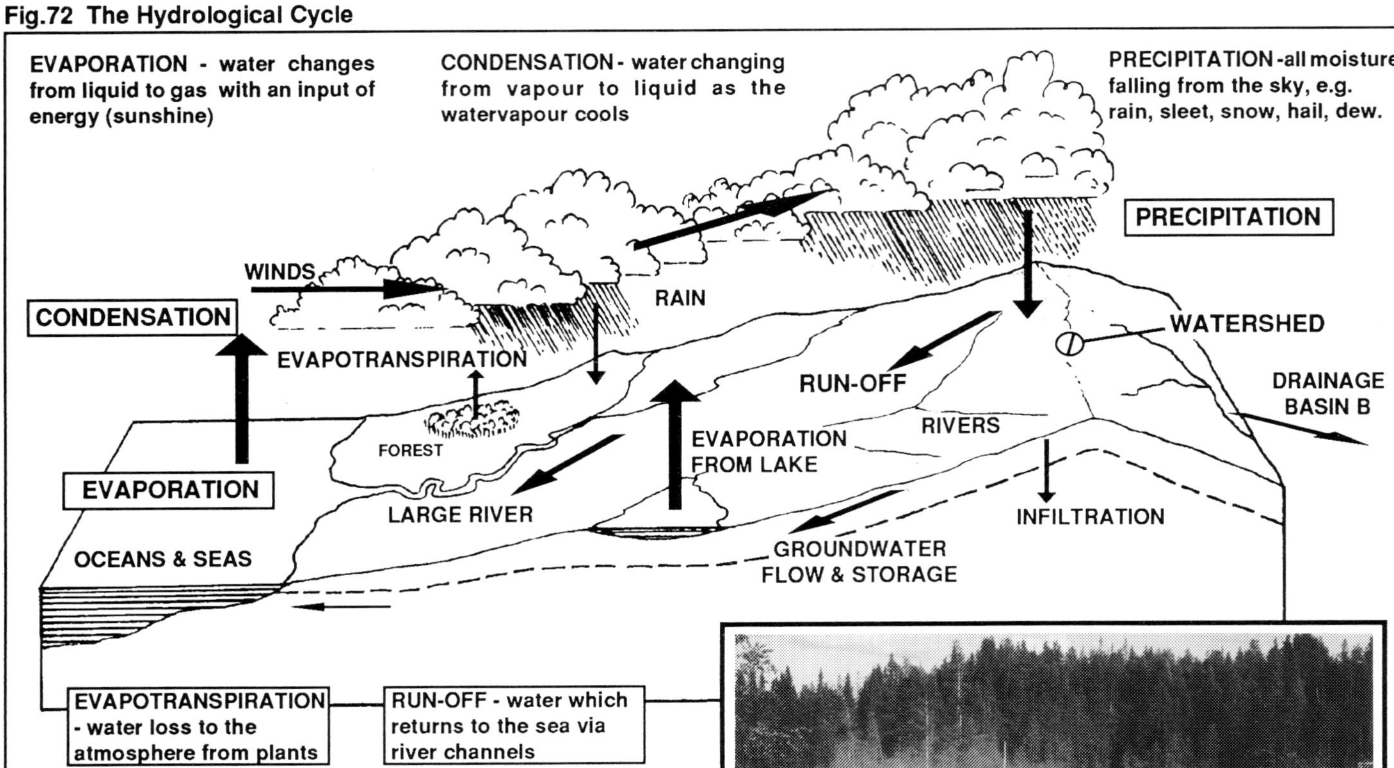

The water or **Hydrological Cycle** is another example of a **system** (with Inputs, Processes and Outputs) this time linking land, water and atmosphere (Fig.72).

Warm air passing over large water areas picks up water vapour or moisture by **evaporation**. As warm, moist air moves inland, pushed by the wind, it is forced to rise over higher land. As it does so, the air cools and the water vapour condenses, forming clouds. Some of the moisture will be dropped as **precipitation** - all forms of moisture which fall from the sky.

Three results are possible as precipitation falls to the ground:

a. It may evaporate - returning to the air.
b. It may soak into the ground due to the **permeability** of the local rock (ability to allow water to pass through it).
c. It may run-off to join a stream or river and perhaps flow back into the sea again.

Water that soaks into the ground may soak in deep down (**infiltration**) or may remain near the ground surface re-emerging later as a spring (**storage**). Surface water will flow into a stream and then into a river (Fig.73). Rivers flow into lakes or back into the sea and in so doing are powerful agents of erosion, responsible for shaping scenery; eroding, transporting and depositing rock debris in other areas constantly (Figs. 74-77).

Examples of the movement of water within the cycle include rivers, ocean currents, winds (carrying clouds), evaporation, evapotranspiration (from vegetation), run-off, infiltration and precipitation.

Fig.73 Water power
Fig.74 The main rivers of the UK.

THE MAIN RIVERS OF THE UNITED KINGDOM

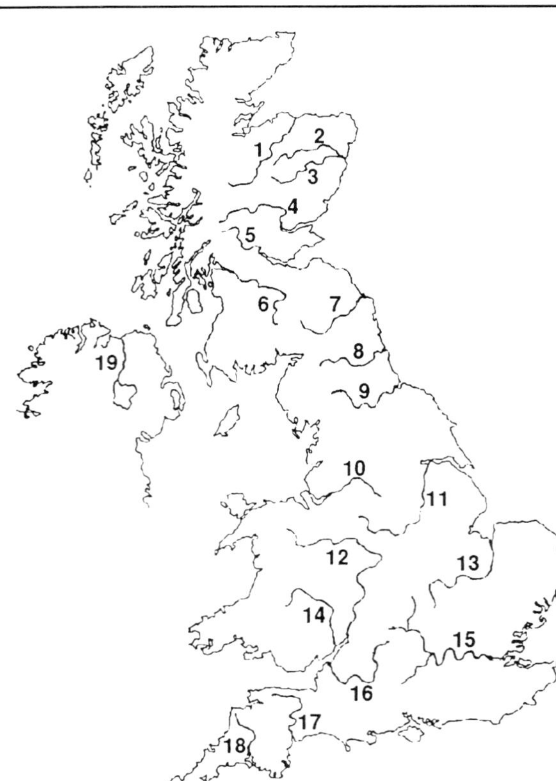

Fig.75

A LONG PROFILE OF A RIVER

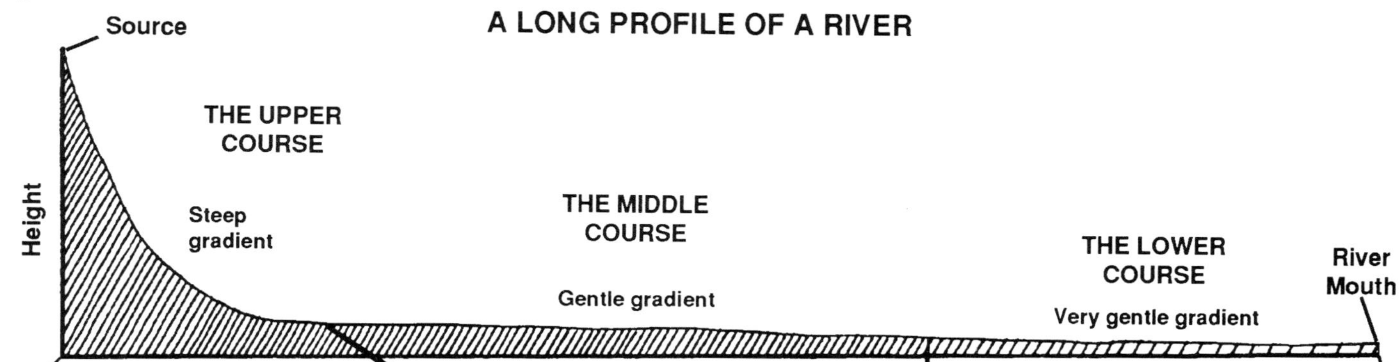

The Upper Course

Many small tributaries or hillside 'burns' cut straight down into the landscape. Vertical erosion takes place.

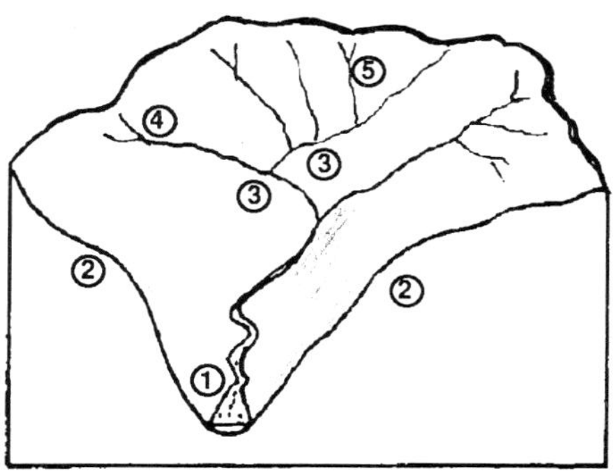

The river has no floodplain:

1 Narrow river flowing like a torrent, through boulders.
2 Steep, V-shaped valley sides right down to the riverside.
3 Interlocking spurs.
4 Many tributaries feeding into the main river.
5 Waterfalls and rapids common

The Middle Course

As the volume of water increases in the river, lateral (sideways) erosion begins to take place.

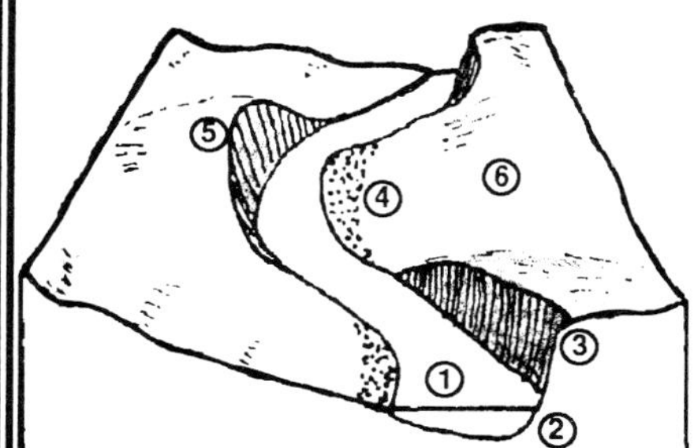

The river has a floodplain on one side:

1 The river flows fastest on the outside of a meander.
2 The river is deepest on the outside bend.
3 The riverbank is undercut by a strong current creating river cliffs.
4 Mud, silt and sand are deposited by slower water on the inside of the bend.
5 Steep valley slope.
6 Gentle slope of valley.

The Lower Course

The river meanders across a wide floodplain formed from silts, mud, gravels and sands deposited by the river.

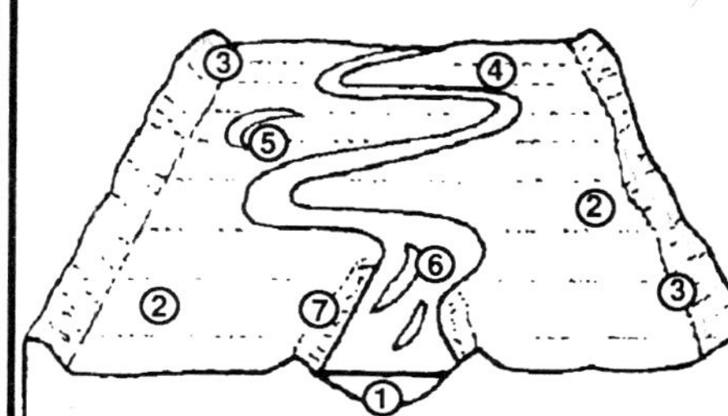

The river has a floodplain on both sides:

1 A wide river flowing down a very gentle gradient.
2 Wide flood plain on both sides of main river.
3 River bluffs indicate edge of floodplain.
4 Large meanders common in the lower course.
5 Ox-bow lake in abandoned river channel.
6 Eyots (silty islands in the river), show that river braiding is taking place.
7 Levees (raised river embankments) form during floods.

Fig.76 Features of river valleys

Rivers as agents of erosion and deposition use water power to carry out their task of modifying the landscape. The amount of water in a river is called its **volume**. A river's volume and speed generate **energy** which the river uses to erode the landscape. The velocity (or speed) of the flow of water is directly proportional to the degree of erosion and is determined by the gradient of the slope down which the river flows.

The idealised river (Fig.75) profile can be classified as having three main sections - The **Upper**, **Middle** and **Lower** courses, each with its own characteristic features (Fig.76). Other interconnected factors which influence the rate of erosion and/or deposition include **climate** (amount and distribution of annual precipitation), **Rock structure** and **type**, and **vegetation** (plants may help bind the soil together and stabilise the soil along the valley sides).

All rivers have a **source** (a starting point, - a marsh, a melting glacier, a lake, etc) and a **mouth** where they enter the sea or ocean, join a lake or sink underground.

The hydraulic force of the water is not enough on its own to create massive erosion. Rivers carry a **load** which acts like teeth, wearing and tearing away at the banks and river bed (Fig.77). Rivers in **spate** (or flood) carry out their tasks at an increased rate, often carving new channels and changing their course in a very short space of time.

Fig.77 Rivers are powerful agents of erosion

Fig.78 River processes

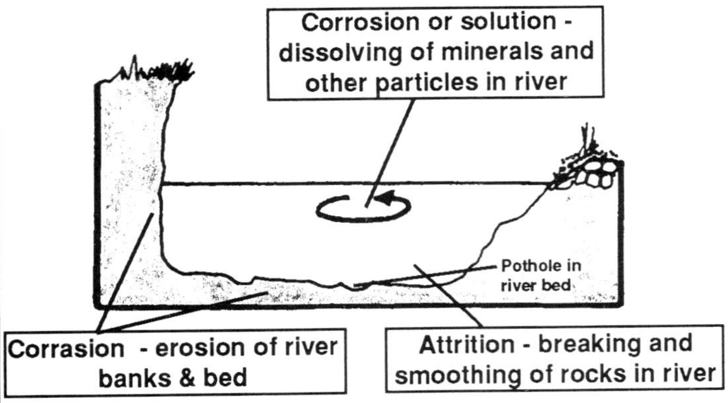

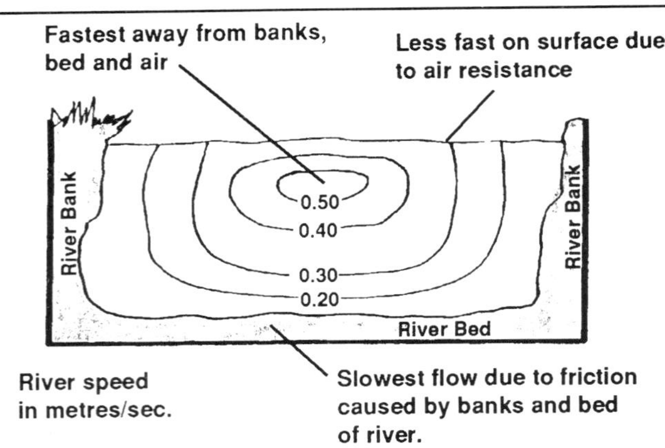

There are four main processes of river erosion.

Hydraulic action or the sheer force of the water as the current hits river banks. Where the river is straight the point of maximum velocity may be found in midstream (Fig.78). But where a river flows around a meander, water is forced into cracks and any existing air within them is compressed. Pressure is increased and the bank may collapse.

Solution or corrosion occurs continuously and is influenced by the acidity level of the water and the local geology & soil cover.

Corrasion occurs where a river picks up material and uses it to abrade (sandpaper) its banks and river bed. Most effective during spate periods, corrasion also leads to the formation of potholes in river beds (Fig.79). Pebbles caught in the hollows in the river bed swirl around, grinding holes into the river bed.

Attrition occurs where the materials in the river bed (called the **bedload**) collide with each other and break into smaller fragments. In time, the angular fragments become smaller and rounder as they are transported downstream.

Fig.79 Potholes in a river bed.

Fig.80 River transportation processes.

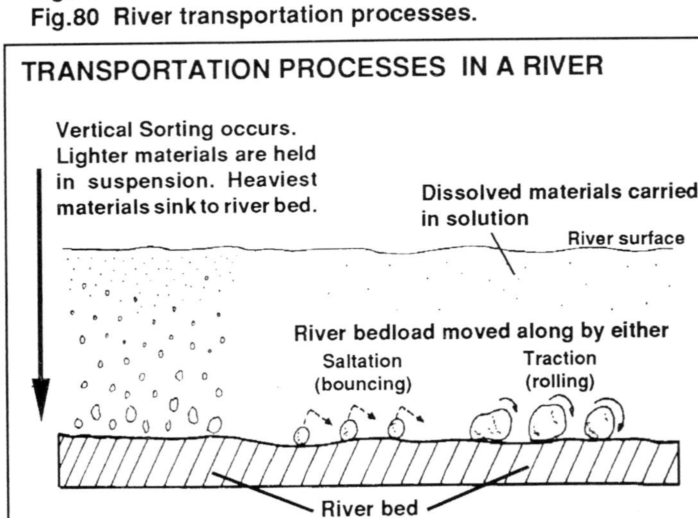

As rivers transport their load downstream, the banks and bed together with the rock debris are eroded and used in the erosion processes (Fig.80). Rivers create many spectacular features - the most famous of which are waterfalls such as Niagara Falls. **Waterfalls** form where a river flows across a resistant layer of rock and fall onto a layer of softer rock below (Fig.81). The underlying layer of rock is eroded as water and bedload falls onto it. This creates a plunge pool and an overhang which eventually collapses. In this way a waterfall retreats upstream.

Fig.81 Formation of waterfalls

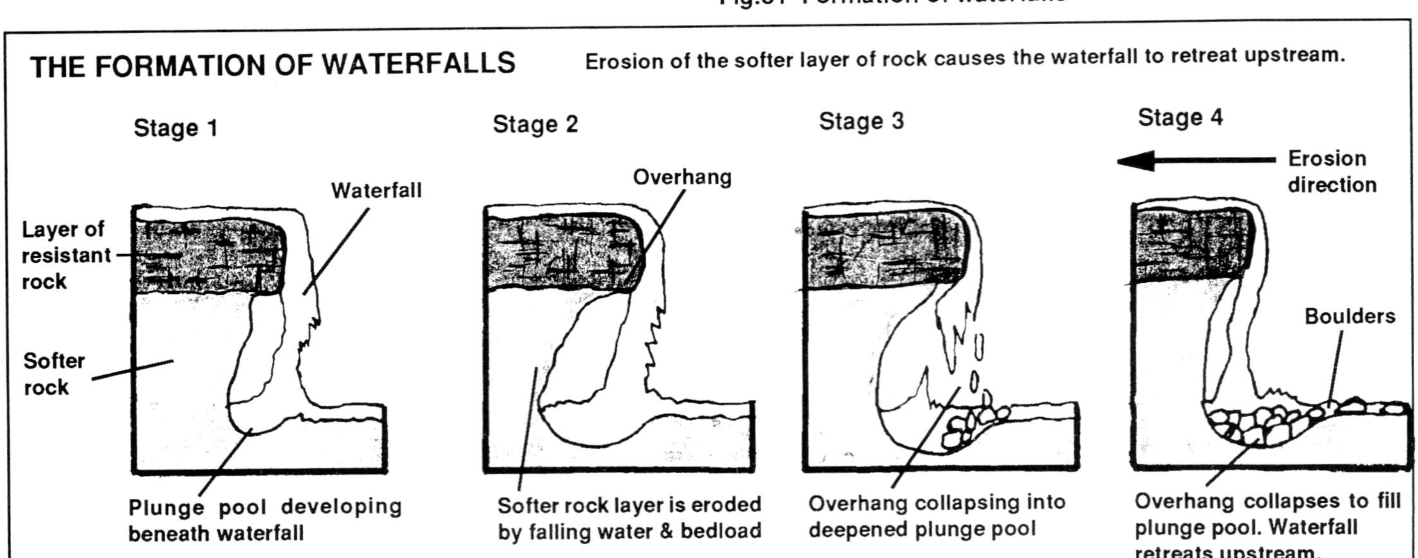

Fig.82
River
Meander

Fig.83
Stages in
Meander
formation

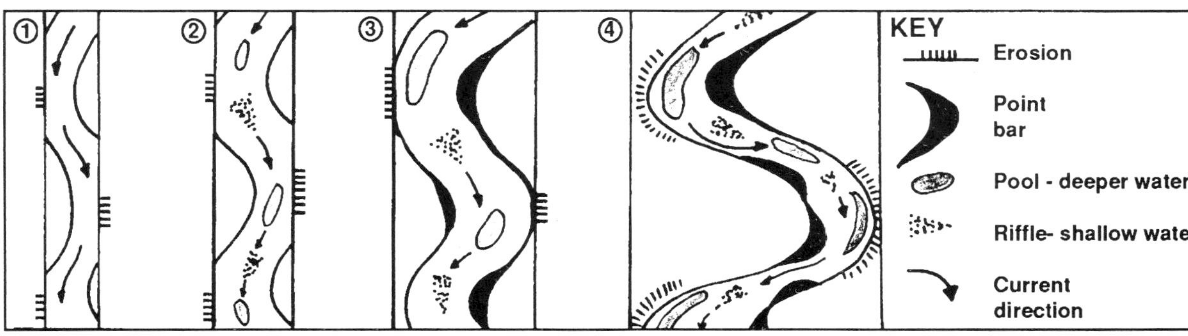

As the velocity of a river decreases it loses its capacity to carry all of its load. Deposition then occurs, starting with the largest materials. Deposition occurs where:-

a. A river widens and **meanders** as it begins to cross a break of slope or a flood plain (Figs.82 & 83)
b. A river enters the sea or a lake
c. A period of low precipitation is experienced.

Vertical erosion caused by a river in the upper course gives way to **lateral erosion** in the middle and lower courses. Ox-bow lakes form at large meanders where erosion undercuts the outside bank and shallow water aids deposition on the inside bank of a river (Fig.84).

Fig.84 Stages 1 & 2 of the formation of an Ox-bow lake

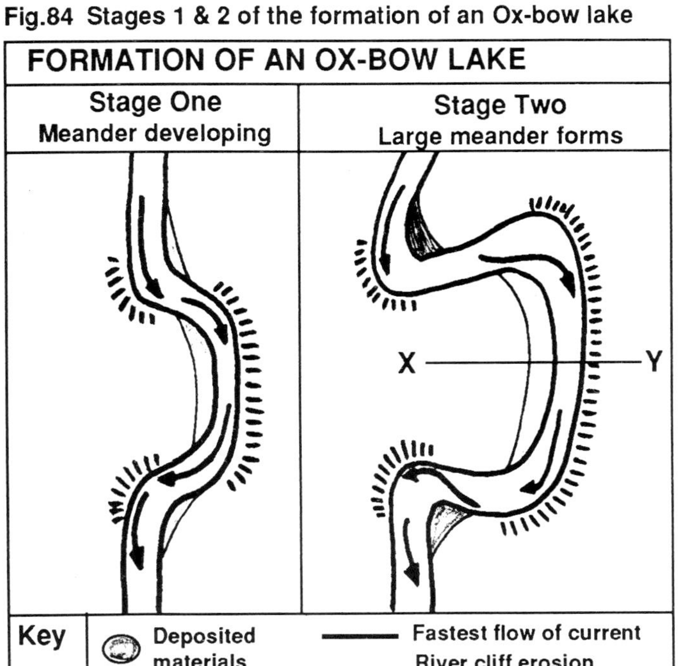

Assignment Fifteen

1a Make a simple copy of Fig.72 to illustrate the system called the Hydrological Cycle.
1b List the inputs, processes and outputs to this system.

2 Write definitions of each of the following terms:- Watershed, Precipitation, Run-off, infiltration, storage.

3 Using an atlas, make a key to Fig.74 -naming rivers 1-19.

4a Give examples of water storage other than groundwater.
4b Give examples of water movement.

5a Describe, using simple diagrams, the features of a river in its Upper, Middle and Lower courses.
5b Describe at least four changes in a river as it flows downstream.

6 Is the river in Fig.77 in its upper, middle or lower course ? Justify your answer.

7a Describe the ways in which a river erodes.
7b Explain why a river's load increases in amount but decreases in size as it flows downstream.

8 **Either** Explain the formation any **two** of the following river features: meander, waterfall, floodplain **or** Complete the diagrams (Fig.84) to illustrate the formation of an Ox-bow lake.

9 Explain the difference between vertical and lateral erosion.

10 Make a simple annotated fieldsketch of Fig.82 to describe the main features of a river meander.

19. EXAM STYLE QUESTIONS

PHYSICAL LANDSCAPES

1 Explain the variations in erosion and deposition along the river valley shown in the diagram.

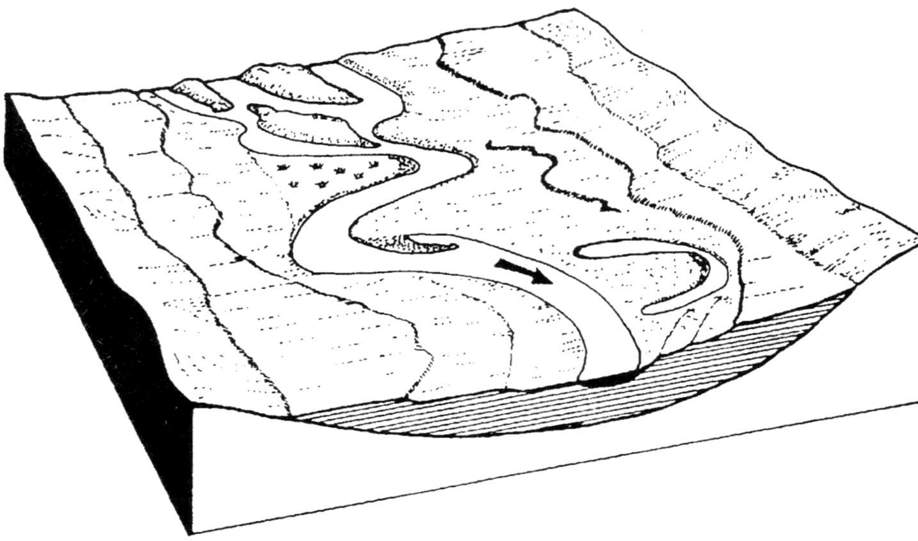

2 Describe fully the physical landscape shown in the sketch below.

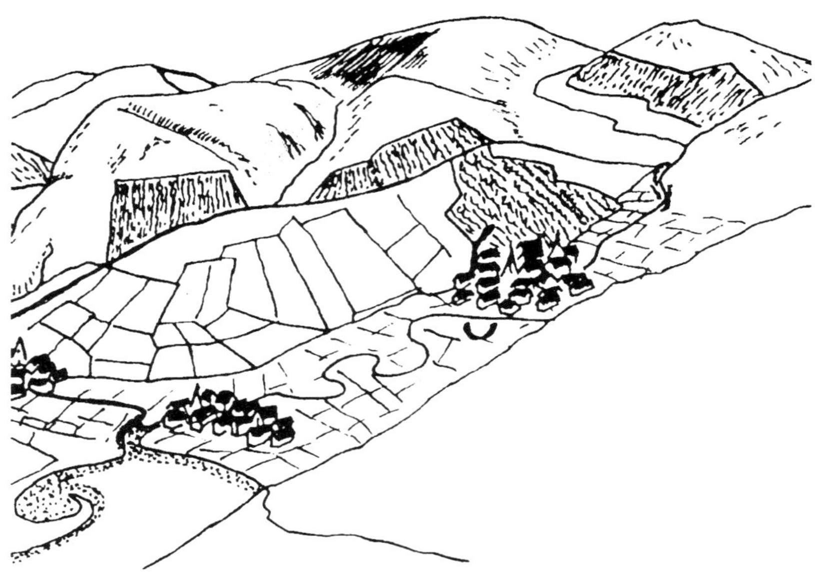

3 Select **one** landscape feature from the sketch. With the aid of a diagram explain how it was formed.

4 Select **two** of the following features and describe how they were formed:-

braided stream; ox-bow lake; meander; floodplain.

VALLEY FLOOR AFTER GLACIATION

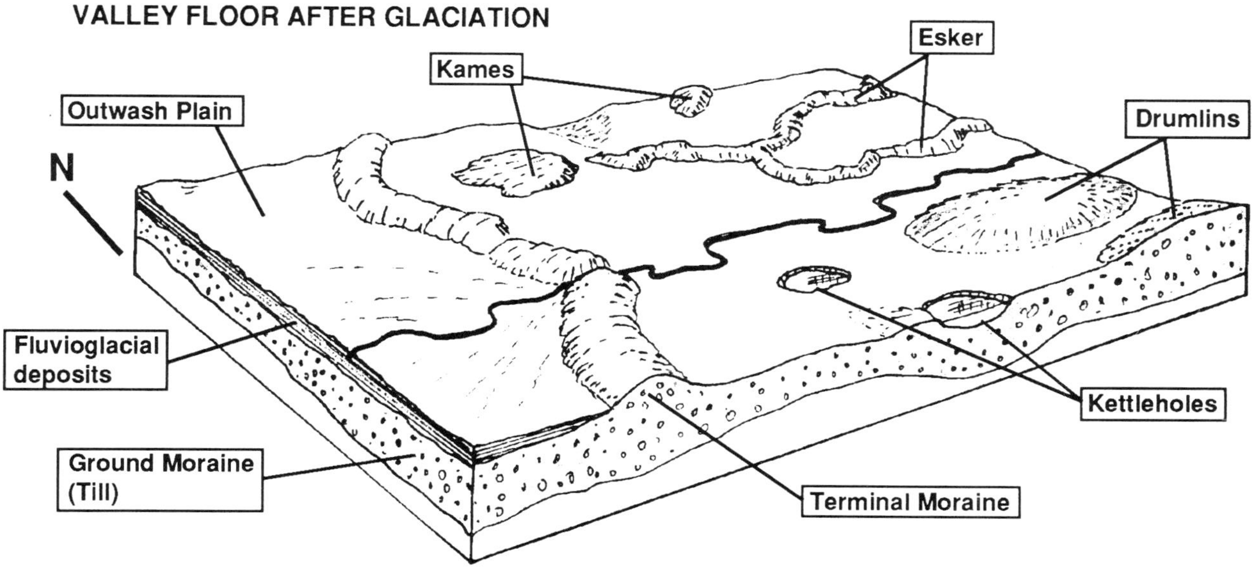

Refer to the diagram above.

5 In which direction was the ice flowing when it formed this landscape? Explain your answer.

6 Explain how one of the labelled features in the diagram was formed.

7 What limitations can upland glaciated landscapes place on land use?

8 Indicate how upland glaciated landscapes can suffer from environmental damage through overuse.

Ordnance Survey Mapwork Questions

These questions can be answered by referring to any of the following map extracts:

a. **Banff and Macduff** 1:25 000 Extract No 830/0148-9
b. **Beinn Eighe** 1 : 50 000 Extract No 831/19 & 25
c. **Gairloch** 1 : 50 000 Extract No 826/19
d. **Stirling** 1 : 50 000 Extract No 732/57-58

9 Compare a **model river** to any of those listed below.
a. Banff and Macduff - River Deveron GR 6761
b. Beinn Eighe - River Grudie GR 9565
c. Gairloch - River Kerry GR 8272
d. Stirling - River Forth GR 8294

10 Describe the Physical features shown in the area indicated.
a. Banff and Macduff - GR 6761, 6861, 6762, 6862
b. Beinn Eighe - GR 9460, 9560, 9461, 9561
c. Gairloch - GR 8271, 8371, 8272, 8372
d. Stirling - GR 8496, 8596, 8497, 8597

11 Describe the relationship between physical landscape and land use in the area indicated.

12 Name the landscape feature in the following Grid Square and explain how it was formed.
a. Banff and Macduff - GR 6761
b. Beinn Eighe - GR 9465
c. Gairloch - GR 8573
d. Stirling - GR 8194

13 For the following Grid Reference, indicate which of the following land uses would be most suitable. Explain your answer, referring to the possible consequences of your chosen development.
Forestry; Arable Farming; Pastoral Farming; Recreation Centre

a. Banff and Macduff - GR 6760
b. Beinn Eighe - GR 9767
c. Gairloch - GR 7878
d. Stirling - GR 8195

RURAL LAND USE: Competition

Key Idea: There are many competing demands for the use of rural landscapes

Fig.85

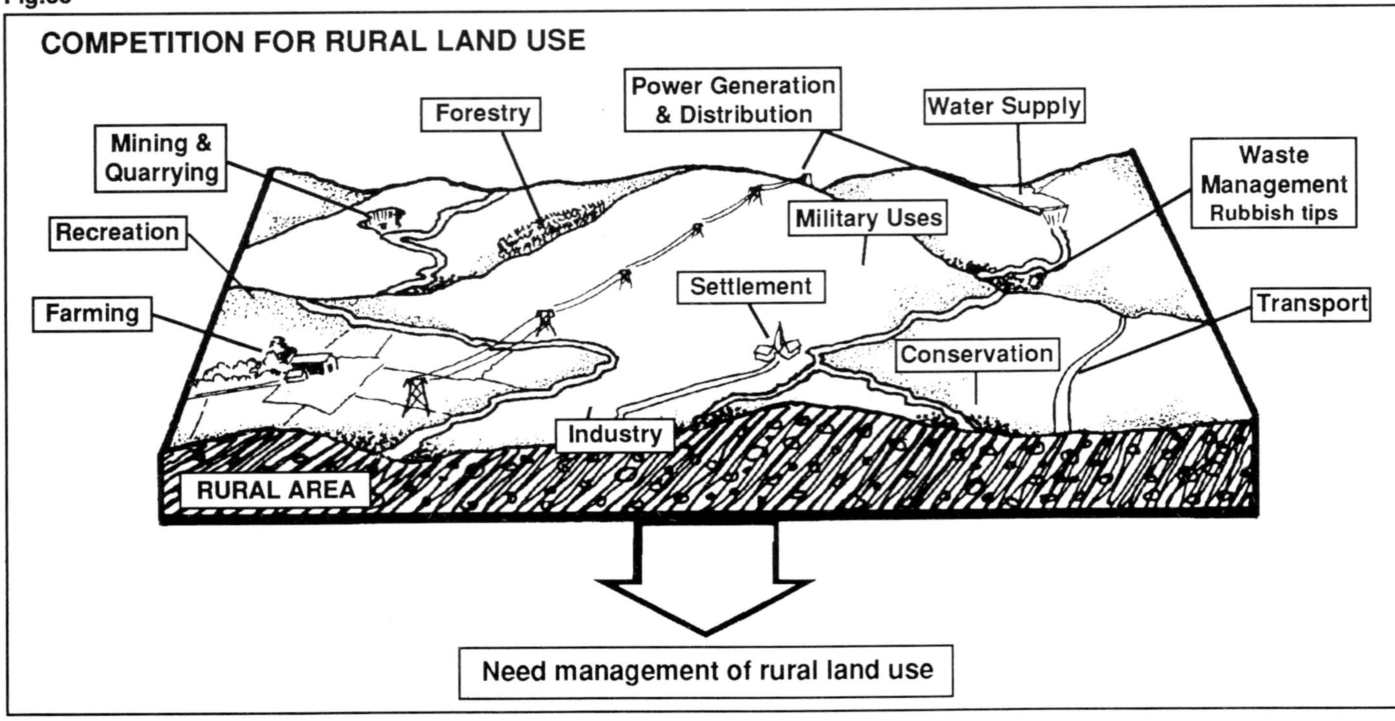

Rural areas are less densely populated than urban areas. They are recognised as countryside or greenspace and have some or all of the following characteristics:-

- **a.** Low density of population
- **b.** Low housing or building density
- **c.** Large amounts of open space with forested and farmed land
- **d.** Low density of communication network
- **e.** High dependence on primary industries for income, e.g. agriculture, mining, forestry
- **f.** Higher degree of 'remoteness' than urban areas

In reality many rural and urban areas often merge, either where a large settlement expands into surrounding rural areas or where an existing rural settlement experiences a large population growth and expands into surrounding countryside.

There are three main types of rural areas to consider:

a. Extensively used rural areas -
where there is limited demand on rural land. Land uses may be carried out on an extensive scale, e.g. hill sheep farming, deer stalking areas, large scale forestry, etc.

b. Intensively used rural areas -
in some areas there is considerable pressure and competition for rural land. This can result in its intensive use and in some areas can affect the rural environment and people, e.g. in and around Aviemore, Scotland where recreation, forestry, farming, settlement and conservation are in conflict over the use of a scenic area of countryside.

c. Rural areas affected by **population changes** -
many rural areas experience both negative and positive influences determined by population fluctuations.
In many developing countries, such as India or Brazil, human competition for rural land is too great to sustain life for everyone. Areas such as this become over-populated and this often leads to rural - urban migration. Many rural people migrate to urban areas (**urbanisation**) in search of an improving quality of life, work and diet.
In many developed countries, such as the USA and UK, competition for land in urban areas is more intense than in rural areas. This results in high urban land values and a decreasing quality of urban life. This can lead to **counter-urbanisation** where people migrate from large urban areas such as London or Chicago to rural areas.

In rural areas throughout the world, there are many competing ways for which the land can be used. Fig.85 illustrates some of the main ways rural land is used. Farming is considered to be the main user of rural land but other land uses such as forestry, recreation, settlement and conservation are growing in importance.

Often different land uses compete for the same area of land and conflicts can arise. Farmers, for example, can be in conflict with walkers who wish access to their farmland. The construction of new motorways or large suburban shopping centres may be in conflict with conservationists who wish to protect rural land areas from destruction. In many rural areas there is a growing need for the management of land use.

Fig.86 Competition for land in the Lake District.

Fig.87 Fieldsketch of fig.86

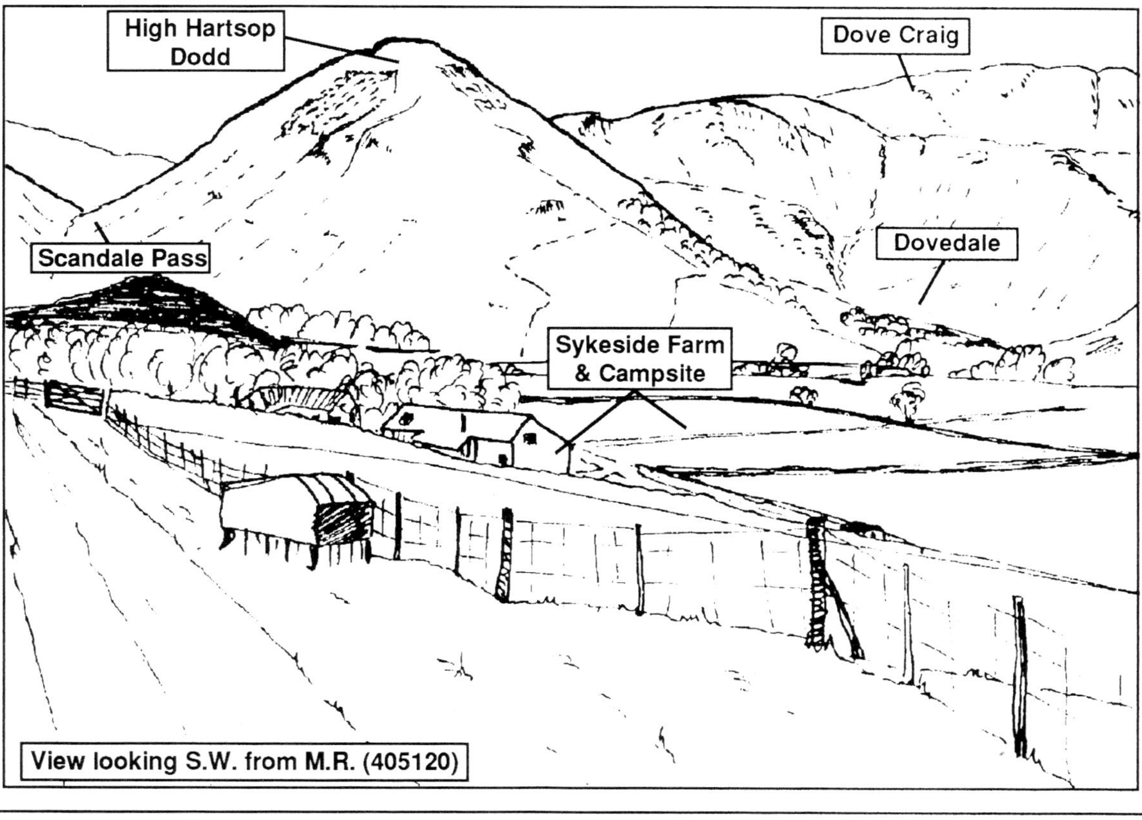

Assignment Sixteen

1 Which of the following areas do you consider to be a **rural** area ? Explain your answer.
A village in the Highlands of Scotland, part of the Amazon Rainforest in Brazil, an oasis in the Arabian desert, a country park on the edge of Glasgow, a famine-stricken area in Mozambique, a parish in Kent, a valley in the Peak District.

2 Write a definition of the following terms:
rural, rural land use, extensive rural area, intensive rural area, urbanisation, counter-urbanisation.

3 Give at least two examples of each of the types of rural land use shown on Fig.85.

4 Complete your own copy of Fig.87 by labelling the sketch to illustrate:-
i. the range of rural land uses
ii. any potential conflicting land uses
within the area of the Lake District shown.

5 In which ways can rural land use be managed ? Give examples in your answer.

RURAL LAND USE: *Farming*

Key Ideas: There are many competing demands for the use of rural landscapes. Farming systems provide food supplies and raw materials.

The United Kingdom has 56.78 million people living within an area of 230, 650 km giving a population density of 236 people/km . With so many people living in a relatively small area, farming is both an essential industry and a major rural land user.

Farming is a primary industry and can be considered to operate as a system with inputs, processes and outputs (Fig.88). Inputs to the farming system include physical and human influences. **Physical inputs** include weather & climatic factors such as temperature, wind, precipitation and sunshine, landscape or relief factors such as altitude, slope, aspect (the direction a slope faces) and site and location of the actual farm. **Human inputs** include those to do with the farmer, such as age, experience and knowledge; economic factors such as markets, capital, transport systems, new technology and Government policies. Other human inputs or influences include the type of tenure (degree of ownership) held by the farmer and the size of the farm.

In areas where the land is difficult to farm, such as hill or upland areas, the physical inputs may be more influential in decision-making than the human inputs. In fertile lowland areas , especially those in close proximity to **good transport**

Fig.88 The Farming System

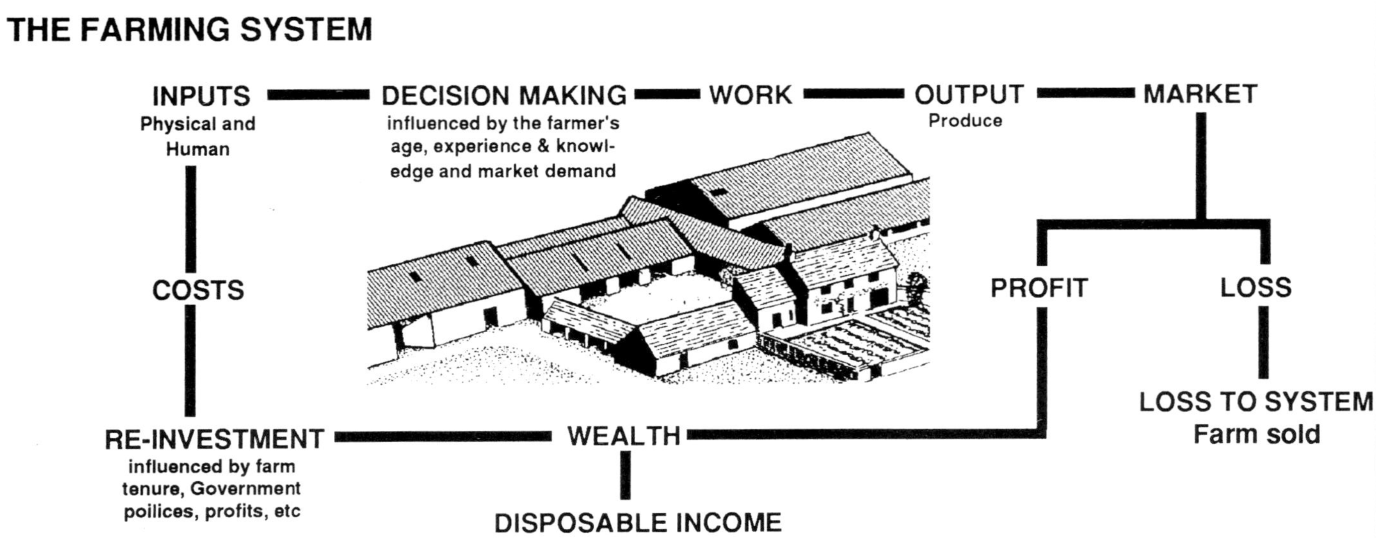

PHYSICAL INPUTS TO THE FARMING SYSTEM	
Altitude	Crop growth is controlled by the decrease in temperatures with height. Temperature decreases by 1°C for every 150m. The growing season is shortened as altitude increases and soils are generally poorer.
Temperature	Temperatures must be above 6°C (called the Threshold temperature) for plant growth. The growing season is defined as the number of days between the last severe frost of spring and the first of autumn.
Precipitation	The seasonal distribution of precipitation is important together with type of rainfall. Plants must have a minimum of 250mm ppt for growth.
Wind	Very strong winds increase evapotranspiration & the soil can dry out. Wind damage is often a problem for crop growing. Shelterbelts of trees are useful in combating wind destruction.
Slope	The angle of slope affects the use of large machinery, depth of soil, soil moisture and its acidity level (pH) and therefore the range and type of crops which can be grown.
Aspect	The Sonnenseite (sunny south-facing slopes) or Schattenseite (shaded north-facing slopes) slopes influence the range and type of crops which can be grown on them in the northern hemisphere.
Soils	The depth, stoniness, mineral content and pH level are all important factors influencing farming and the land use of farmland. Light, sandy soils are well-drained and warm and well suited to growing fruit & vegetables. Limey soils are often light and dry and give high cereal yields.

HUMAN INPUTS TO THE FARMING SYSTEM	
Transport	Transport factors include the type and costs involved in moving raw materials to the farm and produce to the market.
Markets	Closely linked with transport available. Demand is influenced by the size and wealth of the hinterland, dietary and cultural factors and change in tastes and fashion over time.
Capital	In developed countries such as the U.K. farming has developed as a capital-intensive industry with finance available from banks, private investment and government subsidies.
Technology	Developments in new machinery, fertilisers, strains of seed, animal cross-breeding, etc have all influenced farming. New machinery, e.g. combine harvesters have reduced the need for manual labour but increased the level of investment needed
Government Policies	A vitally important factor influencing farming especially in countries such as the U.K. Government subsidies, training schemes and general policies (e.g. for transport, finance etc) have a strong influence on farming. Many of today's decisions affecting British farmers are made by the European Community (E.C.) and the Common Agricultural Policy (CAP).
Farm Size	There is a trend towards farm amalgamation in order to increase farm efficiency and profitability. This is known as agribusiness (highly capital intensive farming).
Inheritance	In Britain the inheritance of small parcels of land upon death has led to fragmentation of farmland and modern problems of access and use of machinery.
Tenure of farm	Varying degrees of ownership (tenancy, freehold, etc) can influence the efficiency of farming carried out.

networks and large markets, the human-economic inputs are often more important and directly influence decision-making. Figure 89 illustrates the main land uses of Britain.

Hill farming - mainly sheep farming - is distributed within the main upland areas including the Scottish Highlands & islands, the Pennines, the Welsh Mountains and S.W.England (see fig.90 for case study).

Lowland farming in Britain consists of Mixed Arable and Dairying, Arable and Market Gardening. **Arable farming** is concentrated mainly in the drier, sunnier east of Britain (see fig.91). **Market Gardening** is concentrated around Britain's large urban areas. (see fig.92) **Mixed Arable** (with Dairying in some cases) is found all over lowland Britain. Mixed farming is the most common type of farming practised in Britain since it provides both protection against crop or animal failure and the potential for high profits in any successful year (see fig.93).

There are three main contrasts between types of farming system in Britain:

a. **Arable, pastoral and mixed farming.**
   Arable is crop farming on generally more fertile soils. **Pastoral** means animal farming such as dairying or sheep farming. **Mixed** farming is a mix of both arable and pastoral.
b. **Extensive and Intensive farming.**
   Extensive farming is large scale farming with a low yield/large area ratio. **Intensive** farming involves a high yield/small area ratio with high inputs of capital & technology (or labour).
c. **Commercial and subsistence farming.**
   Commercial farming is mainly for profit. **Subsistence** farming is concerned with survival usually on a small scale/area.

Fig.89 Land Use in Britain

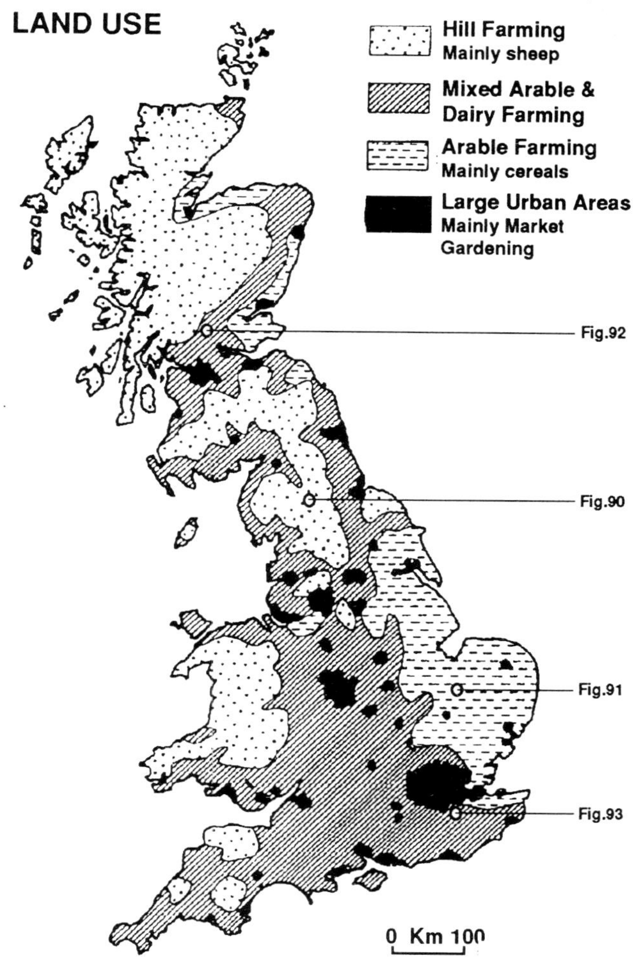

Fig.90

HILL FARMING e.g. Mire Garth Sheep Farm

The high altitude makes for a short growing season, allowing only fodders to be grown. Strong winds and heavy precipitation mean few plants or animals can survive the harsh conditions.
Sheep are the only farm animals capable of surviving on the moors and steep hillsides. Lambing takes place in the more sheltered valleys (or dales).
Mire Garth Farm is a pastoral farm lying in remote Deepdale in the Yorkshire Dales. It has a total sheep population of 4500 and a small herd of 12 beef cattle. In common with most hill farms in Britain, Mire Garth farm must not only survive the environmental handicaps of its location but also contend with a continual oversupply of sheep and sheep products within the country. Government plans to reduce the hill subsidy will mean more hill farms going out of business and others diversifying into farm-tourism (farm holidays, farm open-days, etc).

Mire Garth Hill Sheep Farm, Deepdale by Dent, Yorkshire Dales.

Mire Garth Farm System

- Large farm area (1200 has), Few workers (7), Much capital for land, fence & wall repairs, veterinary help and fodder, High quality livestock, Hill subsidies (Govt)
→ Main work in lambing, shepherding, dipping, harvesting fodders, maintaining walls & fences
→ Very low output per hectare. Very high output per worker. Main produce lambs, wool, mutton, excess fodders
→ All produce for sale at local markets (Settle & Skipton)

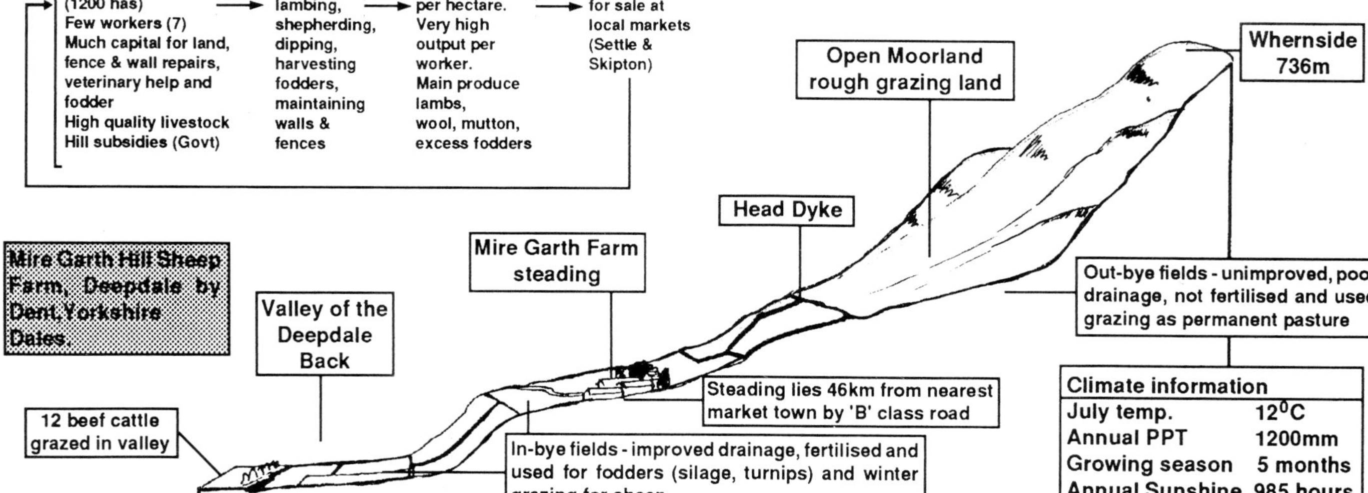

Climate information	
July temp.	12^{0}C
Annual PPT	1200mm
Growing season	5 months
Annual Sunshine	985 hours

FARMING e.g. Woodcock Farm

rtile soil and one of Britain's driest and sunniest climates makes East Anglia some of Britain's most valuable farmland. Woodcock Farm is a good example of an **agribusiness** - the result of the amalgamation of three existing farms, run on a large scale as a specialist grain (or cereal) business producing wheat and barley for the South East of England.

The farm is run by a farm manager for an investment company whose main aim is practicable, profitable farming. To maximise yields the farm uses high technology, fertilisers and herbicides and even has its own plant specialist. The main cereals produced are wheat & barley grown on a four year rotation with oil seed rape as a "break crop". The oil seed fixes nitrogen back to the soil and can be harvested using the same equipment.

The main changes made have include reducing the number of fields from 50 to 12, getting rid of all livestock and reducing the number of workers from 32 to 3. The use of high technology has increased yields of cereals by 18% in 9 years.

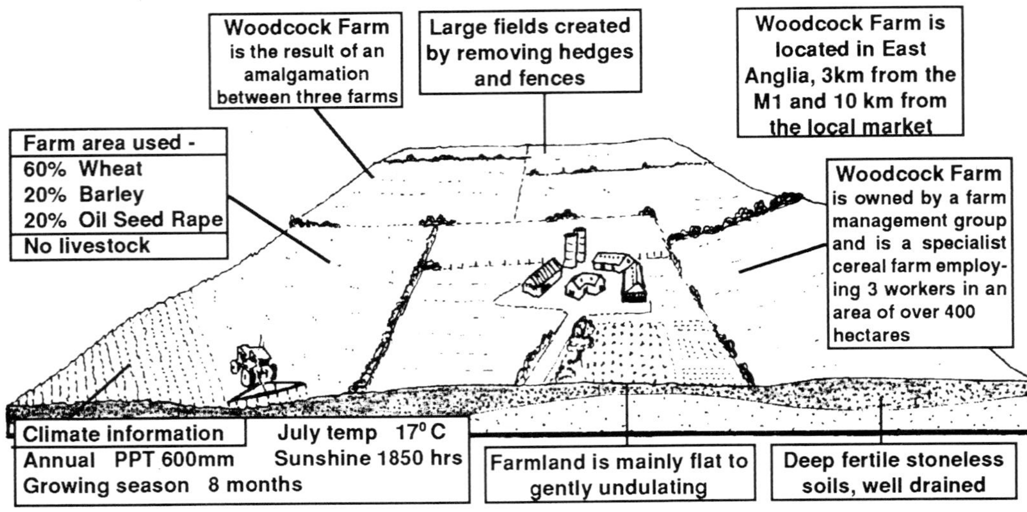

Fig.92

MIXED ARABLE & DAIRY FARMING
e.g. Bieldside Farm

Bieldside Farm has an area of 150 hectares covering fertile valley floor and less fertile valleysides near Stirling in Central Scotland. The farm has been in existence for over 200 years and is the result of two farms being amalgamated into the present larger one.

Bieldside can be described as a mixed arable and dairy farm. The main livestock kept are 70 pedigree Friesian cows and 2 pedigree Friesian bulls. The main fodder crops grown are barley, silage and hay. Arable crops are also grown and include oil seed rape, wheat and Timothy hay. The farm labour force comprises 4 workers using the latest farm technology.

The main farm products include young cattle, bull semen (the most valuable product sold abroad as far as Japan & Saudi Arabia), milk, wheat, oil seed and hay.

The main markets for farm products lies in nearby Stirling Kildean Agrimarket (for milk and livestock and arable crops).

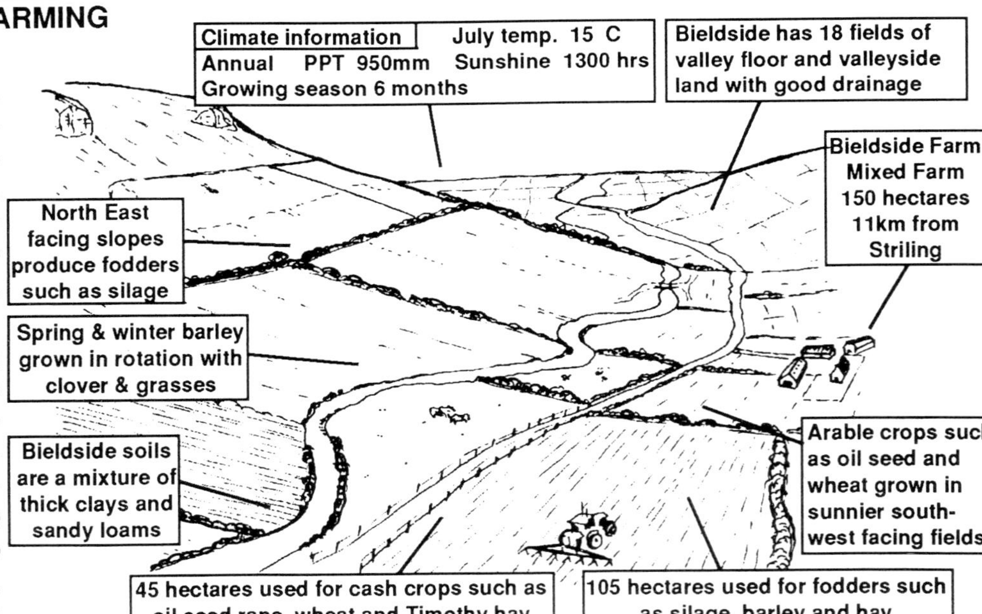

Fig.93

MARKET GARDENING e.g. Greenacres Smallholding

Greenacres Smallholding is located close to the village of Nash 12km from Bromley in London's greenbelt.

The market garden is run by a married couple and extra labour is provided from 12 seasonally employed workers & students.

The smallholding covers an area of 8 hectares and is sited upon fertile alluvial soils with good natural drainage.

Capital investment has been required to replace the 20 centrally-heated glasshouses and to build a visitor's centre with small coffee house and car park.

The main products from the market garden are diverse and planned on an annual cycle. They include fruits & vegetables - tomatoes, cucumbers, apples, lettuces, cauliflowers, cabbages, brussels sprouts, cress, onions, radishes, peas, strawberries, gooseberries, blackcurrants, redcurrants, plums, various flowers such as chrysanthemums, carnations, daffodils, tulips, roses and a wide variety of trees and shrubs.

Plants are grown both in glasshouses and in well-tended small, sheltered fields. Some plants are also grown under closhes (transparent plastic sheeting).

The mild moist climate with a long growing season of over 8 months and sunny summers allows early harvests.

Greenacres Smallholding System

Small plot of land. Many workers - mostly seasonal. High capital investment in buildings, heating, lighting, advertising. High quality seeds → The main work involves care in achieving the optimum growing conditions for all plants, fruit, veg & flowers, trees and shrubs. Other work in harvesting and selling produce → Very high output per hectare and per worker. Main produce includes a wide variety of fruit & vegetables, flowers tress and shrubs. → All produce is for sale at high urban prices. Sales made at the farmshop and in local markets, shop contracts etc.

The proximity of and easy access to a very large urban market (London & its suburbs) makes the smallholding highly profitable.

FARMING PROBLEMS

Farming in Britain faces several major problems in common with many other developed countries:-

- **a.** The overuse of chemicals can lead to excess being washed into rivers and drinking water.
- **b.** The widespread and growing concern over intensive farming methods.
- **c.** The amalgamtion of small farms into large farm units not only puts people off the land but also leads to the destruction of traditional field hedges in order to facilitate the use of large machinery with loss of wildlife.
- **d.** The introduction of high technology leads to the loss of farm work and consequently a reduction in population in many rural areas.
- **e.** The impact of Government policies (both national & E.C.) affects the farmscape of Britain. More land is SET ASIDE and the removal of grants & subsidies will also severely restrict farm development.
- **f.** Major concern over 'factory farming' methods in producing chickens & eggs, lambs and calves etc.
- **g.** Increasing competition for rural land for urban expansion, recreation, industry and transport.

Assignment Seventeen

1. In which ways can farming be described as a **system** ?

2. Explain they ways in which each of the following influence farming and decisions made about farming:-
   Aspect, Markets, precipitation, farm tenure, Government

3. Write definitions for each of the following terms:-
   arable, pastoral, mixed farming, extensive, intensive, commercial, subsistence, agribusiness, market gardens

4. **Either**
   Prepare illustrated revision notes to summarise the farming systems described in Figures 90-93 **or**
   Complete a larger version of the table below after studying figures 90-93

Farm Name	Farm Location	Farm Type	Size	Land, Soils	Inputs	Work	Outputs	Markets	Problems

5. Explain the distribution of farming land use within Britain as shown in Figure 89.

6. Describe the relationship between land use and the physical landscape on Bieldside Farm (fig.92).

7. What are the advantages and disadvantages of
   i. Agribusinesses such as Woodcock Farm (fig.91) ?
   ii. Mixed Farming such as Bieldside Farm (fig.92) ?

8. Many traditional farming areas are suffering a decline in population. Describe the main reasons for this and the likely problems caused for the local communities.

9. Which of the problems facing farming do you consider to be the most important ? Give reasons for your answer.

22. RURAL LAND USE: *Quarries & Greenbelts*

Key Ideas: There are many competing demands for the use of rural landscapes.

Other pressures for rural land come in the form of forestry and newer developments such as the rise of superquarries and urban expansion. Each 'development' has both advantages and disadvantages. **Fig.94**

COASTAL SUPERQUARRIES

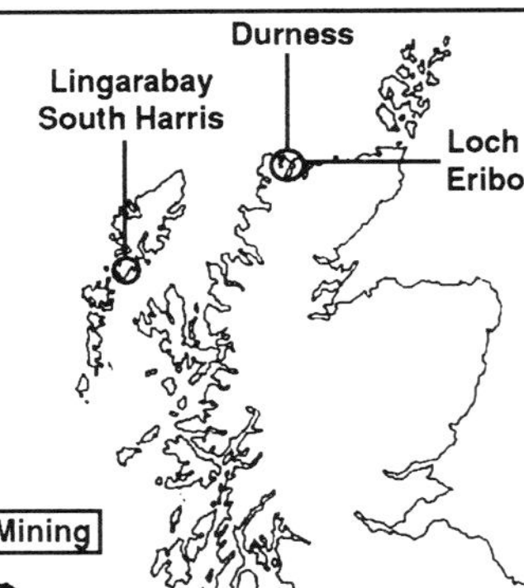

Each year the U.K. uses 6 tonnes of rock aggregate per person in construction projects. New sources of rock are constantly required and attention has now turned to the remote areas of Durness and South Harris as potential sites for coastal superquarries. Quarry companies have carried out feasibility surveys into two main sites. One large site at Loch Eriboll by Durness is forecasted to produce 20 million tonnes of rock per year for up to 1,000 years. Lingarabay on Harris would produce 10 million tonnes per year for 60 years.
Clearly both projects are planned on a megascale and would have a major impact on the areas involved. However, there is considerable debate over whether the coastal superquarries should be developed in these remote but beautiful areas.
The rock companies involved say that these remote communities are suffering depopulation and that the quarries would bring new life to them. And there is intense competition to bring superquarries to remote areas of Norway instead.

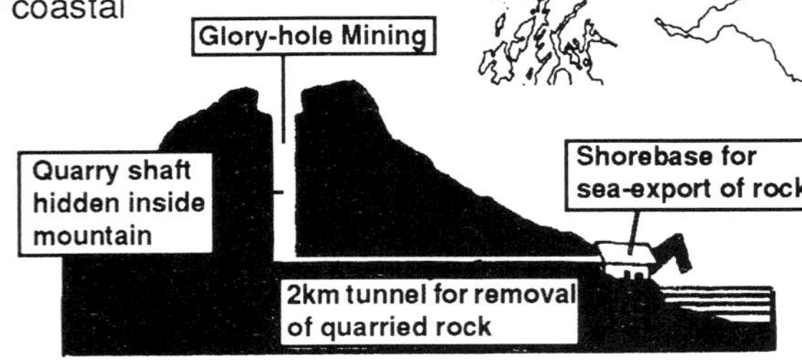

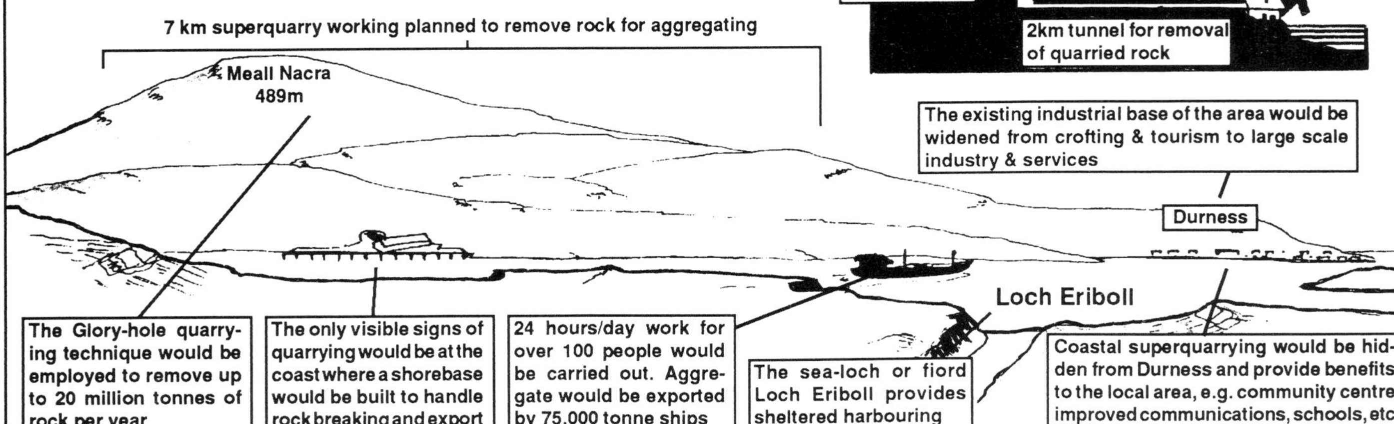

ADVANTAGES OF COASTAL SUPERQUARRIES

Coastal superquarries will bring long term well paid employment to remote areas suffering rural depopulation and loss of young people.
Existing communities will benefit from the input of over £100,000 per year from quarry companies who will also provide community facilities in the form of leisure centres, shops, improved communications and new housing.
Existing communities will be revitalised and rural depopulation will be arrested. Communities will be kept together.
The existing skyline will be preserved through 'glory-hole' mining. There will be no major landscape scars and plant & machinery will be screened. Potential dust and water pollution will be tightly controlled.
Only small, very remote areas of the country will be quarried.
Pressure on the landscapes of the Mendips, Peak District & SE England will be reduced by opening up remote Scottish coastal sites.

DISADVANTAGES OF COASTAL SUPERQUARRIES

The scenic beauty of the area will be affected by air, noise and water pollution. Wildlife and sites of special interest will be scarred and the natural peace & quiet destroyed for money.
Tourism in the local area will be severely affected as the appeal of the area will be reduced by superquarrying.
Coastal areas including waterways will be under pressure from increased traffic. The likelihood of sea accidents and consequent pollution will increase.
Existing rural communities will be destroyed. Road traffic accidents, & crime rates will increase. The 'way of life' will be destroyed.
The area will become overdependent on one industry reducing the variety of the local skills base. Traditional craft industries will die.
Local housing will increase in price and local planning regulations will be modified for 'outsiders'.

Limestone Quarrying

Fig.95

Figure 95 illustrates another common site - that of limestone quarries inland in the Pennines and Cotswold Hills. With the expansion of the construction industry after the Second World war, the demand for cement has meant a massive expansion in limestone quarrying bringing employment to rural areas such as Ribblesdale in the Yorkshire Dales National Park (opposite). Environmentalists claim that Britain's 150 huge quarry sites scar the landscape and cause pollution of air and water.

Fig.96 Urban expansion into rural areas

GREENBELTS AND URBAN EXPANSION

Greenbelts have often been created around large urban areas such as Edinburgh or London to prevent untidy, unplanned urban expansion into rural areas on their fringe. The idea is that Greenbelt areas will limit urban growth by protecting a swathe of land around the edge of cities for rural land uses. Planners restrict the use of greenbelt land to farming, leisure and open space activities. In this way, both the rural economy can be protected from urban developments and the city's services can be concentrated for ease of supply.

Edinburgh's greenbelt is a good example of a 'greenbelt flashpoint' where several attempts are being made to breach or leapfrog the restrictions of the protected rural-urban fringe. One of the biggest developments is located at 'The Gyle' (Fig.97) where a large out of town shopping & commercial centre has been constructed close to the Edinburgh City By-pass. With giant car parks, over 60 major retail outlets and modern purpose-built office complexes, the latest 'greenbelt' development has not only caused a great deal of argument about the value of Greenbelt Legislation but is also a major competitor for Edinburgh's CBD.

Greenbelts are a good example of the way in which Governments can take direct steps to ease problems of competition over rural land.

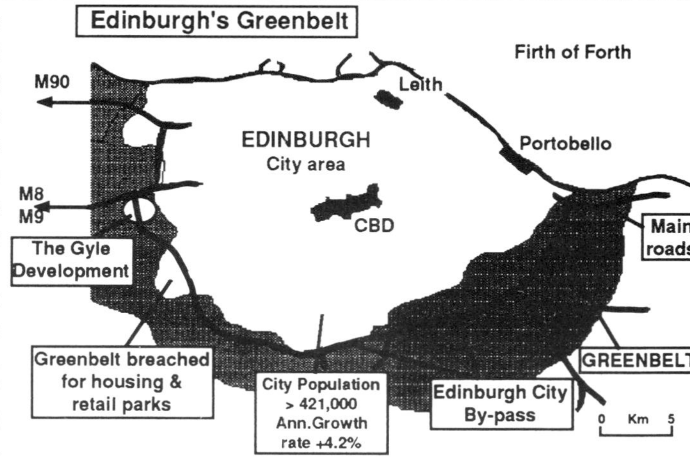

GREENBELT LEGISLATION

1938	Green Belt Act (concentrated on developing London's greenbelt)
1947	Town & Country Planning Act introduced Development Plans
1968	Town & Country Planning Act introduced Structure Plans
1970	Department of the Environment created as overseeing body

The main aims of legislation were to concentrate urban development within strict boundaries (held in check by Greenbelt Legislation); to stabilise the social and economic growth of large urban areas by restricting their expansion and to protect rural economies & land use from urban land speculation.

Edinburgh - expanding city

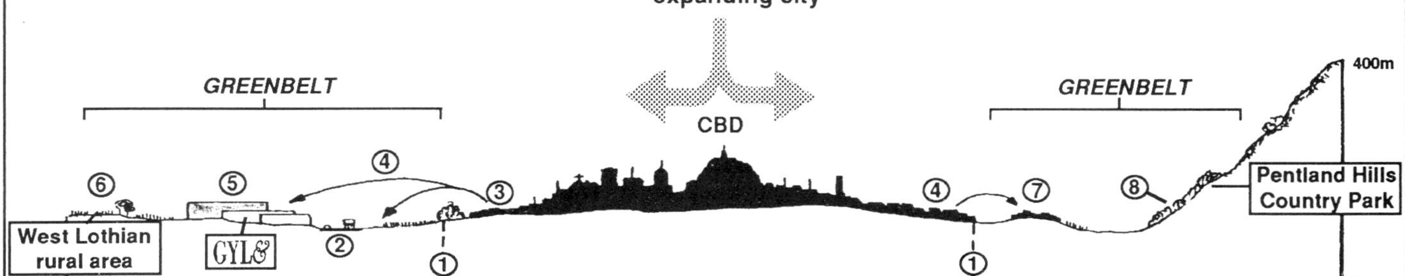

Transect of Edinburgh's Greenbelt & Rural-Urban Fringe

The City By-pass route built through the Greenbelt encourages new development along new communication corridor, especially at major intersections.
Expanding city suburbs becoming congested as planners attempt to restrict suburban growth.
Farmland under pressure from urban expansion, increasing land prices near to ring road intersections and increasing air and noise pollution.
Original Greenbelt beginning at rural-urban fringe (river valley, steep slopes, estate boundary, etc)

Greenbelt breached as new commercial and residential developments extend the city suburbs across the rural-urban fringe.
Large 'Out of town shopping and commercial centre' encroaches on the Greenbelt and provides stern competition for City Centre shops & offices.
Attractive rural areas under pressure from urban recreation - golf courses, ski slopes, rambling, mountain biking, picnics - within Edinburgh's Greenbelt.
Greenbelt leapfrogged as new commuter housing is developed with good Ring Road access.

Fig.97

Assignment Eighteen

1 In which ways do the following exert pressure on rural areas :-
   i. Coastal superquarries
   ii. Expanding urban areas ?

2 Research the Loch Eriboll Superquarry issue using Fig.94 Do you think that the coastal superquarry project should be given the go-ahead or should it be shelved ? Justify your point of view.

3a What are the main aims of Greenbelts ?

3b Make your own copy of the Transect of Edinburgh's Greenbelt & Rural-Urban Fringe (fig.96).

3c Use the transect information to complete a key for the numbers 1 to 8.

4 For either fig.95 or 97, annotate a simple fieldsketch in order to describe competition for and pressure exerted upon rural land.

23. RURAL LAND USE: *Monster country*

Key Ideas: There are many competing demands for the use of rural landscapes.

Competition for rural land use becomes a live issue in many Highland areas blessed with scenic beauty (Fig.98).
The Drumnadrochit area is a very good example of intense competition for land for conflicting purposes. The area owes much of its natural beauty to glaciation. The small village of Drumnadrochit and its linked settlements of Lewiston and Balmacaan are situated in a classic U-shaped valley on the shores of Loch Ness - world famous for its elusive monster "Nessie" (Fig.99). The area attracts over 300,000 tourists annually and is linked to Inverness by the A82.

At present there are traffic congestion problems and a need for a by-pass. The beauty of the area together with its natural landscape make the routing of by-pass a very emotive issue (Fig.100). In addition there are also proposals for three new developments in and around the village - a Waterlife Centre on the lochside, a golf course and a 70-house residential estate to meet demand for commuter housing. Locals are divided in their views of the plans. Some locals welcome the opportunities for the further growth and development of the Drumnadrochit area. Others, including various environmental groups, are concerned over the impact on the beauty of the area (Fig.101).

Fig.98

The HIGHLAND BLETHER

TROUBLE IN MONSTER COUNTRY !

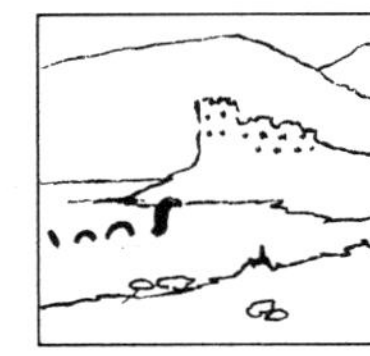

The world famous village of Drumnadrochit, on the shores of Loch Ness is set to become the epicentre of a major battle over rural land use. Developers are proposing 3 new projects destined to maintain the popularity (and coffers of local businesses) of the area. Plans to by-pass the village and relieve traffic congestion, air & noise pollution and reduce the threat of accidents to local schoolchildren may not now be as popular as once thought. Environmentalist groups are marshalling their arguments against a proposed Waterlife Centre, a Golf Course and plans to build bridges across beautiful Urquhart Bay or through a site of special scientific interest known as 'The Cover'.
"By-passing the village at the time when we are considering plans for its development is crazy talk," states Jim MacLeod, local publican and postie. "We need all the visitors we can get in Drumnadrochit." But other residents such as Nathan Thackery disagree. "I didn't move here to benefit from destroying nature." Let battle commence......

Fig.99

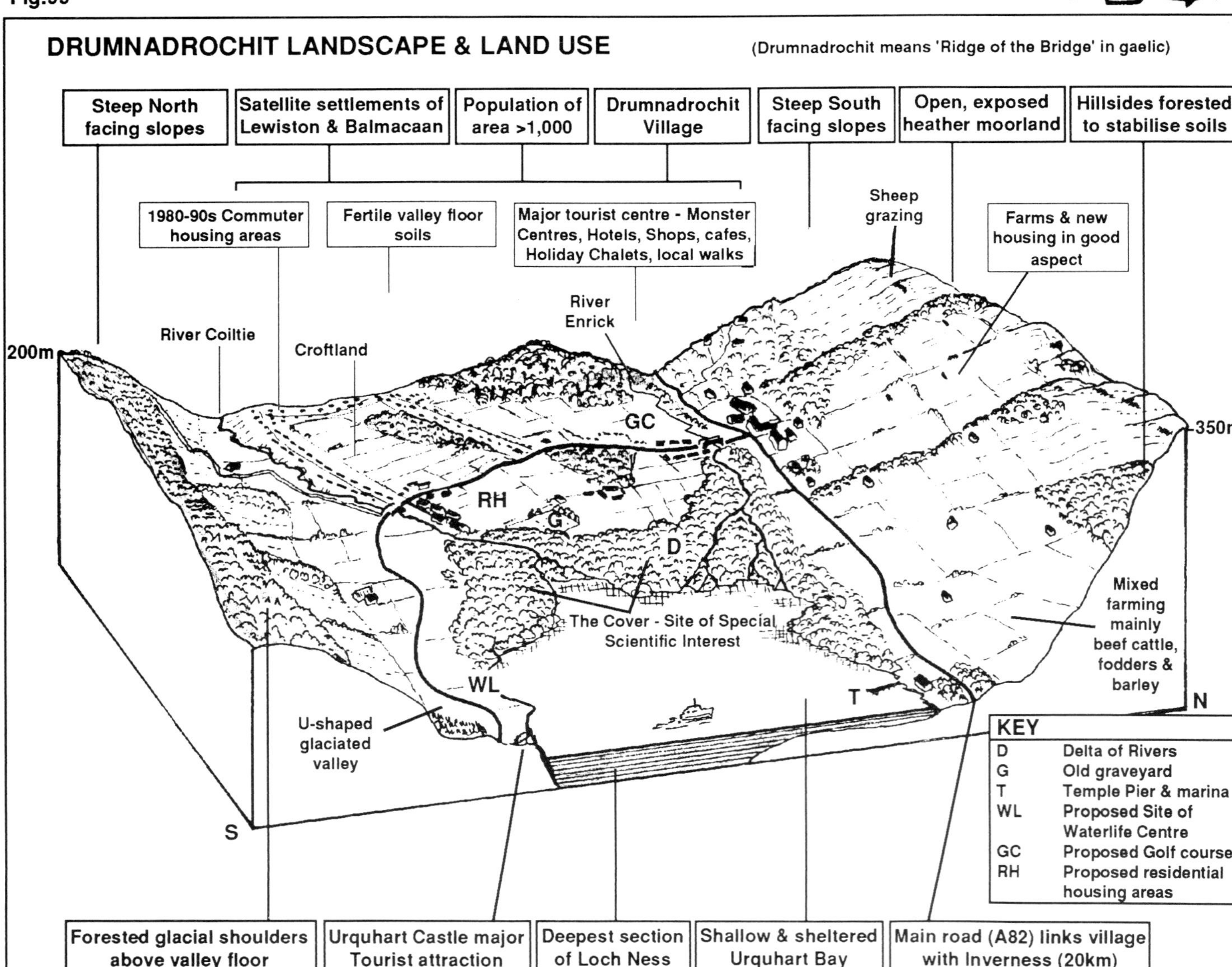

Fig.100

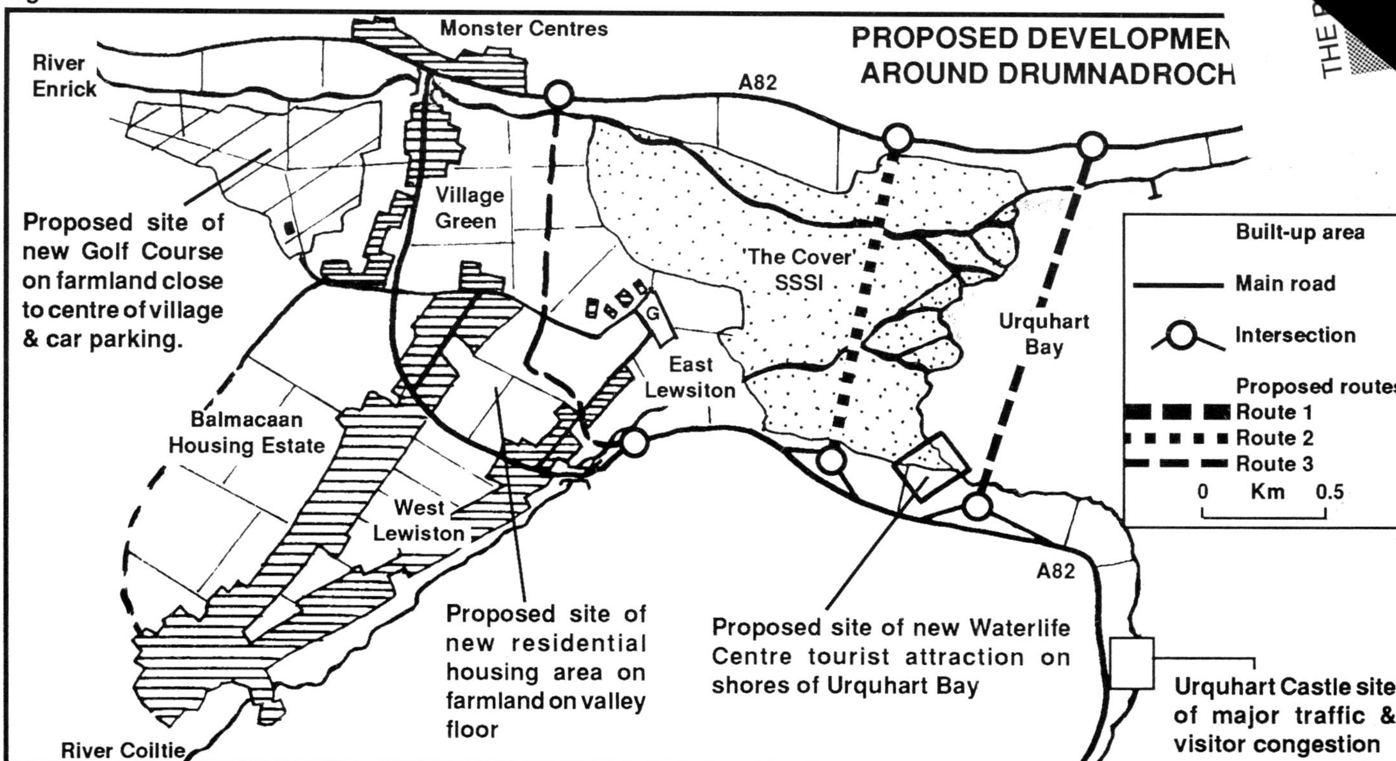

Information	Route 1	Route 2	Route 3	Waterlife Centre	Residential Housing	Golf Course
Proposals	1.45km By-pass from Temple Pier across Urquhart Bay on stilted roadway above water.	1.20km By-pass from Kerrowtown Fm across 'The Cover' on piled roadway.	1.42km By-pass from the Monster Centre across farmland, through East Lewiston.	A exhibition & underwater visitor centre on shores of Urquhart Bay. Car parking, shops and restaurant.	70 detached and semi-detached houses with access roads, parking bays, play areas and all services.	A 9-hole golf course with clubhouse built on farmland. Open to locals and visitors all year.
Houses affected	None. 2 nearby.	None. 1 nearby.	Two demolished.	None. None nearby.	None. 11 nearby	None. 22 nearby.
Farmland used	21.4 hectares	112.35 hectares	131.25 hectares	25.1 hectares	52 hectares	28 hectares
Environmental impacts	2 embankments, 1 cutting, 1km bridge, 2 intersections, 3 junctions. Affects Urquhart Bay, sailing & fishing rights. Visual impact on Bay & views over Loch Ness. Limited pollution of Bay in construction.	3 embankments, 2 cuttings, 2 bridges, 2 intersections, 3 junctions. Affects 'The Cover" (SSSI), wildlife &fishing rights. Environmental conflicts likely. Limited pollution of rivers in construction.	3 embankments, 2 cuttings, 2 bridges, 2 intersections, 4 junctions, 1 flyover. Affects valley floor farmland and old shelterbelts. Visual problems screened by plantings. Traffic problems at Monster Centres at construction.	Exhibition & underwater Visitor Centre to be built on lochside. Visual impact on Urquhart Bay & views over Loch Ness. Recycling of water may disturb existing aquatic life (& monster ?). Addtional sewage disposal problems, traffic congestion and loss of amenity farmland.	Visual impact on rural area. Destruction of existing shelterbelts & old wall pattern. 3 junctions, screening by plantings. Affects valley floor farmland, access for existing householders, local schools and extra service provision needed (sewage, water)	Little affect on existing trees, wall pattern or roads. Visual impact small and rural-ness maintained. 1 junction, 1 clubhouse, 1 car park. Minimal affect on service provision in area.
Jobs created short/long-term	125 / 1	75 / 1	70 / 1	25 / 18	75 / 0	15 / 4
Total costs	£23.9 million	£15.87 million	£12.55 million	£4.1 million	£3.25 million	£3.79 million

Fig.101 View looking NW over Urquhart Bay to Drumnadrochit

Assignment Nineteen

1 Describe the relationship between land use and landscape in the Drumnadrochit area.

2 Copy and complete the table below:

Proposed Development	Costs	Environmental Costs	Groups For/Against

3 Select any one proposed development and describe its possible social, economic and environmental consequences on the area around Drumnadrochit.

4 Examine the case for and against the proposed Drumnadrochit By-pass. Do you think there should be a by-pass ? Give evidence to support your answer.

24. RURAL LAND USE: *Land for Leisure ?*

Key Idea: There are many competing demands for the use of rural landscapes.

Land for **leisure** activities in rural areas has increasingly been in demand in the last 50 years. With over 50 million people pursuing a wide variety of leisure interests, there is increasing pressure on the areas of Britain they visit (Fig.102 and 103).

Leisure is how people enjoy themselves when they are not working. Experts believe that the greater the leisure time the higher the quality of life. But leisure activities (Fig.104) cost money and the time that unemployed people have is not regarded as leisure time.

Scotland is a small country with a variety of leisure locations (Fig.104) popular with residents and visitors alike. Local authorities have developed a wide range of **amenities** for leisure, including sports centres, theatres, parks, etc. Scenic areas such as Glen Affric and the Loch Lomond area are very popular leisure locations.

Many areas directly benefit from leisure - increased wealth, employment, amenities, improved communications, etc. But leisure activities also bring disadvantages to areas - traffic & people congestion, erosion & damage to sensitive areas, changes to the rural way of life, pollution, etc.

There is a great debate raging today over the best way forward in developing leisure activities and the areas affected by it. Some people consider that scenic areas such as Wester Ross (Fig.105) should become National Parks and as such, should be protected from unplanned 'development' by legislation. Others suggest that National Park status will increase the problems for these areas - attracting even more visitors, fuelling local conflict over land use and encouraging the setting up of 'out of bounds areas'. But problems of rural access and protection will not go away as land is increasingly needed for leisure.

Fig.102 Severe erosion on Cairn Gorm

Fig.103 Coastal leisure - Blackpool beach in summer

Fig.104

LEISURE & RECREATION : BRIEFING PAPER 1

Leisure time is the time available to people when not working, sleeping or subsisting. The last 50 years has seen a great increase in the amount of leisure time, for a variety of reasons including -

* workers have more and longer paid holidays
* the average number of hours worked per week has fallen
* more people own cars
* greater wealth
* greater awareness of the benefits of leisure activities
* the provision of leisure facilities

People may use their leisure time in any way they choose. Leisure may be **passive** - e.g. relaxing watching videos or listening to music - or **active** - e.g. sports, dancing or playing an instrument.

The type of leisure people select depends on such factors as age, sex, fitness, personal interests and abilities, mobility & finances. The availability of **amenities** is also a major factor in their choice. Leisure locations also vary from **urban-based**, e.g. cinemas, pubs, sports centres, dance halls, to **rural-based** locations e.g. forest and country parks, lochs, hills, long distance footpaths, etc.

Increasing personal mobility and awareness of the countryside and open spaces means an increasing pressure placed upon scenic areas and major competition for rural land for leisure activities.

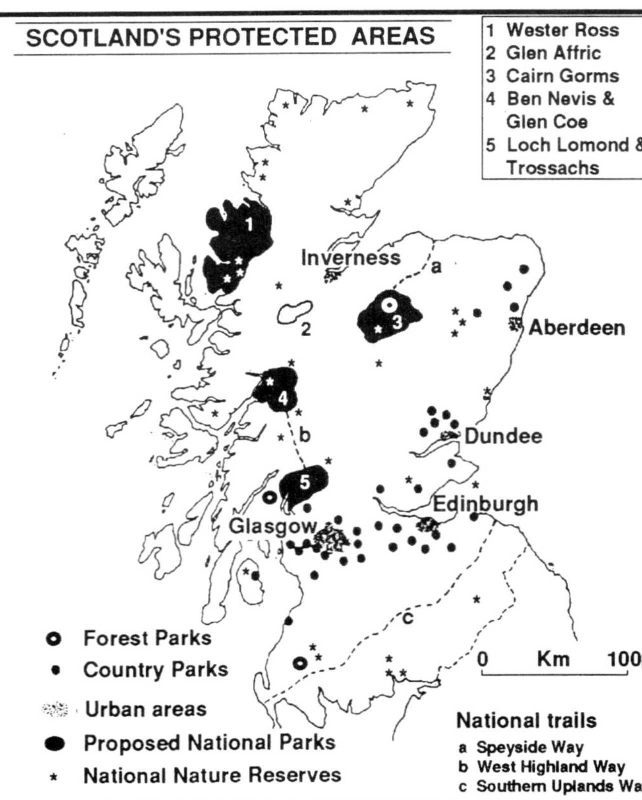

Fig.105

LEISURE & RECREATION: BRIEFING PAPER 2

Wester Ross is a landscape of rugged coasts, sheltered sandy bays and high quality mountain landscape. This remote area lies 70km west from Inverness and has a low population density)of less than 8 people per km ²). The isolation and scenic beauty of Wester Ross make the area extremely popular with a growing number of visitors. Cars, caravans and motorhomes together with tour-buses make the road system unable to cope with summer traffic. Increasing demands have been and are being made on the rural land resources of the area arising from a range of land uses including housing, leisure activities, forestry and hydro-electric developments, etc.
Turning the area into a National Park is being discussed as one method of protecting Wester Ross from its tourist appeal. But is this the best solution to a growing rural problem ?

WESTER ROSS BASE MAP

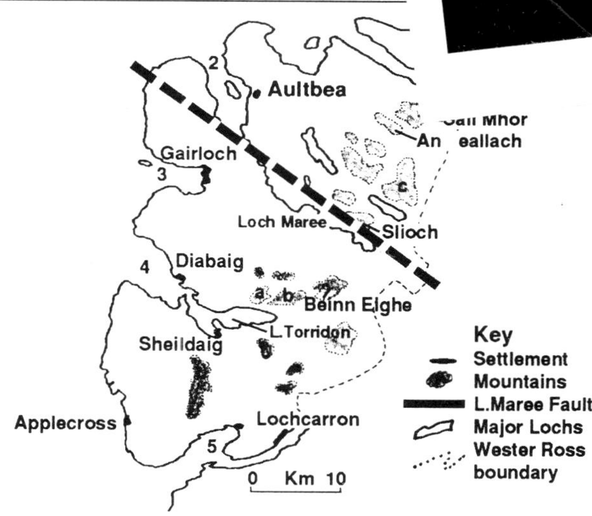

WESTER ROSS: RURAL LAND RESOURCES & USES

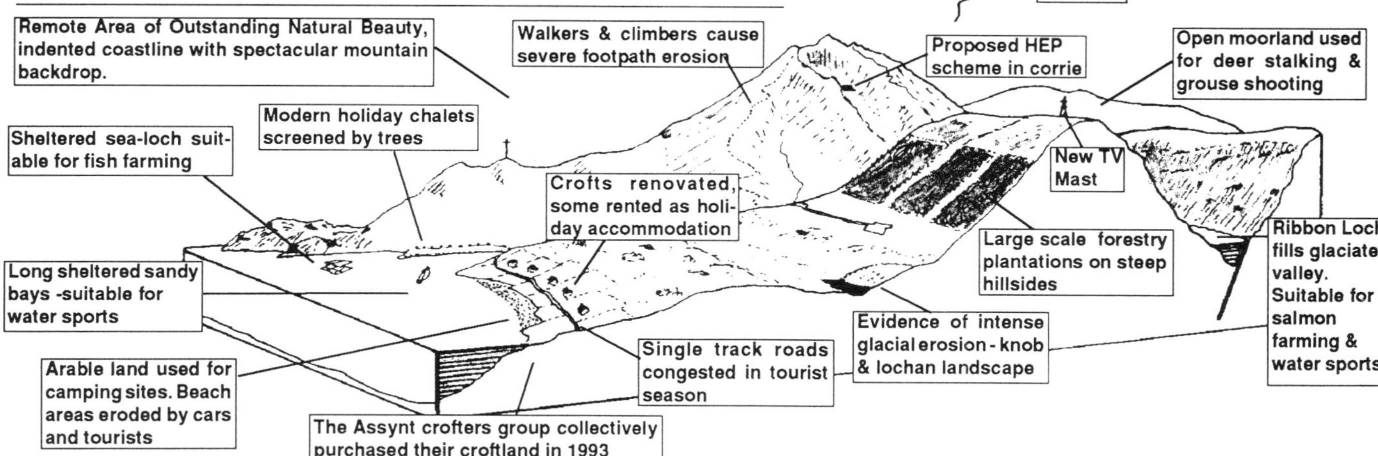

IN FAVOUR OF WESTER ROSS NATIONAL PARK

National Park Status would give legal protection to the area thwarting any unplanned, unsightly, unsuitable developments within Wester Ross.
Government investment would be available to provide upgraded visitor amenities, e.g. accommodation , leisure & visitor centres, tourist info,etc.
Improved communications including upgraded TV & Radio, roads and rail links would be developed.
The **local environment**, its flora & fauna and scenic beauty would be preserved for the nation and the future.
Local people would benefit from increased facilities and from jobs in tourism (& construction of amenities). Unemployment rates would fall. The local economy would be boosted.
Rural depopulation would cease and communities would grow.
The **most sensitive areas** would be protected - parts of these could be 'out of bounds' to preserve their beauty.
A **wide range of leisure activities** would be provided for visitors - hill walking, sailing, fishing, golf, pony trekking - all giving jobs to locals.

AGAINST THE WESTER ROSS NATIONAL PARK

National Park Status would lead to many restrictions being placed upon local initiatives and existing farming, forestry and fish farming industries.
European Community Objective One status already exists for the Highland area and as such Wester Ross will benefit from investment in its infrastructure, industrial base and employment anyway.
Giving **National Park status** would encourage even more visitors to the area, increasing existing problems of summer congestion, pollution, footpath erosion and general disturbance to flora and fauna.
Local people would not necessarily benefit from National Park status - 'holiday cottage syndrome' would mean young locals moving away since many local houses would be bought by urban dwellers.
The **'Right of Access'** may be lost to areas of Wester Ross - locals & some visitors would not readily accept restrictions to their movement.
Locals argue strongly that it is **conservation** (maintenance of the living landscape) and not preservation that is urgently required in Wester Ross.
A **wide range of leisure activities** already exists.
Local culture would be under threat from increased numbers of visitors.

Assignment Twenty

1 Describe the effect of visitor pressure as illustrated in figures 102 & 103.

2 Write definitions for each of the following terms:- leisure, recreation, passive leisure, active leisure, amenities, National Parks.

3a Describe the types and distribution of Scotland's Protected Areas (fig.104).

3b Explain the distribution of Country Parks in Scotland.

4a Make your own copy of the Wester Ross Base Map (fig.105).

4b Complete a Key to the map for the following:-
Sea Lochs **1-5** Mountains **a-c**.

5 Suggest ways in which **conflicts** may arise in popular areas such as Wester Ross when:-
 i. leisure activities share the same rural area, e.g. hillwalking & deer stalking, or coach tours & cycling
 ii. various land uses share the same rural area, e.g. farming & tourism, or forestry & picnicking.

6 National Parks are designed to preserve beautiful landscapes & local wildlife, and provide access for visitors.
 i. List the advantages & disadvantages of National Parks.
 ii. Do you think Wester Ross should be granted National Park status ? Justify your answer fully.

25. EXAM STYLE QUESTIONS

RURAL LAND USE

1 Examine the block diagram.
Which of the proposed development applications for **site X** is the most appropriate ?
(a nature reserve; a caravan and camping site; an RAF bombing range; a quarry)

Support your conclusion with a detailed argument.

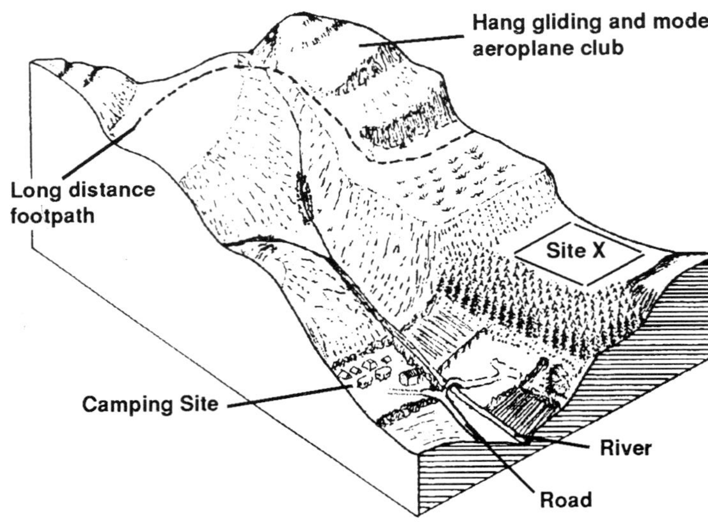

2 The varying demands of land use in glaciated upland areas may result in conflicts of interest. Quoting a specific example you have studied, describe the conflict and the steps taken to resolve it.

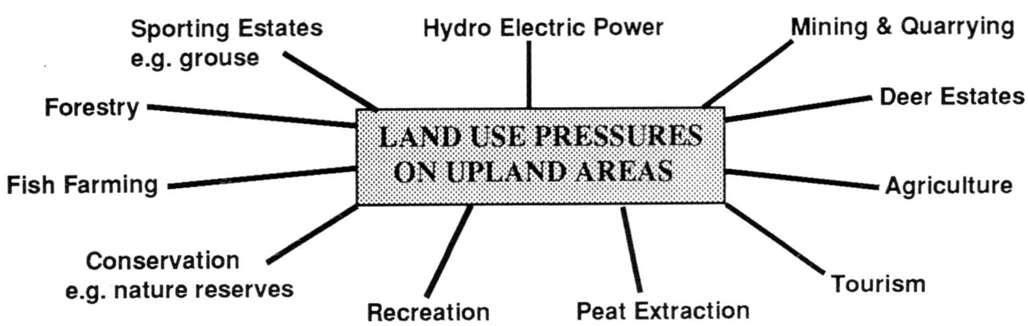

3 Several areas in Scotland (including Wester Ross and Loch Lomond) have been identified as possible National Parks. Put the case for and against National Parks as a method of protecting upland areas.

Definition: National Parks are areas of beautiful and relatively wild country which are protected for the nation's benefit. Established farming is maintained; wildlife and buildings are protected; whilst providing access and facilities for visitors.

4 Describe how the farming landscape in the sketch appears to be under pressure from non-farming activities.

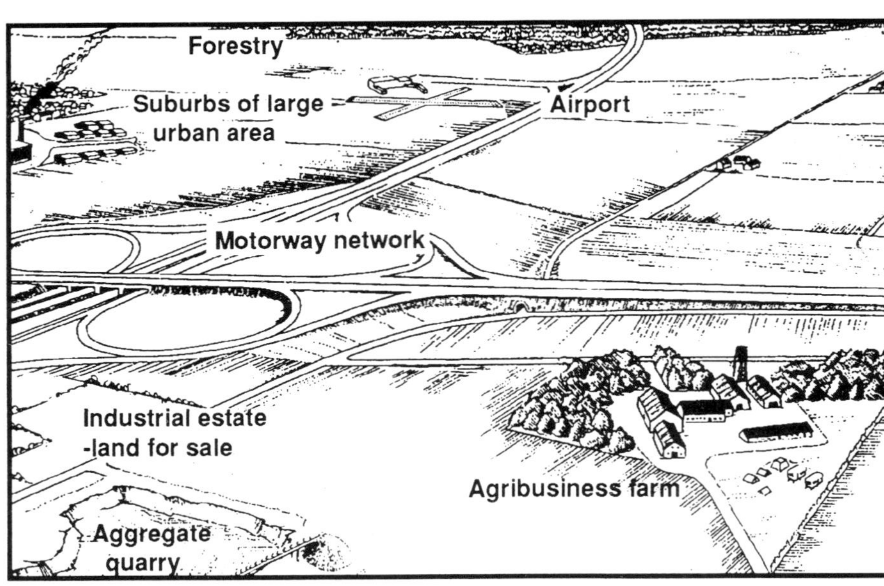

Competition for Rural Land Use

5 Among a number of **trends in British Farming** consider the following list:-
i. The number of farms has fallen rapidly since 1960 and is still falling.
ii. Average farm size has risen markedly since 1960 and is still rising.
iii. The number of farm workers has more than halved since 1960 and is still falling.
iv. Average field size has increased since 1960 and continues to increase.

Explain the reasons behind these trends in British farming.

6 Describe the measures that the **European Community** has taken in recent years to reduce farming surpluses.

7 Study the model of a large intensive commercial farm (**agribusiness**) in Southern England.

Explain the pattern of land use on the farm.

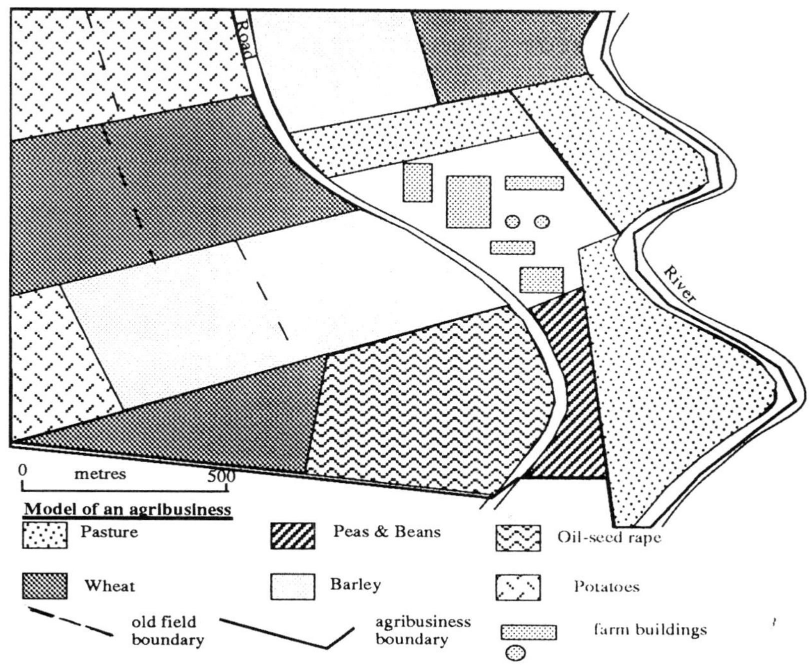

8 Agribusinesses aim to increase productivity a much as possible to make the maximum profit. What steps would you expect an agribusiness to take to increase its productivity?

9 Explain why environmental groups are often critical of agribusinesses.

10 Examine the two sketches of farming landscapes below.

Describe and explain the differences in land use between the two areas.

FARMING LANDSCAPE X

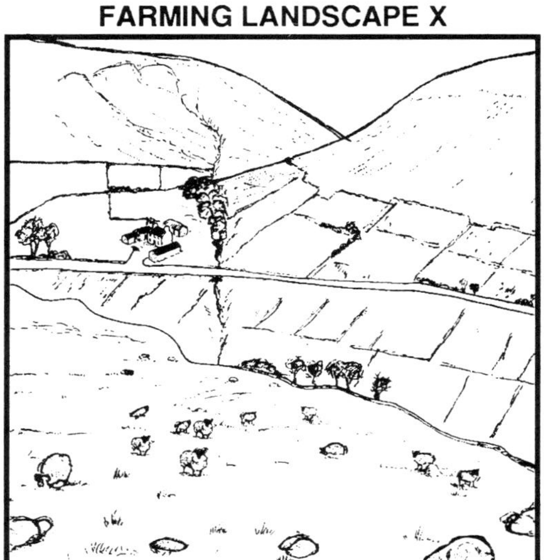

FARMING LANDSCAPE Y

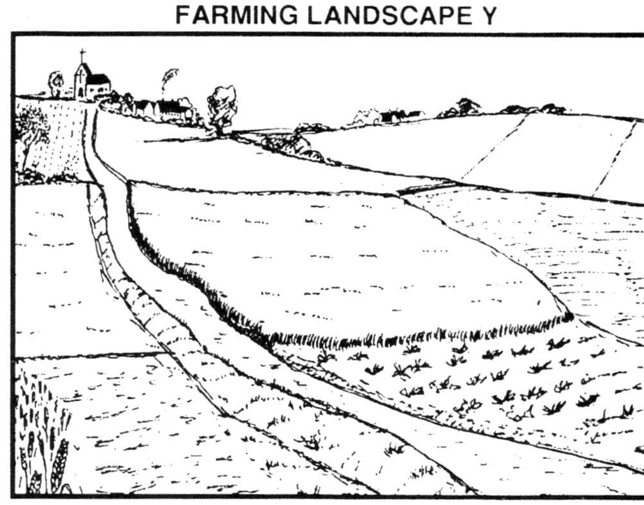

11 What are likely to be the main differences between farms in the two areas shown?
(mention: size, labour, buildings, products, machinery)

12 Refer to figure 89 on page 48
Describe and explain the distribution of **arable** farming in Great Britain.

26. WEATHER: Measuring the weather

Key Idea: Elements of weather can be identified, observed, measured, recorded and classified

Fig.106 River in spate after heavy rain

Weather is the state of the atmosphere at a local level, observed and measured on a time scale from miuntes to months. Weather studies emphasise the aspects of the atmosphere which affect human activity (Fig.106). These elements of weather include temperature, precipitation, sunshine, air pressure, wind, cloud and visibility. The study of weather , the science of **meteorology**,(Figs.107-108) involves the daily observation and measurement of weather elements from a large network of 'weather stations' - some at sea, most on land. The British Meteorological Office (at Bracknell, near London) collates weather data using computers and skilled experts. Weather studies and fore-casting have recently been greatly advanced through the use of satellites.

Fig.107 Weather recording

MEASURING & RECORDING THE WEATHER

Temperature

Stevenson Screen

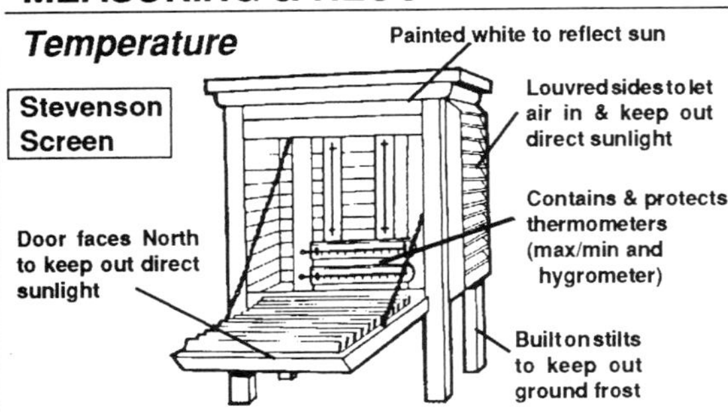

Temperature is measured using thermometers. **Maximum and Minimum thermometers** are used to give daily highest and lowest readings and there-fore the daily or **diurnal** range and average. The thermometers are usually stored in the **Stevenson Screen**, well protected from direct sunlight and frost, as well as interference from people or animals. Temperature readings are shown using **line graphs** and described using the following scale:

THERMOMETERS

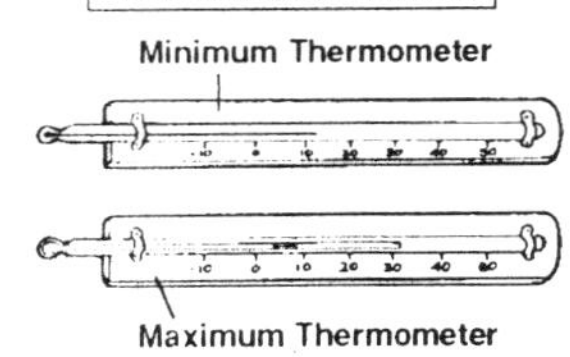

Temp°C	25	20	15	10	5	0	-5	-15
Description	Very Hot	Hot	Warm	Mild	Cool	Cold	Freezing	Very Cold

Humidity

Hygrometer

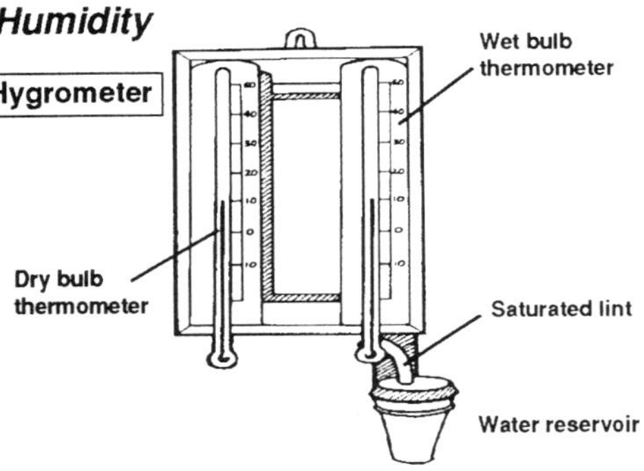

Humidity is the amount of water vapour or moisture in the air. Warm air holds more moisture than cold air. When air holds all the moisture it can, the air is said to be **saturated**. If temperatures then fall slightly **condensation** will occur and water droplets will form resulting in cloud or fog. This temperature is known as the **Dew Point**. Precipitation only occurs in saturated air. Meteorologists are interested in the amount of water in the air relative to the amount in saturated air. This is known as the **Relative Humidity** and is given as a percentage. A relative humidity of 100% means saturated air and a high probability of precipitation. Meteorologists use a Relative Humidity table for calculating the Relative Humidity.

RELATIVE HUMIDITY TABLE (%)

Dry Bulb Temp. °C	Depression of the Wet Bulb .5	1.0	1.5	2.0	2.5	3.0	3.5	4.0
0	91	82	73	65	56	48	39	31
1	91	83	75	66	58	50	42	34
2	92	84	76	68	60	52	45	37
3	92	84	77	69	62	54	47	40
4	92	85	78	70	63	56	49	42
5	93	86	79	72	65	58	51	45
6	93	86	79	73	66	60	53	47
7	93	87	80	74	67	61	55	49
8	94	89	81	75	69	63	57	51
9	94	88	82	76	70	64	58	53
10	94	88	82	76	71	65	60	54

To calculate the Relative Humidity, subtract the wet bulb from the dry bulb temperature (the depression of the wet bulb) and use the table to calculate the Relative Humidity %.

Precipitation

Rain Gauge

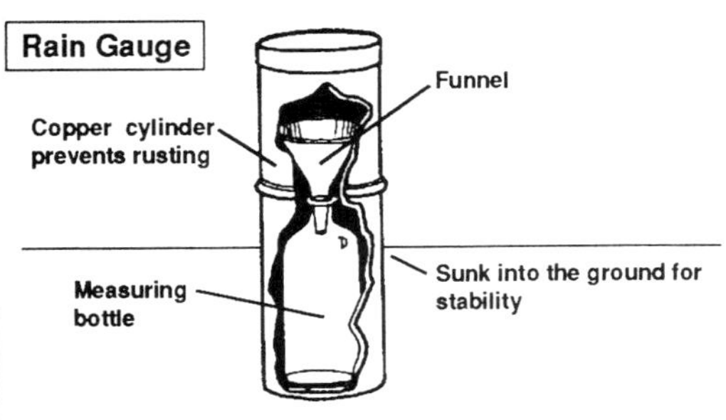

Precipitation is moisture falling from the sky and is measured by using a **Rain Gauge**. Rainfall, snowfall, hail and sleet, etc are captured and fed into the measuring bottle from the funnel. The Rain Gauge is sunk into the gorund for stability and is usally located away from shelter, e.g. trees, buildings, walls, etc. Precipitation is measured in millimetres and illustrated by **bar graph** and described using the following scale:-

PPT in one day (mm)	12	6	3	1	0
Heavy	Long Periods of ppt	Showers	Light Drizzle	Trace	Dry

Sunshine

Heliograph

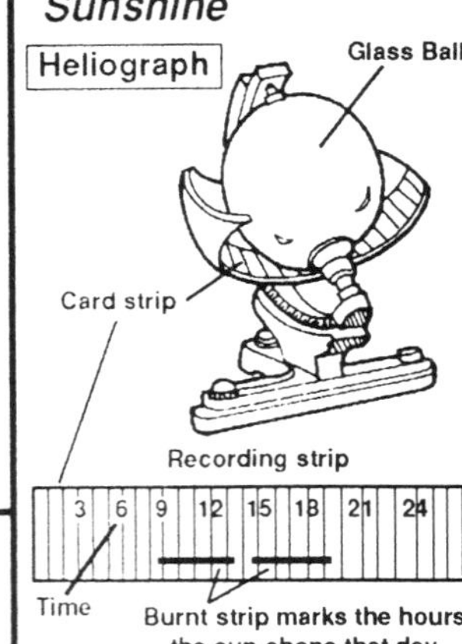

The amount of sunshine is meas-ured by a **Sunshine Recorder** (or a Heliograph). The amount is given in hours read from the recording strip through which the sun's rays were magnified and burnt on to a strip of card.

Wind Speed and Direction

Anemometer

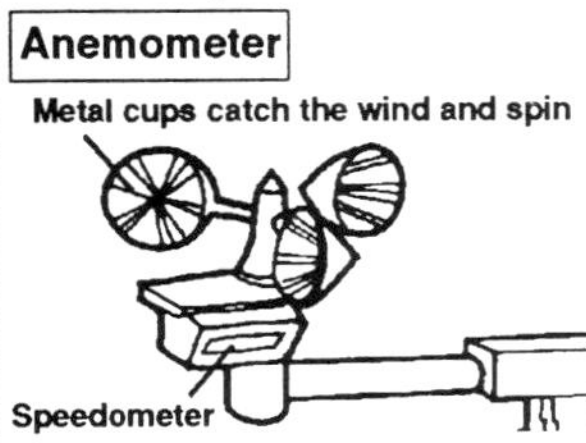

Wind vane

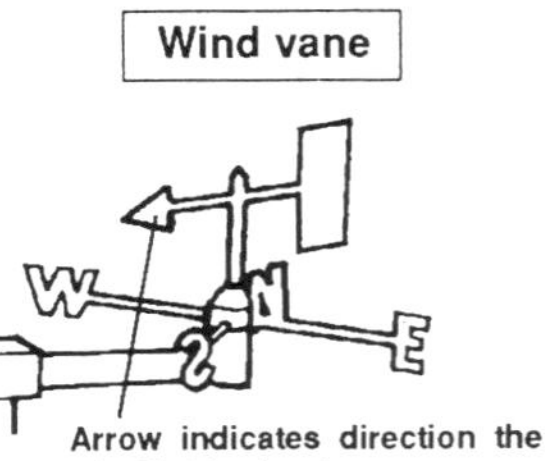

Wind speed can be measured very accurately with an **Anemometer** and is given in knots, km/hr or force. The **Beaufort Scale** is used to estimate the force of the wind.

Wind direction is measured using a **Wind Vane**. Wind direction is given as the direction **from which** the wind blows and is usally given as a compass direction, e.g. South-West.

Both wind instruments are usually sited several metres above ground away from shelter such as trees, buildings or wals.

Fig.108

Air Pressure

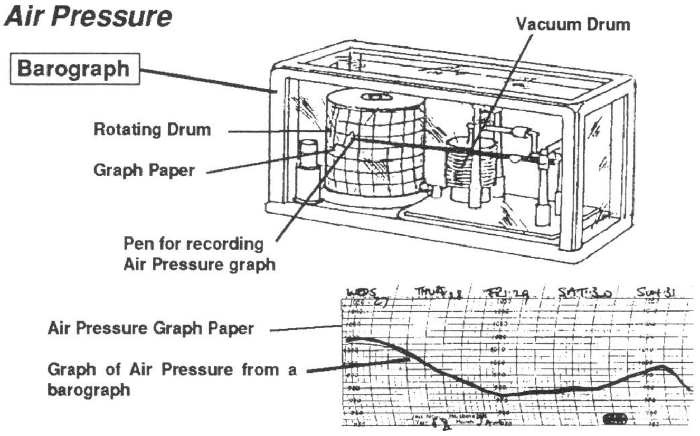

Air Pressure is the weight of air pressing down upon the surface of the Earth. The instruments used to measure air pressure are **barographs** and **barometers** and they are very sensitive to slight changes in pressure. A barograph measures and records air pressure all the time. A pen traces air pressure on a graph which revolves once a week. Air pressure is measured in **hectopascals** (formerly millibars) and the instruments are usually kept indoors away from inclement weather or interference.

Observing Visibility

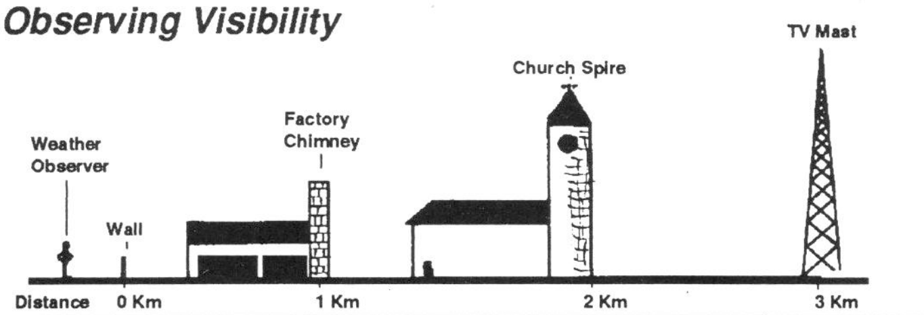

See less than 1 Km = FOG	See 1-2 Km = MIST	See over 2 Km = CLEAR DAY

Visibility is the furthest distance that can be seen and is given in kilometres. Measured by eye, visible distances are fixed on landmarks or tall buildings.

Observing Cloud Cover

Cloud cover is the amount of cloud obscuring the sky. It is calculated according to how many eighths of the sky, or **oktas**, are covered in cloud.
For example,
0 oktas means the sky is completely clear,
8 oktas means the sky is completely covered
9 oktas means the sky cannot be seen.

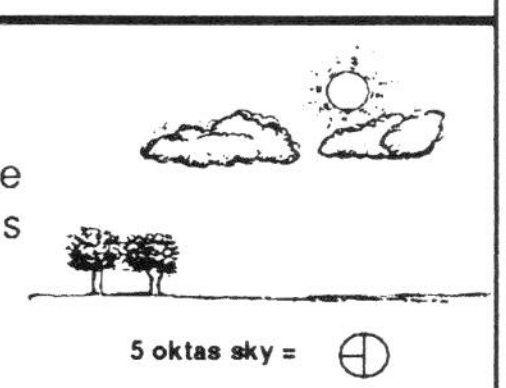

See table opposite for more details

Observing Cloud Type

Clouds consist of millions of ice crystals which form when condensation occurs. The many different types of cloud can be classified into 3 main groups - High, Medium and Low level clouds. Each is formed under different circumstances and is associated with different types of weather.

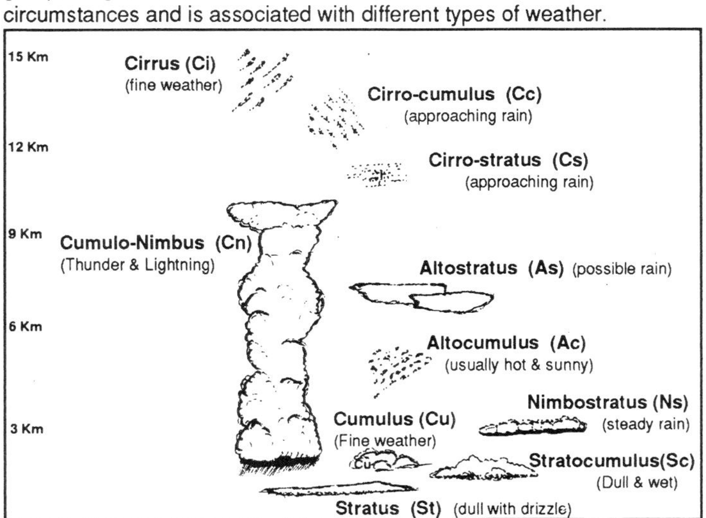

Weather Station Symbols

Station Symbols are used as a short-hand summary of the weather recorded at a weather station and have the following coded meaning. In the case of this weather station

Temperature 10°C, Wind SW, speed 25 knots, Weather drizzle, 6 oktas cloud cover

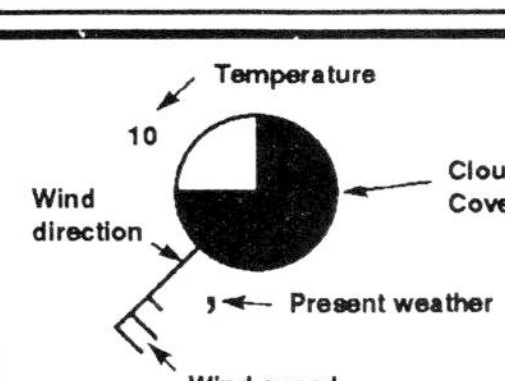

Weather Symbols

Wind Speed

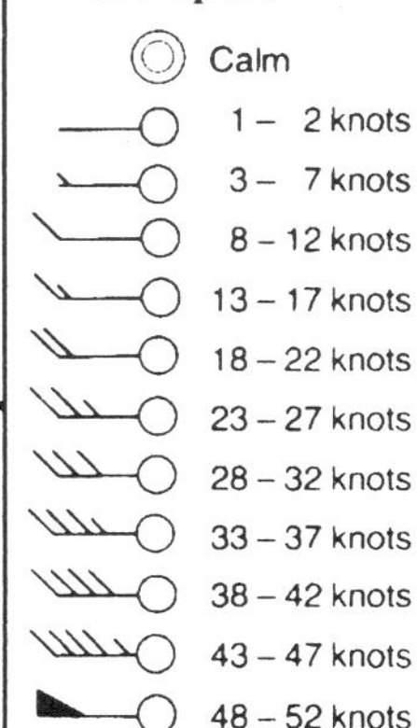

Cloud Coverage

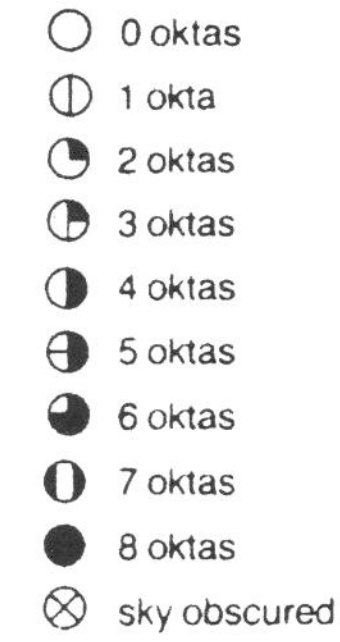

Low Cloud (CL)

Symbols for low cloud are

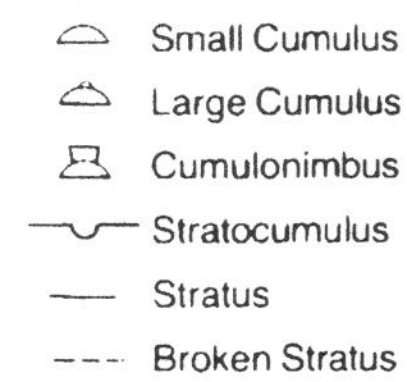

The symbol for low cloud is found below the station circle.

Medium Cloud (CM)

There are only three types of medium level clouds used in station models -

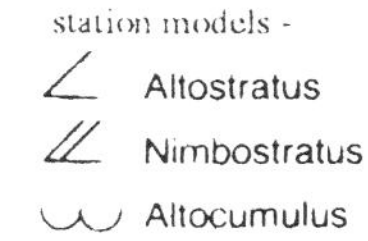

High Cloud

Symbols for high cloud are

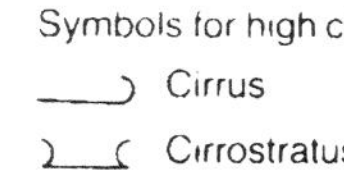

Assignment Twenty-One

1 What kinds of problem could result from the flood in figure 106 ?

2 List six elements of weather.

3 Explain the meaning of the following terms :- weather, relative humidity, precipitation, air pressure, cloud cover, visibility.

4 Using the information given in Figs.107-108, complete a larger version of the following table:-

Weather Element	Instrument used	Units of measurement	Location of instrument

5 Copy the table below and calculate the Relative Humidity using Fig.107

Dry Bulb Temp C	Wet bulb Temp C	Relative Humidity %
6	5	
10	6.5	

7a Decode the following Weather Station Symbols

7b Draw Station Symbols for the following data:

C. Temp. 22 C, Rain, 6 oktas Wind SW, 15 knots

D. Temp. -5 C, Fog, Sky Obscured, Calm

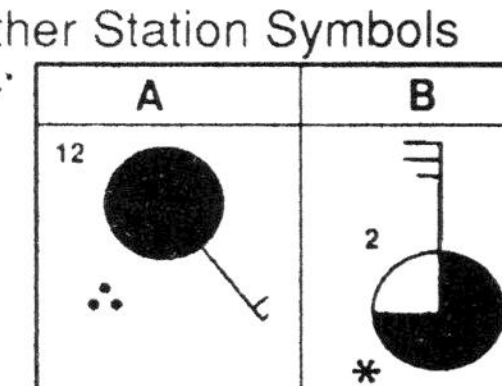

27. WEATHER: Streams and fronts

Key Idea: Elements of weather can be measured & recorded and dynamic patterns identified

Fig.109 Air masses and weather in the U.K.

Polar Maritime (Pm) originates from Northern Canada and the Arctic Ocean. Pm is a very common air mass over the U.K. It brings cool conditions throughout the year. Pm air warms up slightly in crossing the Atlantic Ocean and can give heavy showers over highland usually separated by bright intervals. Good visibility with strong to gale force winds.

Arctic Maritime (Am) originates from the Arctic Ocean. Am brings very cold conditions in winter, cold in spring, rare in summer. Am air warms up very slighlty in crossing the North Atlantic and can bring Scotland snow in winter, hail in spring both as heavy showers lasting several days. London may be at freezing point in winter with limited precipitation. Strong to gale force in the north of the U.K.

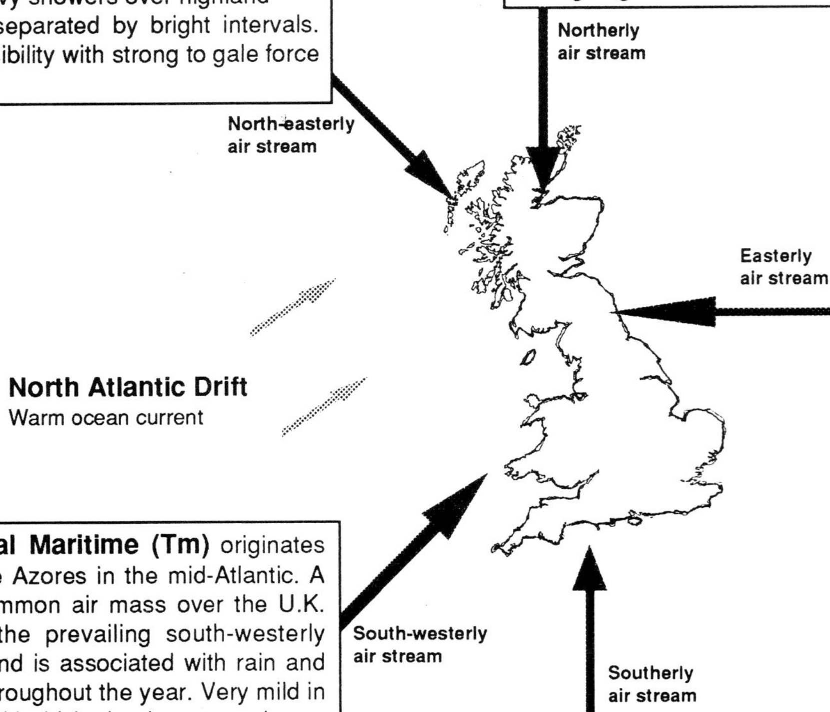

Polar Continental (Pc) originates from Siberia in winter. Pc gives very cold conditions in winter (SE England below 0 C). Begins cold and dry but warms up in crossing the North Sea and can give heavy snow in Eastern U.K. with bright, clear conditions over the western areas. Pc may last several days and the wind chill factor is severe. In summer, Pc may bring settled dry and warm conditions with light winds.

Tropical Maritime (Tm) originates from the Azores in the mid-Atlantic. A very common air mass over the U.K. Brings the prevailing south-westerly winds and is associated with rain and cloud throughout the year. Very mild in winter with thick cloud cover and poor visibility (hill and coastal fog). Little frost in winter under Tm conditions. Summers are warm with occasionally heavy thunderstorms. Tm brings moderate to strong winds.

Tropical Continental (Tc) originates from over the Sahara, bringing southern air conditions occuring mainly in summer over the U.K. Summer conditions are very hot and dry with little wind. Winter conditions associated with Tc are warm, dry and sunny.

The weather in the U.K. is directly affected by the winds which blow over the country. These winds originate from **air masses** - areas of almost stationary air that tend to assume the temperature and humidity characteristics of the areas they lie over.
When an air mass moves to another area it becomes an **air stream**- carrying with it the temperature and humidity of its source area. Air streams are named after their source areas (Fig.109). Five air streams influence weather in the U.K. :-

Pm	Polar Maritime	Cold & Wet
Am	Arctic Maritime	Very Cold & Wet
Pc	Polar Continental	Cold & Dry
Tc	Tropical Continental	Warm & Dry
Tm	Tropical Maritime	Warm & Wet

The U.K. lies at the confluence of these five air streams and as a result, has a very variable weather pattern.
When one air stream meets another they do not readily mix because they have different temperatures and humidity. The junction between air streams is known as a **front** .

The warmer, lighter air stream always rises over the colder, denser air stream. As the warmer air rises it cools and any water vapour condenses into water droplets forming clouds. There are three main types of front (Fig.110) :-

Warm Front - where warm air is advancing and is forced to rise over cold air bringing steady rain.
Cold Front - where advancing cold air undercuts warm air bringing heavy rain.
Occluded Front - where a cold front undercuts a warm front bringing very heavy rain.

The winds and air streams that influence the weather over the U.K. depend upon air pressure. Air pressure is illustrated on weather maps using **isobars** (Fig,111).
Isobars indicate where areas of high and low pressure are located.

Anticyclones - high pressure (above 1013 hp), where falling air circulates outwards, in a clockwise direction.
Depressions low pressure (below 1013 Hp), where rising air circulates inwards in an anticlockwise direction.

Fig. 110 Fronts

COLD AND WARM FRONTS

Wherever warm air meets colder air it always rises over the colder, denser air producing a **Warm Front** (& usually prolonged rain).

Where cold air meets warmer air it undercuts the warmer, lighter air producing a **Cold Front** (& usually heavy rain followed by showers).

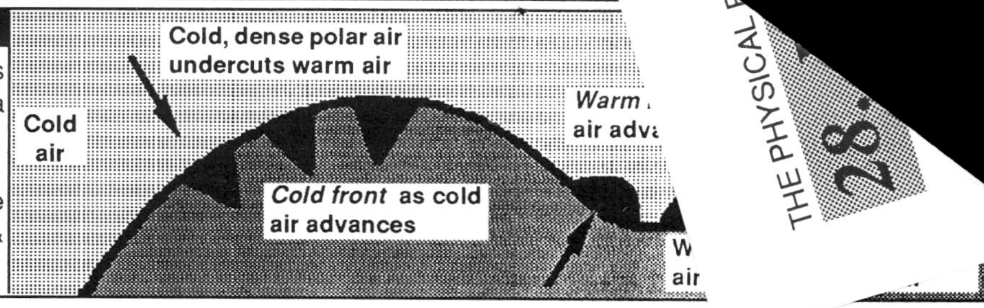

Air streams from both Polar and Tropical areas converge upon the U.K. with regularity creating frontal situations such as those illustrated here. Where the warmer tropical air dominates, low pressure develops as warm air rises, lessening the weight of air pressing down on the surface of the Earth. Low pressure systems slowly develop creating an anti-clockwise windflow, rain and low cloud.
Winds blow from High pressure areas to Low pressure areas at an angle due to the rotation of the Earth

FRONTS AND SECTORS

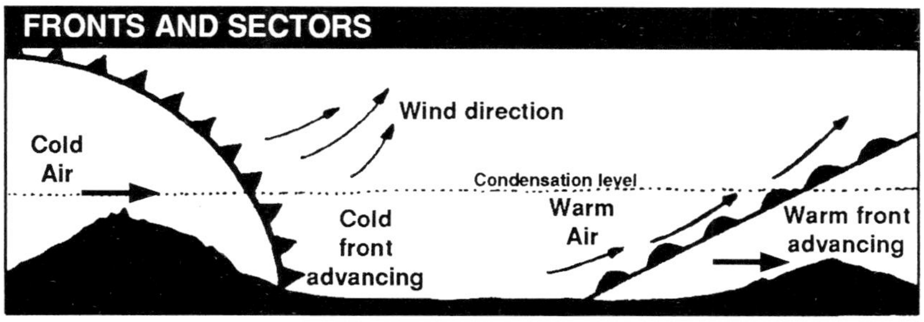

FRONTS IN A WEATHER SYSTEM

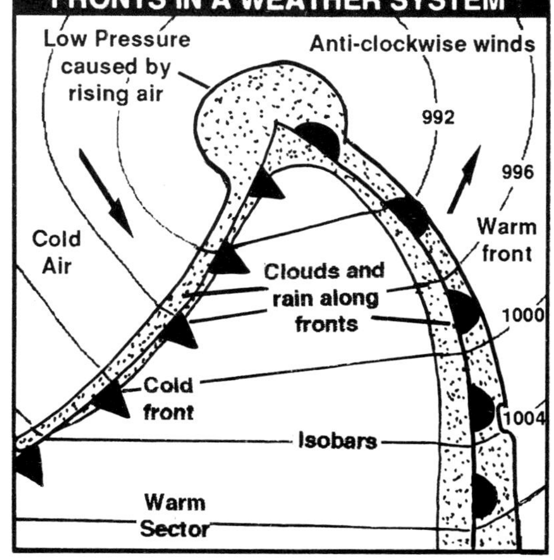

ANTICYCLONE HIGH PRESSURE SYSTEM

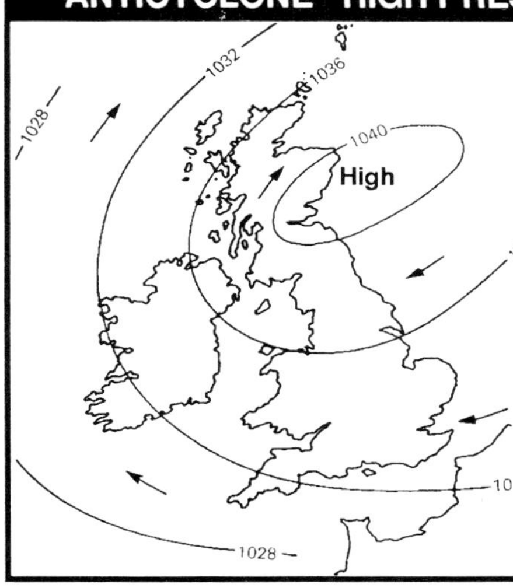

Winds blow in a clockwise direction around High Pressure systems

Isobars are well spaced, there are light winds. Anticyclones are slow moving.

Settled, dry and sunny weather

In winter anticyclones bring very cold, frosty and foggy weather. In summer, they bring hot weather.

DEPRESSION LOW PRESSURE SYSTEM

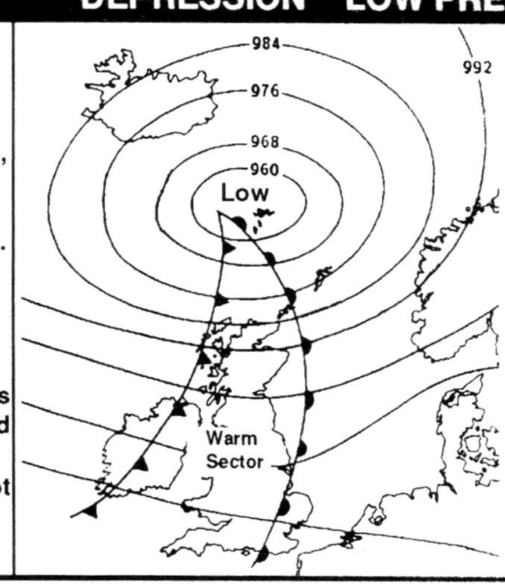

Winds blow in an anti-clockwise direction around Depression (Low Pressure systems)

Isobars are closely spaced - strong to gale force winds are experienced

Unsettled, dull and wet weather throughout the year

Depressions move quickly and are associated with warm and cold fronts

Fig.111 High and Low Pressure Systems

Assignment Twenty-One

1 What are the main influences on the weather of the U.K. ?

2 Explain the meaning of each of the following terms:- air mass, air stream, front, isobar, depression.

3 Using a simple outline map, prepare a summary of the main air streams and their associated weather over the U.K.

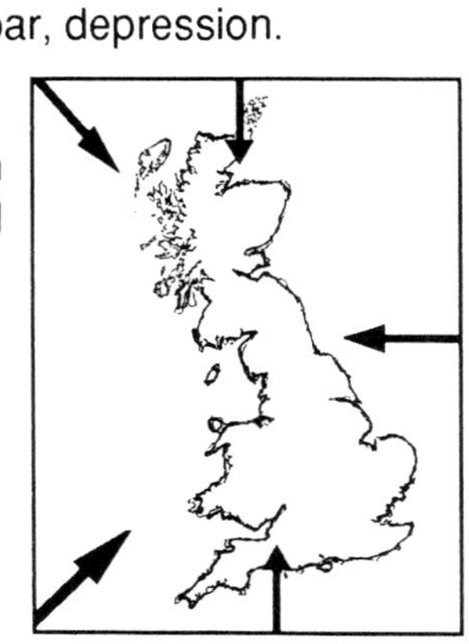

4 Explain the weather brought to the U.K. by
i. Arctic Maritime (Am)
ii. Tropical Maritime (Tm)
iii. Polar Continental (Pc)
air streams

5 Explain each of the following:-
i. Gale force winds in a depression
ii. Drought in an anticyclone
iii. Falling barometers in a depression
iv. An occluded front
v. Lack of frost in a depression

6a When do depressions form and why ?
6b When do anticyclones form and why ?

7 For any day of your choice, research and collect weather data (from station readings, media sources, satellite photos, weather maps (synoptic charts), etc).
Identify and explain the main influences on the U.K. weather that day.

WEATHER: Development of a depression

Key Idea: Elements of weather can be measured & recorded and dynamic patterns identified

Depressions develop along the junction between the Tropical and Polar air streams between latitudes 40 and 45 N.°This junction is known as the Polar Front (Fig.112).
Warm, southerly air wedges under the colder, northerly air and as it does so warm air rises creating a drop in air pressure. Winds circulate around the low pressure in an anti-clockwise direction. Pressure continues to decrease as first a warm front and later a cold front sweep across the U.K. from west to east, bringing associated weather in a series of stages. Eventually the cold front catches the warm front as the depression fills and an occluded front forms. Figure 112 illustrates the passage of a depression over the U.K.

THE DEVELOPMENT OF A DEPRESSION OVER THE UNITED KINGDOM Fig.112

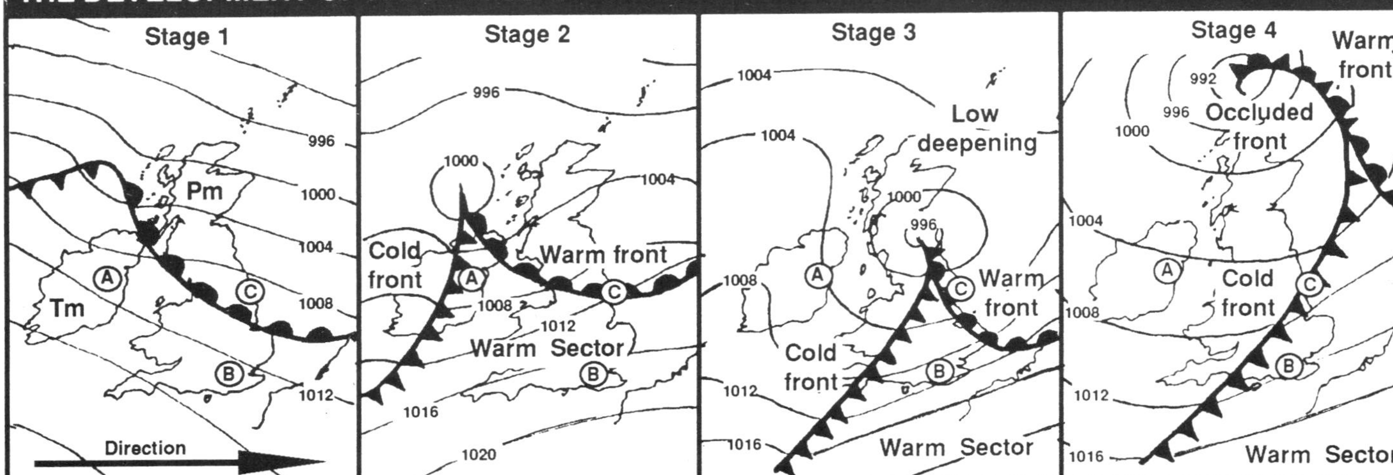

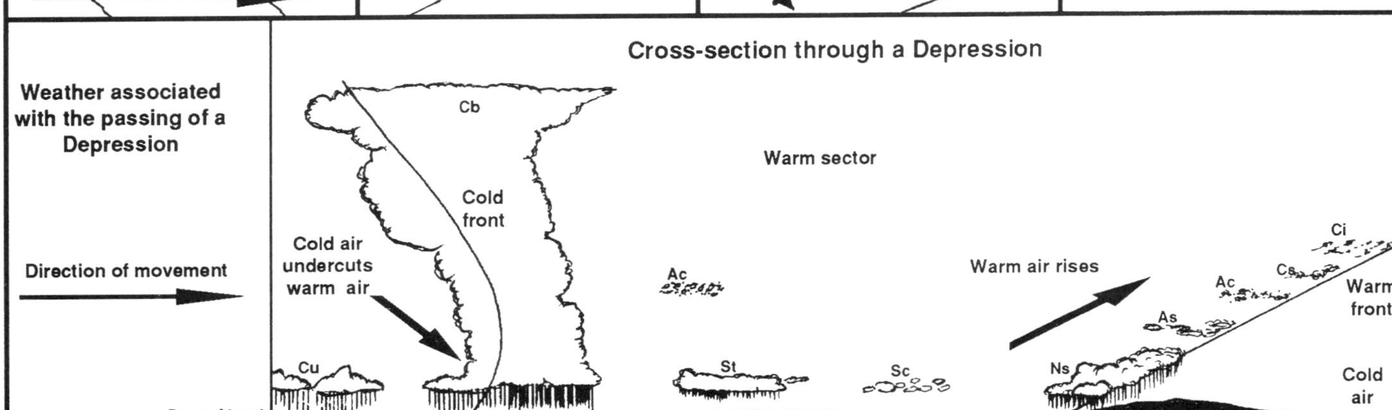

Distance (Km)	after the cold front	about 45 km	about 175 Km	145 - 175 Km	about 500 Km
Air Pressure	rising more slowly	sudden rise	steady	fall ceases	steady fall
Wind Direction	NW	veering SW to NW	SW	veers SE to SW	SE
Wind Speed	blustery slowly decreasing force 3-4	strong to gale force 6-8	decreasing force 2-4	strong force 5-6	slowly increasing force 2-4
Temperature (e.g in December)	cold e.g. 3°C	sudden decrease, e.g 4°C	warm to mild e.g. 10°C	sudden rise e.g. 11°C	cool e.g. 6°C
Relative Humidity	rapid fall	high in precipitation	steady and high	high in precipitation	slow rise
Cloud	decreasing Cc and Cu	very thick giant Cb	low to clear St, Sc, Ac	low and thick cloud, Ns	high and thin cloud Ci, Cs, Ac, As
Precipitation	heavy showers	short downpours of heavy rain & hail	drizzle to stop raining	prolonged rainfall	dry
Visibility	Good, poor in showers	poor	often poor	decreasing rapidly	Good

Climate and Weather

Weather is concerned with daily atmospheric changes.

Climate is the average weather recorded over a period of thirty years. The average weather for any place on the planet can be illustrated using an annual climate graph showing details of the temperature and precipitation pattern.

Fig.113 Climate Graph annual average weather

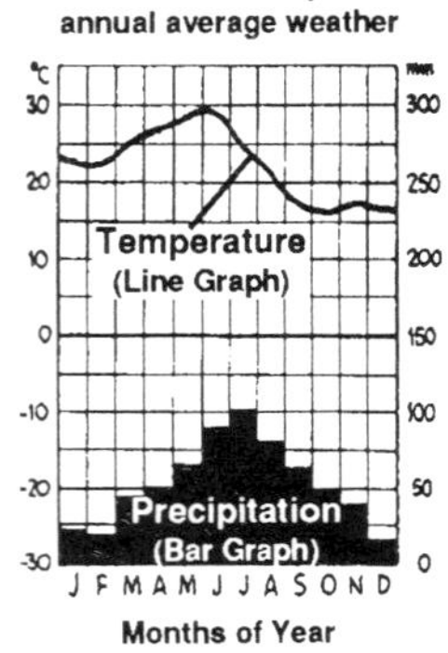

Assignment Twenty-Two

1 Describe the development of a Depression over the U.K.
2a Study Fig.112.
State the relationships between the passage of fronts and:- i. air pressure ii. precipitation.
2b Compare the weather experienced at **A** and **C** throughout the passing of the depression.
2c Explain the difference in weather experienced.
3 Write a weather forecast for **B** for Stages 1-4.
4 Describe the relationship between weather and climate.

29. EXAM STYLE QUESTIONS

WEATHER

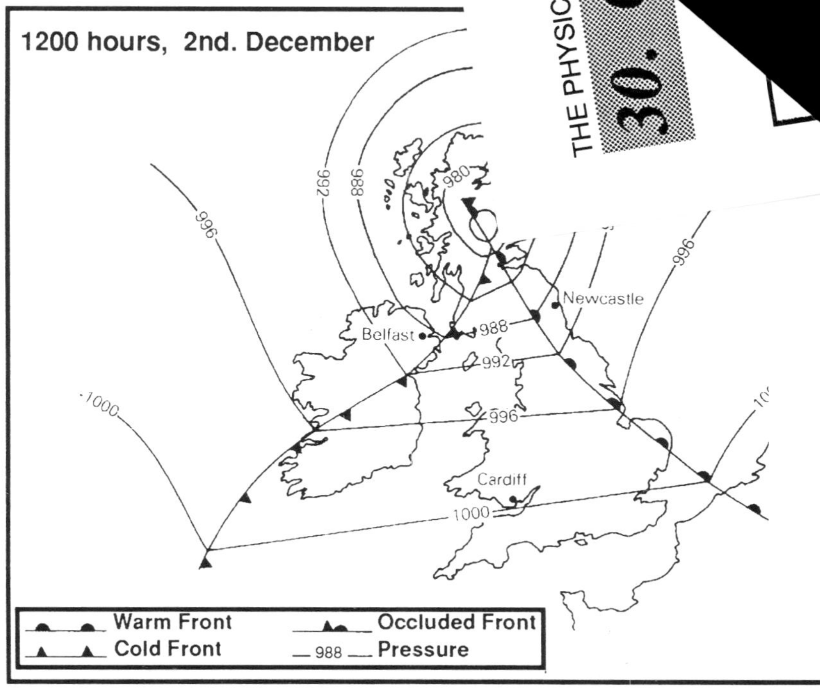

1 Explain in detail the difference in weather conditions being experienced at **Belfast** and **Newcastle** at the time the synoptic chart was constructed.

2 Which of the following station circles is most likely to be a summary of the weather at Belfast.
Explain your answer.

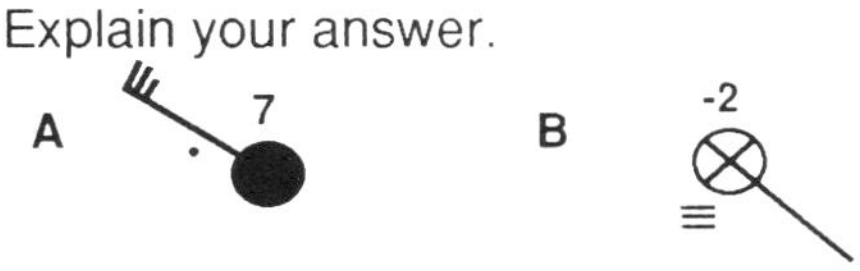

3 The weather system shown over the British Isles is moving rapidly North East. Describe what is likely to happen to the weather in **Cardiff** in the 24 hours after the chart was drawn.

4 Study the following weather forecasts for Newcastle. One is for 1200 hours on 2 December and the other is for 1200 hours on 4 December.

Match each forecast to the correct day, giving reasons for your choice in each case.

Forecast **A** : Prolonged rain, heavy in places, overcast , moderate southeasterly winds, cool, maximum temperature 8°C.

Forecast **B** : Showery conditions, generally light, occasional bright spells, northwesterly winds, cool, maximum temperature 6°C.

5 Describe ways in which various recent meteorological developments such as satellite photography, radar images and computers can make weather forecasting more accurate.

6 Name the five weather instruments labelled on the diagram and indicate what each instrument measures.

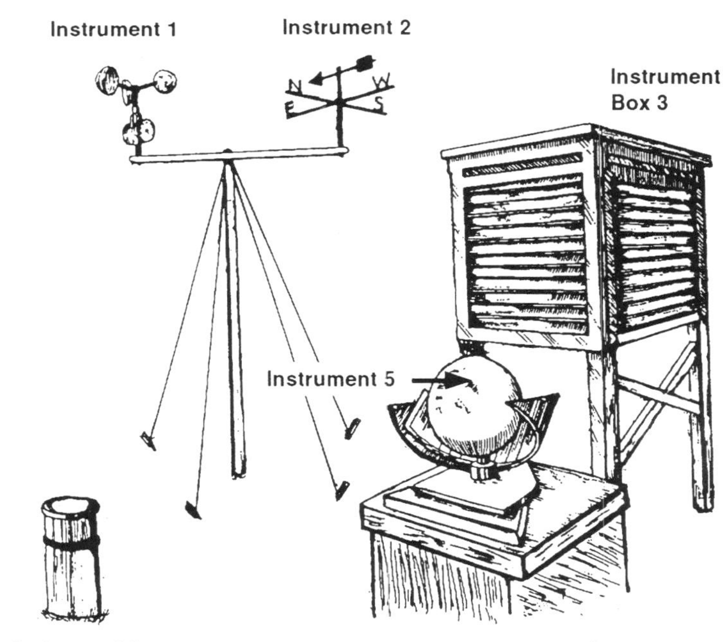

7 What factors should be taken into account when considering a site for a ground weather station?

8 An anticyclone is a high pressure weather system.
Describe the weather anticyclones tend to bring to Britain in
(a) winter
(b) summer

See p 65
CLIMATE FACTORS
e.g. LATITUDE + ALTITUDE

LIMATE: *Major climate zones*

Key Idea: The world can be divided into major climatic zones

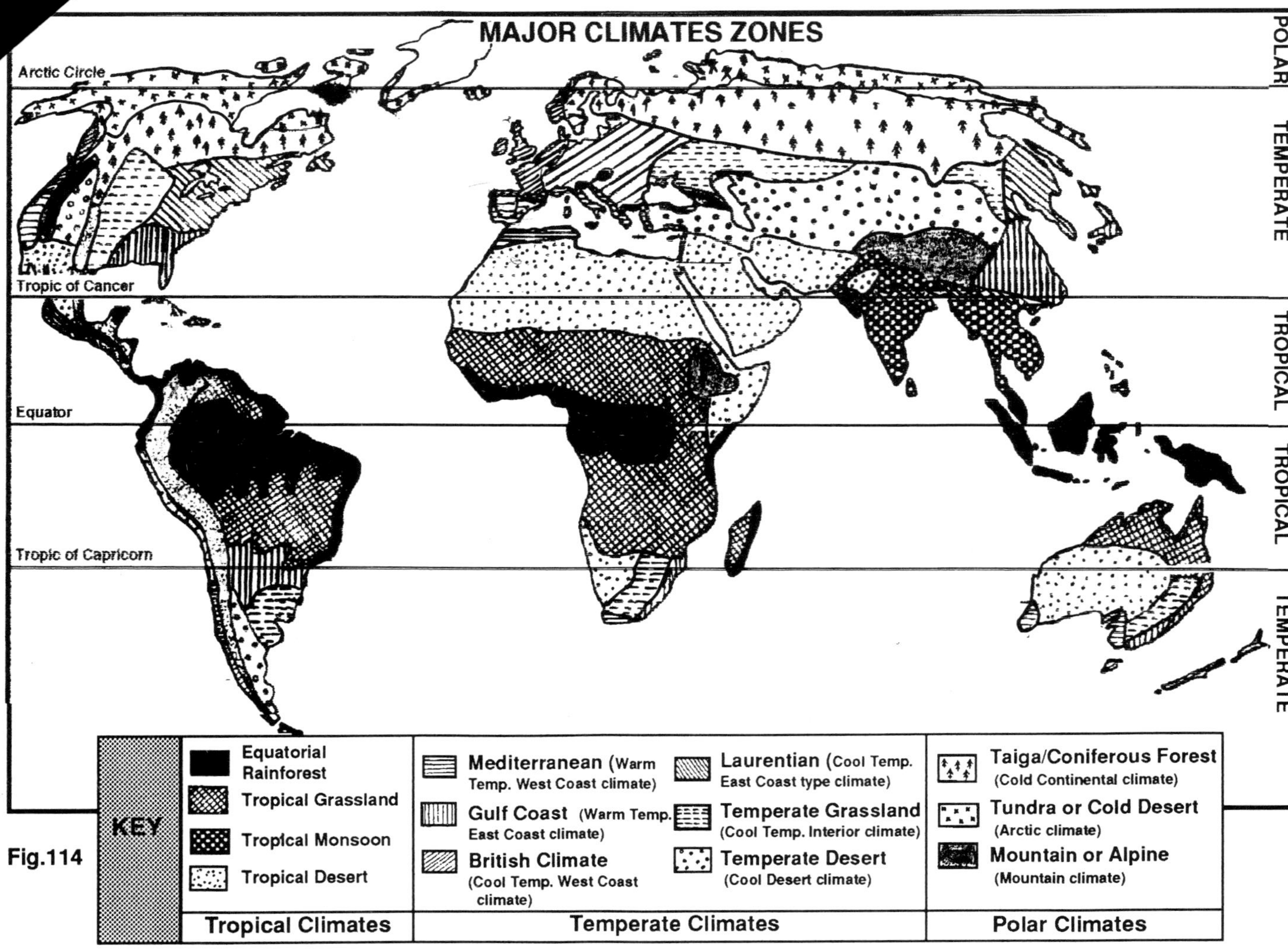

Fig.114

The major climatic zones shown in figure 114 represent large areas of the Earth which have broadly similar climate characteristics. The climate of each area strongly influences the natural vegetation and therefore the formation of soils.

The world's climates may themselves by classified into three main sectors:-

Polar climates	Climates of areas located roughly above latitude 60 North
Temperate climates	Climates of areas located roughly between latitude 60 and the Tropics of Cancer and Capricorn
Tropical climates	Climates of areas located within the Tropics, centred around the Equator.

Each climatic zone, for example, the Tundra area can be referred to by its climatic name, in this case, Arctic, and by its natural vegetation name, Tundra or Cold Desert (sometimes known as the **biome**).

The climate of an area may be influenced by a range of factors which may interlink. The most important of these factors are:

Latitude - increasing distance from the Equator and therefore from the most direct rays of the sun affect the average annual temperatures of an area. In general the further from the Equator, the colder the area. The growing season decreases with latitude.

Altitude - increasing height above sea-level has the same general effect as increasing latitude.

Marine influence - because the sea cools the land adjoining it in the hot season and warms it slightly during the cool/cold season, the overall effect is to reduce the annual range of temperature and increase annual precipitation. Marine climates are therefore generally wetter and more **equable** (having a small range of temperature).

Continentality - Away from the moderating influence of the sea, the land overheats in the hot season and cools quickly during the cool/cold season. The overall effect is to increase the range of temperature and decrease the annual precipitation. Continental climates are therefore more **extreme** (having larger ranges and low precipitation).

Ocean Currents - warm ocean currents, e.g. the North Atlantic Drift, warm affected coastlines, even in high latitudes such as Norway (ice-free coasts all year). Cold ocean currents cool affected coastlines and can make them drier, e.g. the Canaries current of the Saharan coast in Africa.

The areas examined in figure 115 illustrate a variety of influences on their climate and therefore on their natural vegetation and human use.

Fig.115

Tundra or Cold Deserts

Tundra areas are located in the extreme north of Alaska, Canada and Siberia as well as coastal Greenland and Iceland. These areas experience an Arctic climate. The short, summers may have continuous periods of sunlight but monthly temperatures do not easily reach freezing point. Winters are very severe, long and dark with temperatures regularly falling below -35°C. The annual range of temperature is approx. 32°C - smaller than areas inland due to the moderating influence of the sea which freezes for over 8 months.

DISTRIBUTION OF TUNDRA AREAS

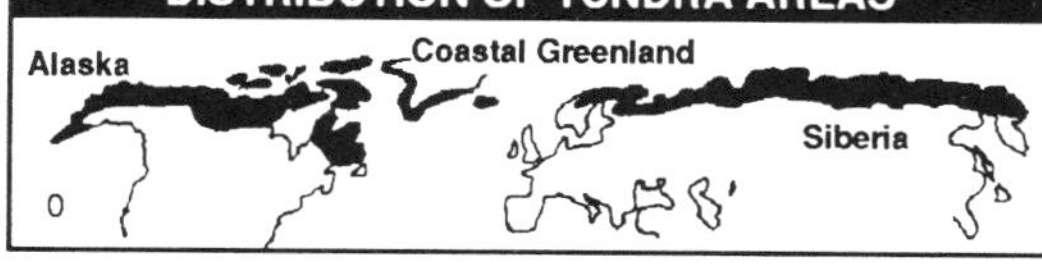

Precipitation is very low and well under the desert limit. Most precipitation falls as winter snow with rain during the brief summer.
Tundra areas are cold, almost barren treeless plains with continuous permafrost. White-out conditions are common during severe winters.
Summer temperatures are only high enough to thaw a thin top layer of soil which is known as 'muskeg' - a marshy plain or swamp.

THULE, Greenland (7.

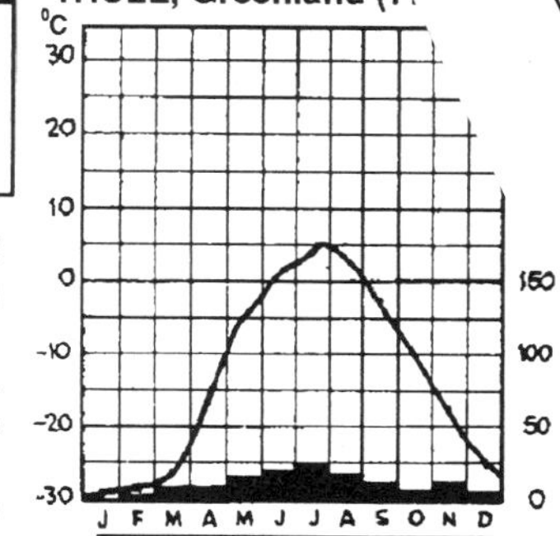

Temp.Range = 32.5°C
Annual PPT = 88mm

Mediterranean Areas

'Med' or Warm Temperate Western Coast areas are found along the west coasts of continents between 30° and 40° north and south of the Equator. The "Med' climate is often considered to be a mixture of hot desert and mild, marine climates. The climate is famous for its hot, dry summers and mild, wet winters. Summers are hot with the sun high in the sky and little cloud cover. Winters are mild due to the moderating influence of the sea. "Med' areas with cold offshore ocean currents often have coastal fogs, for example in California.

DISTRIBUTION OF MEDITERRANEAN AREAS

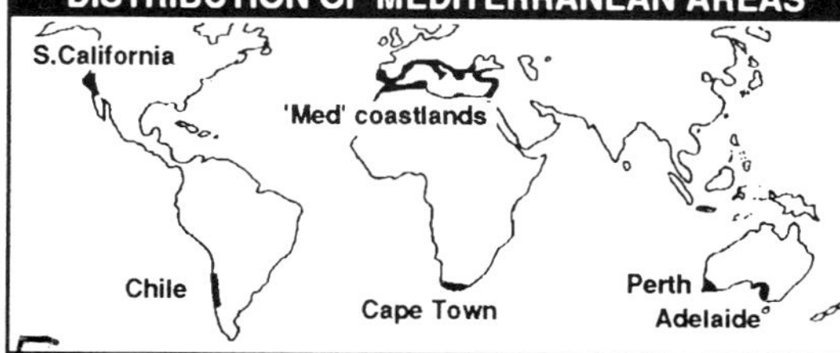

Precipitation is unevenly distributed with a summer drought and winter maximum. The annual precipitation often exceeds 750mm and is mainly rainfall. The highest temperatures, and evaporation rates occur during the time of minimum ppt and can cause problems for plant survival & agriculture.

ATHENS, Greece (38N, 23E)

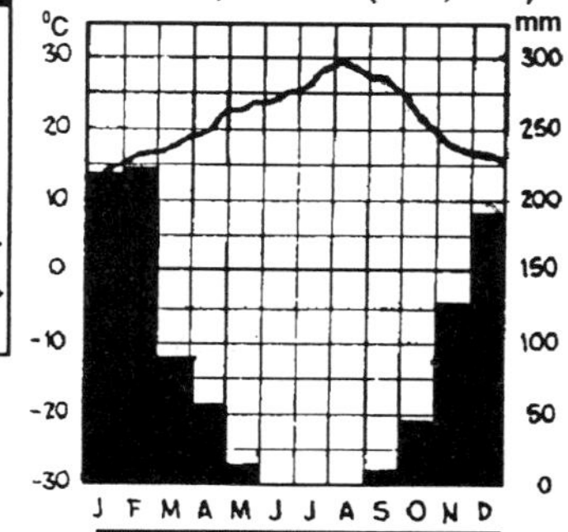

Temp.Range = 15.2°C
Annual PPT = 769mm

Tropical or Hot Deserts

Tropical or Hot Deserts are usually found on the west coast of continents, between 15° and 30° north or south of the Equator, in the trade wind belt. Hot deserts are defined as areas with less than 250mm of annual precipitation which have no month below 6°C.
Hot Deserts have extreme climates with very high temperatures (often over 35°C) and a temperature range of over 25°C. Daytime temperatures are high due to overhead sun, lack of cloud cover and high insolation from bare ground, rock or sand.

DISTRIBUTION OF HOT DESERT AREAS

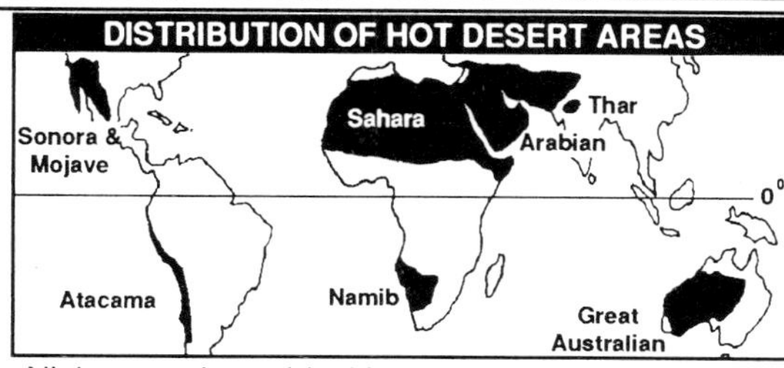

Nights can be cold with temperatures often below freezing. Precipitation is both extremely low (often less than 90mm) and unpredictable. Many hot deserts receive rainfall in one major downpour but rapid surface run-off, low infiltration rates and high evaporation minimise the effectiveness of the rain for plants.

JAZA IR FARAZAN, Saudi Arabia (45N, 10E)

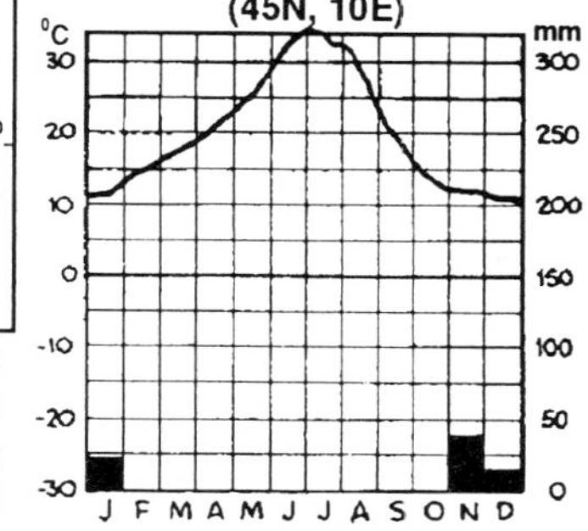

Temp.Range = 9.8°C
Annual PPT = 77mm

Equatorial Rainforest

Equatorial Rainforests are located in lowland areas along the Equator. They are found in humid areas, extending roughly 6 degrees north and south of the Equator. Although rainforests account for only 8% of the land area of the Earth, they host 50% of all the growing wood and at least two-fifths of the flora and fauna of the planet. The climate of the Equatorial Rainforest is uniform. Temperatures remain high and constant all year round because the sun is always high in the sky. The temperature range is very low (2-3°C) and there is often

DISTRIBUTION OF EQUATORIAL RAINFOREST AREAS

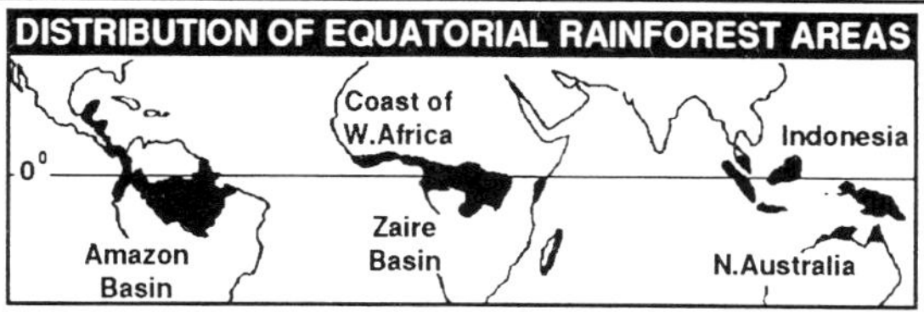

a slight increase in temperature during 'drier' spells. Annual precipitation falls as convectional rain and is both high and evenly distributed throughout the year. The high temperatures in combination with heavy precipitation give the rainforests a very humid climate where evapotranspiration is rapid. Daily, there are about 12 hours of daylight and 12 hours of darkness, a minimum temp of 22°C and a maximum of 32°C.

MANAUS, Brazil (3S, 0W)

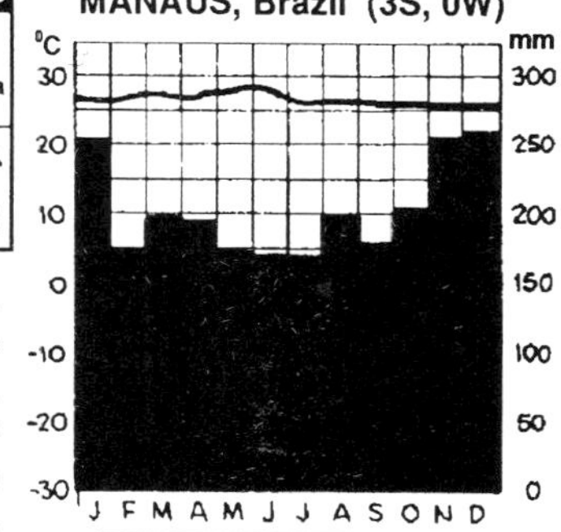

Temp.Range = 2°C
Annual PPT = 2056mm

Assignment Twenty-three

1 Make brief notes on each of the following influences on climatic zones:-
latitude, altitude, continentality, the seas and oceans.

2 Using fig.114, copy and then complete a larger version of the table below:-

Sector	Continental Climates	Marine Climates
Polar		
Temperate		
Tropical		

3 Give the meaning of each of the following terms:-
biome, equable, extreme, desert, humid, tundra.

4 Using fig.115, explain
i. the distribution of Rainforests and Hot Deserts
ii. the large range of temperature in Thule
iii. the low precipitation experienced in Jaza

5 Compare the desert climates experienced in Jaza and Thule.

6 Which climatic zone (fig.115) would be easiest to live in ? Explain your answer.

31. CLIMATE: *Tundra - cold deserts*

Key Ideas: The physical environment offers a range of possibilities for and limitations on human activities. The physical environment is a resource which has to be used with care

The Tundra or Cold Desert landscape is a variety of very cold, high mountains, intensely glaciated areas and low coastal plains (Fig.116). The word 'tundra' means barren treeless plain' and is a landscape with a very low rate of plant growth. Tundra areas have long, severe winters, short growing seasons and limited precipitation. The ground lies permanently frozen apart from the top 50-80cm which thaws in summer, forming 'muskeg' or marshy areas (Fig.117).

All tundra vegetation has adapted to the harsh conditions and lack of moisture. The tundra has fewer species of plant than any other climatic area and all are low growing to gain protection from strong wind. The main species include lichen mosses, grasses, some shrubs and flowers such as saxifrage and poppies. Most plants have small leaves to reduce transpiration and short roots to avoid permafrost. Mosses and cotton grasses survive in marshy areas. On south facing slopes and in areas of better drainage, flowers survive. On north facing slopes and in peaty, poorly drained areas, heathers grow.

Adjacent to seasonal rivers, dwarf trees such as stunted birch may grow but only to about 25cm high. In turn the tundra soils suffer from a lack of organic materials and consequently are poor, shallow and lacking in plant nutrients. Plants survive the harsh winter under deep snow but suffer from a lack of photosynthesis due to lack of sunlight.

The fragile tundra vegetation and soil can be disrupted by human activity such as tourism or mineral extraction (Fig.118). Caterpillar vehicle tracks may scar the tundra surface for over 35 years in some areas. The difficulties of the harsh climate and isolation of tundra areas such as Siberia and Northern Canada have so far limited the extent and amount of major human activity in tundra areas. However many experts believe that the tundra areas hold untapped, natural resources such as oil, gas and metals and as such, offer major opportunities for their development as the technology to combat the harsh conditions and remoteness is improved. The oilfields of North Slope Alaska offer one such example.

Fig.116 **A Tundra landscape**

Summer Tundra
Very short, cool summers, sunlight for up to 3 months, landscape thaws, muskeg and marshy hollows.

Winter Tundra
Very long, severe winters, darkness for up to 3 months; landscape completely frozen and snow-covered.

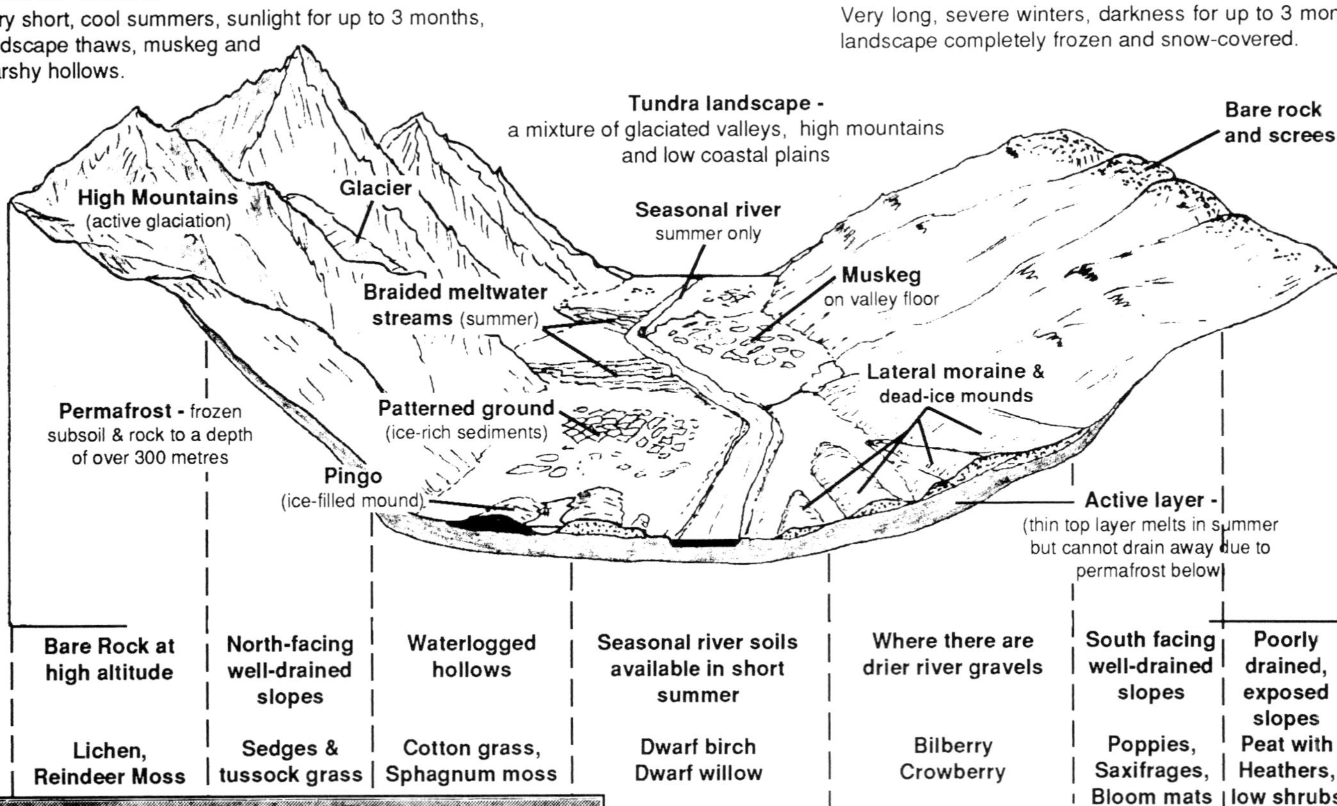

Fig.117 Permafrost in Alaska

Tundra Soil Profile

A soil profile is a section down through the topsoil, subsoil and bedrock of the area under study. Each Soil Profile can be divided into 3 main layers or Horizons, e.g.
A Horizon - Top soil
B Horizon - Subsoil
C Horizon - Bedrock (or original material known as Parent Material)

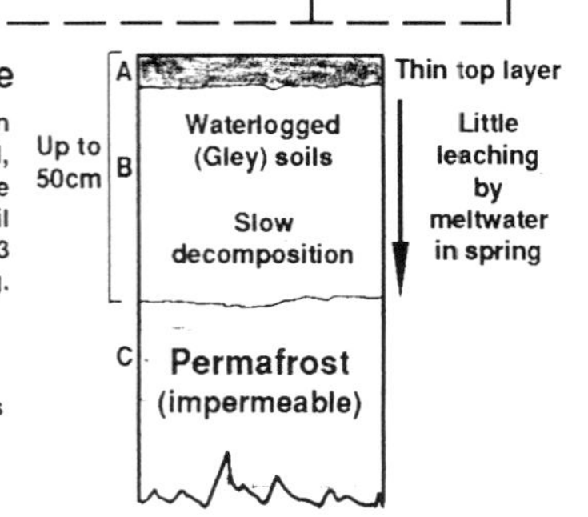

Fig.118 Oil related developments on Alaska's North Slope

OIL DEVELOPMENTS ON NORTH SLOPE ALASKA

Oil was discovered on Alaska's North Slope in 1968 - a wilderness previously undeveloped due to its remoteness and the severity of its climate and landscape. The rapidly expanding petro-economy (oil dependent) of the USA made the development of Alaska's oilfields an important priority. Oil companies such as Shell, Esso and Texaco in partnership with the US Government invested billions of dollars in overcoming the physical, human and environmental problems in developing the oilfields. A 1300km pipeline was constructed despite great difficulties across Alaska to the ice-free port of Valdez. Oil was, and still is, exported from there to Seattle via supertanker. Over the last 30 years, oil developers have had face many challenges including those posed by the landscape, harsh climate, traditional Inuit peoples and conservationists concerned about the environmental effect of oil development.

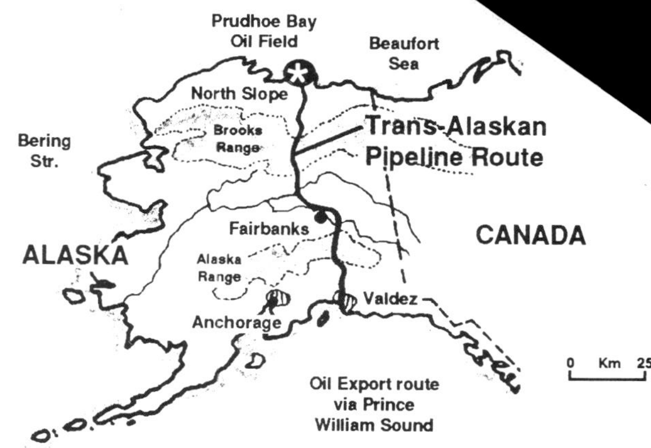

THE ROUTE OF THE TRANS-ALASKAN PIPELINE SYSTEM (TAPS)

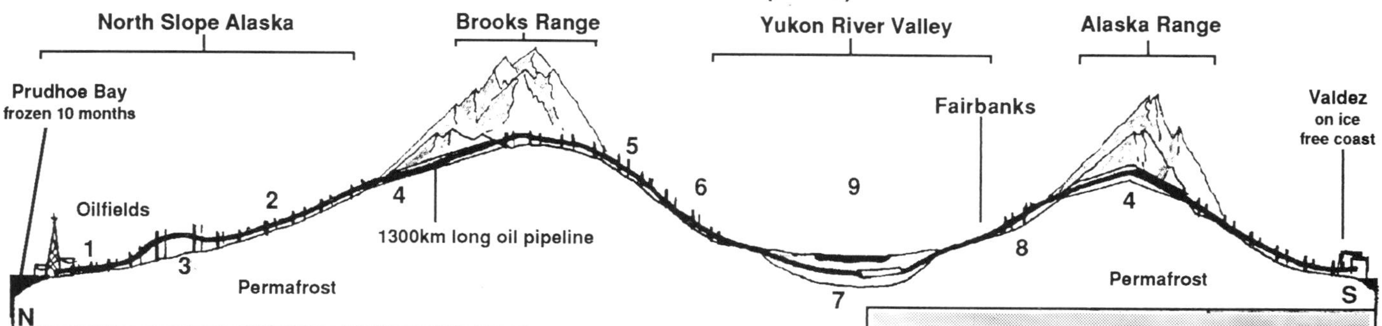

KEY TO PIPELINE DIAGRAM

1. **Oil pumped 1300km through pipeline at 80°C.**
2. **Pipeline built on stilts to stop the heat of the oil melting the perma frost and causing leakages.**
3. **3m high caribou underpass.**
4. **Pipeline follows tunnel drilled through solid rock**
5. **Anti-leak valves fitted every 100m**
6. **2 million barrels of oil & natural gas are pumped through the pipe line per day. Oil takes 5 days to travel the length of the pipeline.**
7. **Pipeline laid under the Yukon River in special concrete casing**
8. **Pipeline is flexible in order to counteract earthquakes**
9. **Pipeline crosses 350 rivers.**

Oilfield settlement in mid-summer near midnight

PROBLEMS ASSOCIATED WITH OIL DEVELOPMENTS IN ALASKA

Physical Problems

The long, severe winter lasts over 8 months and there can be up to 22 hours of total darkness each winter day.
Temperatures drop to below -50°C causing frostbite, snapping steel tools like twigs and necessitating the 24 hours per day running of diesel engines in order to stop them seizing up. Permafrost makes all construction difficult & expensive. The top layer melts in summer making quagmires and buildings collapse upon it. Other pipeline difficulties arise from earthquakes, 350 rivers, the 1460m rise over the Brooks Range, tanker accidents in and around the narrows of Prince William Sound (Valdez).

Human Problems

The traditional way of life of the Inuits has been changed. Modernlinuits welcome the modern developments brought by oil to the tundra. Inuits live in centrally heated wooden houses; buy food at local shops, own personal possessions such as TV, vehicles, rifles, CD players,etc; children go to school and adults have the opportunity of oil related work. Other traditionalists are less happy. They say that the community spirit has gone forever; traditional skills (hunting & fishing) are being lost; many young people leave the tundra for Los Angeles & New York; the language is being lost. Alcoholism, AIDS, divorce and violence are more common today.

Environmental Problems

Large vehicles destroy tundra soils & vegetation (which takes up to 35 years to regenerate). The migration routes of caribou are interrupted by pipeline developments. The habitats of various wildlife are disturbed including arctic foxes, wolves, brown bears, moose and dall sheep. Unsighlty scars on an area classified as 'wildscape' are common on the North Slope. Oil spillages affect wildlife and vegetation around the oilfields. Major tanker accidents, e.g. the Exxon Valdez accident in Prince William Sound near Valdez threaten coastlines & wildlife. Land once the domain of traditional inuit peoples and wildlife is now industrialised.

Assignment Twenty-four

1a What does 'tundra' mean ?
1b Describe the tundra landscape.

2 Give a full definition of each of the following terms:- muskeg, permafrost, pingo, active layer.

3 Make a simple fieldsketch of the photograph in Fig.116 and label its main features.

4 Describe the main ways in which plants adapt to the tundra climate.

5 Describe the relationship between vegetation and tundra landscape.

6a Make your own copy of the Route diagram of the Trans Alaskan Pipeline and key (Fig.118)
6b Explain why the pipeline is built on stilts.
6c Describe the problems the tundra area creates for the export of oil from North Slbpe Alaska.
6d **"Oil has brought great benefits to Alaska in the last 30 years".**
How far would each of the following people agree with this statement ? Fully explain your answers.
Oil worker, Old Inuit, Young Inuit, Environmentalist.

IATE: *Mediterranean coasts*

physical environment offers a range of possibilities for and limitations on human activities. The physical environment is a resource which has to be used with care

The ... any Mediterranean areas consists of a variety of ... ains, wide river valleys and narrow, sandy coastal plains (Fig.119). These areas have undergone long periods of change, both to their natural landscape and in their traditional land uses.

Mediterranean areas have long, hot, dry summers and short, mild, moist winters. Many areas experience severe summer droughts necessitating large-scale irrigation schemes where agriculture services tourist and urban areas.

The Mediterranean vegetation consists of a mixture of open broad-leaved evegreen forest, evergreen coniferous woodland and scub. At one time these areas were extensively forested. In some areas these persist and are dominated by evergreen oaks such as Cork Oak, and conifers such as Corsican Pine. Many areas, however, have been deforested and a secondary-scrub (maquis or garigue) has developed. Plants adapt to the Mediterranean climate by growing small, waxy, shiny leaves to reduce transpiration; having long tap roots which reach groundwater; storing water in thick bark (such as the Cork Oak) and through completing their life-cycles before the onset of the summer drought. Lack of vegetation cover, especially on steep slopes, leads to erosion of soil and mudslides in winter.

Brown Mediterranean soils are reasonably fertile when there is sufficient moisture for plant growth. Traditional agricultural crops from Mediterranean areas include olives, citrus fruits (such as oranges, grapefruits & lemons) and vines (grapes). In many tourist areas, farms tend to be small and intensively-cultivated and operated on a market gardening basis, supplying, through summer irrigation, fruit, vegetables and flowers to tourist resorts.

The area presents many problems for human activity. The long summer drought can limit agriculture. There are often water shortages especially in rapidly expanding tourist areas. The summer heat and drought can produce very serious forest and scrubland fires - especially common in the south of France and California. The large areas of mountainous land have thin, unproductive soils. The Mediterranean Sea has little tide or current and as such can suffer from algal raft pollution as well as sewage and oil pollution from tourism and tanker traffic.

But the same area also presents the ideal climate for tourism. Europe's most important summer tourist areas are located around the Spanish Costas and Balearic Islands (such as Majorca) - bringing both advantages and disadvantages to these areas (Fig.121-122).

Fig.119

A Mediterranean Landscape

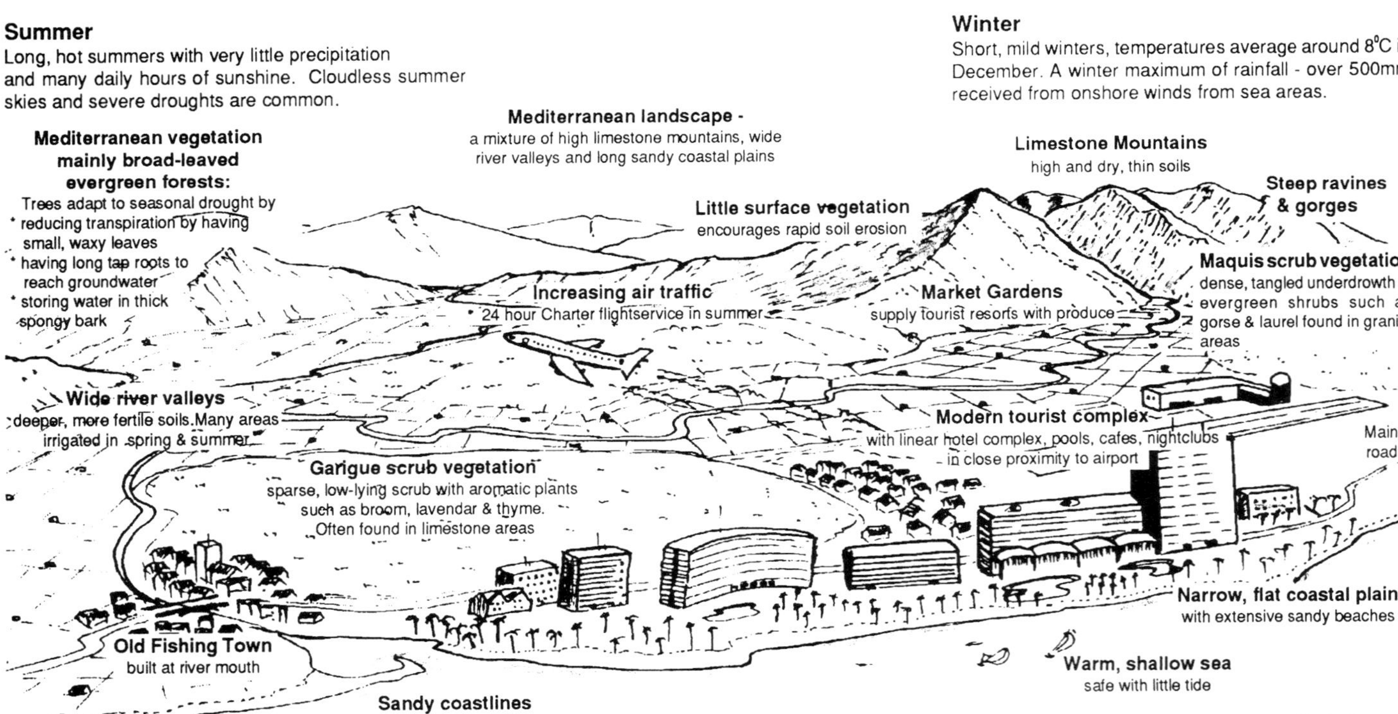

Fig.121 A Tourist Complex in Majorca

A Mediterranean Brown Soil Profile

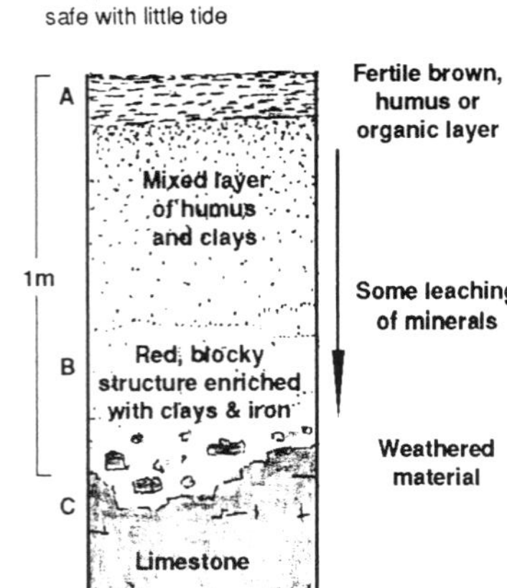

Fig.122 Tourist development in Majorca

TOURIST DEVELOPMENT IN MAJORCA

The warm, dry climate of Mediterranean areas, together with major improvements to communication networks across Europe and a favourable exchange rate with the Spanish peseta, have attracted over 12 million visitors to the island of Majorca.
Indeed, Spain continues to be the most popular tourist destination with an annual 43 million visitors in total. The country, and islands such as Majorca, are economically dependent on tourism for their livelihood.
Tourist developments bring both advantages and disadvantages to any area but the popularity of Majorca (often referred to as a 'tourist-factory') brings its own special problems. The 'Med' in which the island is set is fragile and in many coastal areas there are constant problems of pollution. Many formerly poor rural areas have benefitted from tourism but conservationists remain concerned about the environmental impact of the industry.

The Med is an enclosed sea, with little tide.

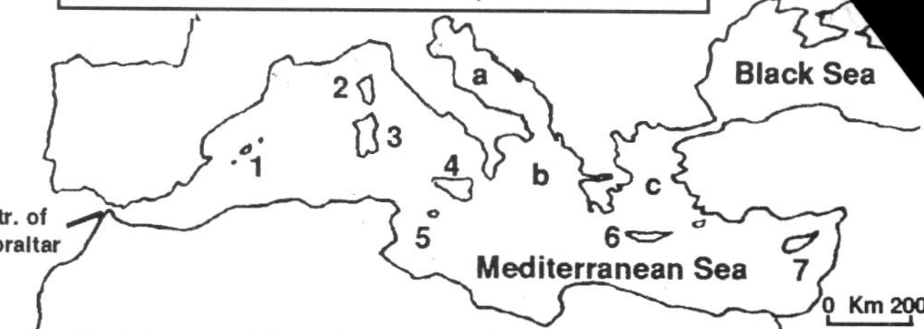

Water entering the sea from the Straits of Gibraltar circulates in an anti-clockwise direction around the Mediterranean. This circulation can take between 30 and 50 years.

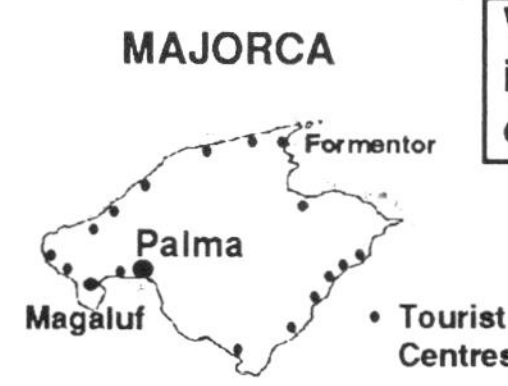

An open sewer runs through the terrace of a cafe-bar in Majorca

TRANSECT OF A MAJORCAN COASTAL AREA

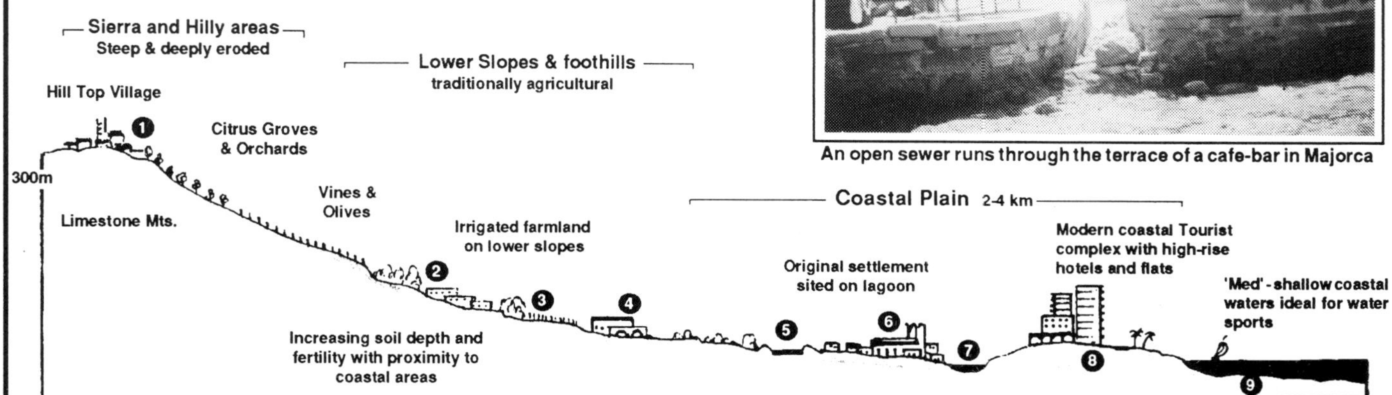

KEY TO TRANSECT DIAGRAM

1. New villas and second homes in village
2. New Timeshare Complex built in rural surroundings
3. Luxury villas and leisure facilities (e.g. tennis clubs)
4. Farmland used for leisure projects, e.g. Water Parks, Golf courses, etc.
5. New motorways & by-passes link tourist coast to airports
6. Commercial land uses abandon Old town for new tourist complex. Old town by-passed by new road.
7. Lagoon partially drained and developed for water sport.
8. Unplanned ribbon development along coast. Problems from tourist congestion, e.g. sewage
9. Pollution problems along coast including sewage, oil and algae (in dry summers).

ADVANTAGES AND DISADVANTAGES ASSOCIATED WITH TOURIST DEVELOPMENTS IN MAJORCA

Advantages include

Improving national balance of payments as tourists bring money into the country as a whole. Improved links with other countries. More cultural exchange. Business contacts & links improved. Increasing local employment in cafes, bars, souvenir shops and boutiques, hotels, marinas and leisure centres, catering, servicing. Decrease in rural depopulation as young people gain employment. Increasing wealth of formerly poor rural areas; higher land values. Higher standard of living for tourist areas and a stimulated local economy. Farmers sell produce directly to tourist industry. Local craft industries develop.
Improved infrastructure of tourist areas. Communication networks developed, e.g. new roads, airports, telecommunication links. Local services improved with better sewage disposal, water and electricity supplies. More entertainment and interest in historical buildings many of which are now preserved using new wealth of area.

Disadvantages include

Tourist areas are congested, especially beaches, cafes, airports, main roads; coastal 'strips' are particularly overcrowded in summer. Adverse visual impact in areas where tower block hotels, car parks, airports and 'building sites' spoil views.
Increasing environmental disruption from tourist-related development, including water pollution along coasts from sewage, noise pollution from airports, nightclubs and heavy traffic, air pollution from traffic jams, etc. Farmland lost to tourist developments. Threat to traditional 'way of life' of areas; traditional crafts and culture give way to foreign ideas.
Much employment is seasonal in nature and jobs may be taken by outsiders to the area. Tourists can create social problems such as resentment amongst locals, threats to local customs, violence and crime may increase. Damage to the habitat of wildlife, vegetation and buildings may occur. Property prices may increase.

Assignment Twenty-five

1a Describe the Mediterranean landscape.
1b Describe the relationship between landscape and vegetation

2 Write the meaning of each of the following terms:- evergreen forest, maquis scrub, garigue, tourist complex

3a Make a simple fieldsketch of the photograph in Fig.121 labelling the following features: limestone foothills, tourist complex, evergreen Cork Oaks, linear hotel layout, water sports centre.
3b Explain
i. the attraction of the area
ii. the distribution of hotels

4 Compare the summer and winter climates of Mediterranean areas .

5 Describe the relationship between land use and the physical landscape of 'Med' areas such as Majorca.

6a Complete a larger copy of the following table giving examples of the impact of tourism in areas such as Majorca.

	Benefits	Losses
Local Economy		
Local Community		
Local Environment		

6b To what extent do you agree with the following statement ?
"Tourism is not the saviour of poor Mediterranean coastal areas but their longterm downfall".

IMATE: Hot Deserts

he physical environment offers a range of possibilities for and limitations on human activities.
The physical environment is a resource which has to be used with care

Hot Desert landscapes (Fig.123) consist of a wide variety of landforms . The main agents of erosion shaping much of hot desert scenery are the weather, wind and water (Fig.124). The great diurnal range of temperature combine to make desert rocks expand and contract. As a result, rocks peel in layers and eventually break down into grains of rock or sand. This process is known as **onion weathering**. The wind blasts sand at rocks, creating arches and pedestal rock formations. The wind also builds up sand into giant sand seas (ergs) which move slowly in sand storms . Although water is limited in desert areas, the lack of vegetation and the high intensity of rare desert rainstorms contribute to shaping the scenery. Desert river courses, often called wadis, can carry flash floods, leading to the formation of canyons, depositing alluvial fans in their wake.

The harsh hot desert environment limits much human activity to the areas around oases (waterholes). In recent years growing pressure for land around waterholes and along desert margins has led to the formation of 'new desert', formed by a process known as **desertification** in areas such as the southern Sahara (Fig.125).

Fig.123 A Stony desert area in Egypt

Fig.124

A Hot Desert Landscape

Summer or Hot Season
Intensely hot and dry conditions. High evaporation rates. Daytime temperatures can reach 50°C; nighttime temperatures often drop below 0°C. Occasional convection storms bring flash floods after heavy downpours.

Winter or Cool Season
Continental desert areas and those with high altitudes can experience a winter or cool season in which temperatures often drop to 10°C or less in day time. Cool winds may affect deserts during their 'winter' but precipitation rates remain low.

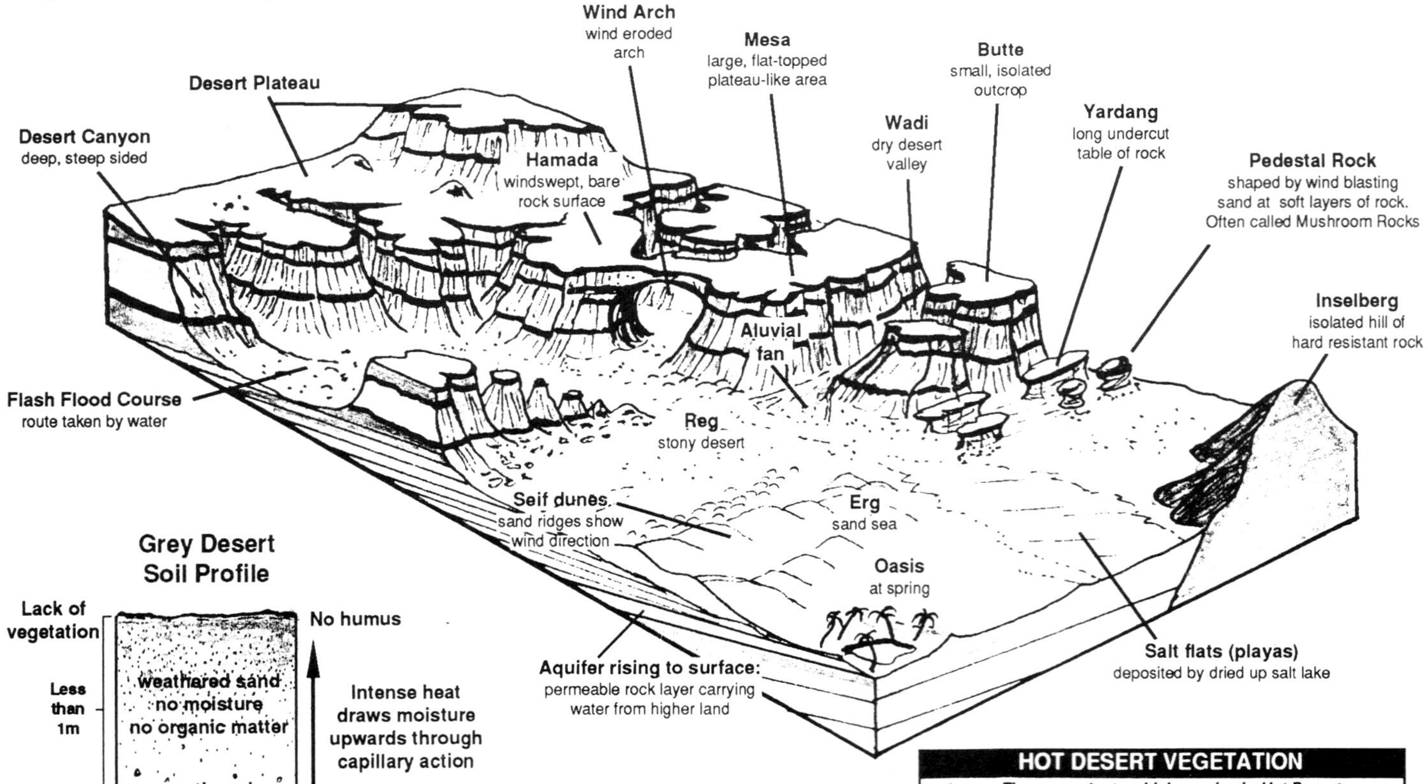

Grey Desert Soil Profile

Intense heat draws moisture upwards through capillary action

Desert soils are potentially productive and capable of sustaining high quality crops with irrigation. Salinisation (salt build up) due to intense evaporation can threaten arable farming.

HOT DESERT VEGETATION

There are plants which survive in Hot Deserts:-
Cactus stores water in its tissues and protects its supply using spikes or needles.
Tumbelweed pulls up its roots and allows itself to be blown into wetter desert areas.
Date Palms grow around oases and have long tap roots reaching down to groundwater supplies.
Desert flowers & shrubs such as the Rose of Jericho can lie dormant in the drought conditions and bloom in short periods in order to release seeds.

Fig.125 Desertification

Trees cut down for fuel & shelter - roots no longer bind desert soils

Overused, overgrazed area around a desert oasis

DESERTIFICATION - the advance of the Hot desert

"This is not just a famine we are looking at - its is severe environmental collapse. As the population has increased and the drought has continued, crop yields have fallen. People have cut down more trees to get the same size of crop yield from a larger area. Trees are used for fuel, for shelter and for fodder for animals. The soil is being stripped and the land wrecked. Animals are dying from lack of grass and others are being sold or eaten. Many people are leaving this area in search of food. This has been going on at an unprecedented rate in recent years - the people have been building a desert.." The Guardian 22.2.91

Each year over 120,000sq.km of land is destroyed by desertification - a gradual process in which land dies and becomes desert. It is found in every continent except Europe and daily affects the lives, economies and environment of many areas worldwide. Desertification is perhaps most severe in Africa where the countries of the Sahel Zone (see map) and Southern Africa are most at risk.

Desertification spreads like land cancer and is the result of a range of factors combining to create dead-areas often referred to as **piospheres**. Once piospheres develop people and animals move to other areas in search of food, water and grazing for their animals. Farmland is often abandoned as patches of desertified land merge and become large areas of new desert.

It is estimated that over 30 million people in Africa are affected and many have become refugees, migrating between rural areas or towards large urban areas in search of help, food and shelter. The United Nations Organisation believes it will take as much as $35billion and over 25 years to help these desertified areas. Meanwhile relief agencies such as Oxfam continue to help the people by supplying short-term aid (food, blankets, medicine, seeds, tools and money). But it is already too late for many areas affected by desertification.

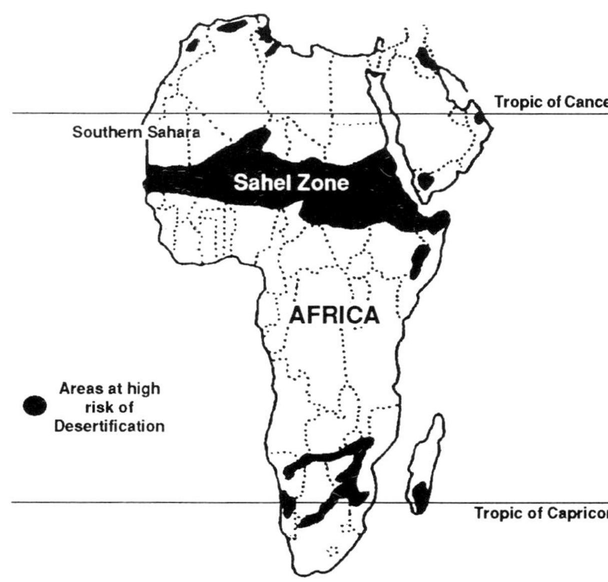

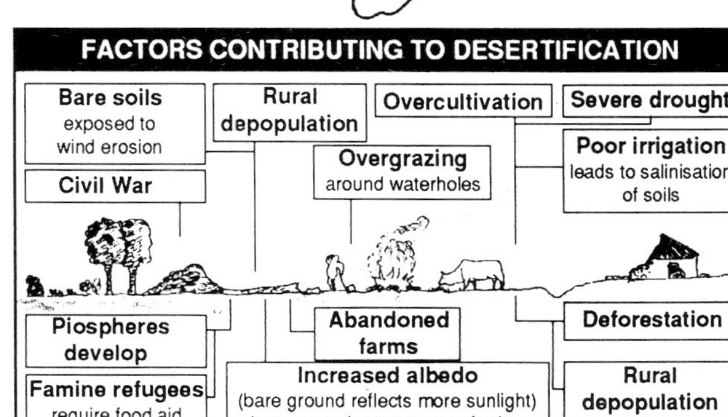

Assignment Twenty-six

1a Describe the processes which shape desert scenery.

1b Describe the Hot Desert landscape using a suitable diagram of your own.

2 Write the meaning of each of the following terms:- Aquifer, butte, mesa, seif, inselberg, erg, reg, hamada.

3a Explain the formation of **two** of the following desert landforms wind arch, pedestal rock, yardang, salt flat, oasis

3b Explain the main plant adaptations to the desert climate.

4 Compare the following :-
i. Hot and Cold Desert climates
ii. The usefulness of Hot Desert and Mediterranean soils.

5 What is **desertification** ? Illustrate your answer.

6a Describe the relationship between the distribution of Hot Desert and areas of desertification in Africa.

6b Make a simple fieldsketch of the photograph top-right of this page, labelling its main features.

6c Identify and explain the main causes of desertification in areas such as the Sahel Zone of Africa.

6d Use the diagram "Factors Contributing to Desertification" to design a flow-chart to illustrate the process.

7a To what extent do you agree that desertification is a problem caused by people ?

7b Research possible solutions to desertification. What can be done to alleviate the problems this process causes ?

ɪMATE: *Equatorial Rainforests*

Γhe physical environment offers a range of possibilities for and limitations on human activities. The physical environment is a resource which has to be used with care

Rainfo... ... in lowland areas, river valleys and coastal plains around the Equator (Fig.126). A small area may hold over 250 different species of hardwood tree and a great diversity of other plants (Fig.127). A multi-layered growth can be observed where tall emergent trees pierce the dense, main canopy; smaller trees and shrubs colonise an understorey layer; lianas and tree creepers grow on the giant buttress roots of the hardwoods and lichen, moss and algae bedeck every surface; the forest floor is dark and damp and covered in all types of fungi. Ferns and orchids can be found on branches. This profuse plant life supports a great diversity of insect and animal life.

Fig.126 A clearing in an Indonesian Rainforest

The overall appearance of plant and animal life thriving in constantly hot, wet conditions conceals the fact that without the protection afforded by the main forest canopy and its supply of nutrients (in the form of dead leaves & fruit), the tropical soils would quickly become infertile and incapable of supporting it. The rainforest in fact only survives by maintaining the supply of nutrients to the soil in which it grows. Where the canopy is removed on a large scale, the intense sunlight and heavy rain combine to remove soil nutrients (**leaching**), destroying soil fertility.

The natural vegetation of rainforests in recent years has been deliberately disturbed by a range of human activities including **slash & burn** (where population pressure leads to the destruction of rainforest), **industrial clearance** (for minerals such as oil, bauxite), **logging** (for timber & paper manufacture) and large scale **cattle ranching** (Fig.128). The rapid scale of forest destruction (over 10m hectares per year) is creating many serious global problems (Fig.129)

Fig.127

A Rainforest Landscape

The importance of rainforests

Rainforests are home to over half of all the growing wood and at least two-fifths of all the plant & animal species on the Earth. The rainforests are thought to be one of the main methods by which the planet converts Carbon Dioxide (CO_2) into carbon (through photosynthesis for plant food) and oxygen released into the air).

One season: heavy precipitation all year round, high temperatures (> 20^{0}C), very low range of temperature (2 ^{0}C).

Features of rainforests:

Forest canopy blocks sunlight & rainfall from the forest floor. The forest floor is dark & very damp, littered with rotting leaves and tree fruits. "Jungle" (thick undergrowth) grows along river banks & in clearings. Tropical hardwood trees are the dominant plants. The tallest trees (or emergents) can grow to over 80m high. Thousands of other plants are found here, including orchids, ferns, fungus, tree creepers, etc. Rivers & streams criss-cross the rainforest areas.

Cross-section through rainforest

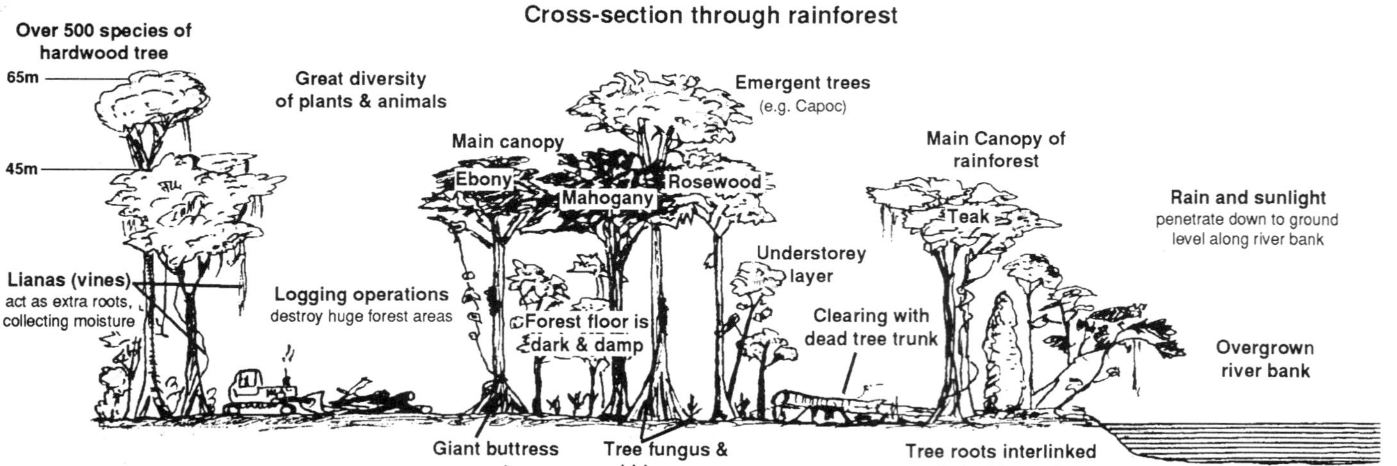

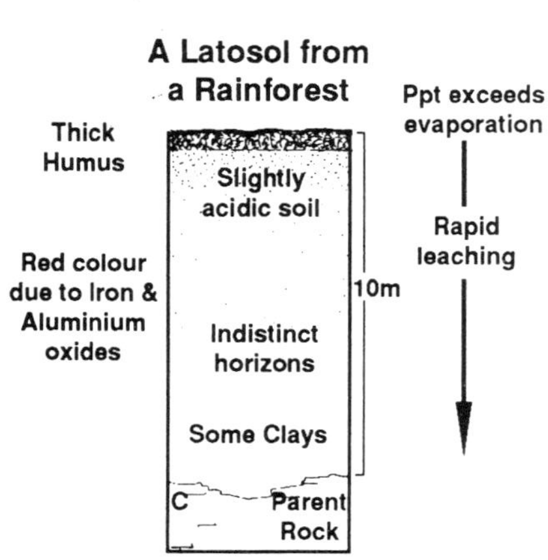

Fig.128 Cattle ranching in cleared rainforest

Fig.128 Deforestation in Equatorial Rainforests

DEFORESTATION IN EQUATORIAL RAINFORESTS

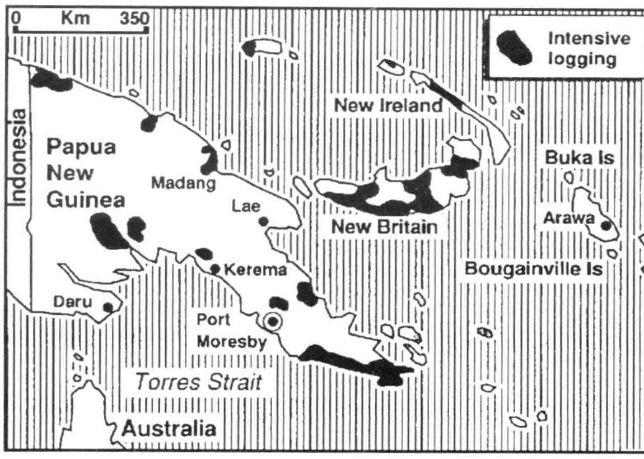

DISAPPEARING FOREST IN PAPUA NEW GUINEA

15 million hectares of lowland forest remain (worth $100 billion).

Half already allocated for logging developments

There are many reasons for the deforestation (clearance) of rainforests. In Indonesian rainforests, the expanding population of some areas is leading to the clearance of over 1 million hectares annually to create space for farm land. Large international logging companies are also clearing rainforest (e.g. on Papua New Guinea, New Ireland and New Britain). In other rainforest areas, such as the Amazon Basin (Brazil) new industrial developments and the construction of communication routes account for an annual clearance in excess of 2 million hectares. In Central American rainforests, huge areas are firebombed then seeded with grass from the air (which grows well in the conditions and in the remaining woodash). Large scale ranches are set up to fatten cattle quickly - the meat being sold to multinational hamburger and food processing companies.

DEFORESTATION IN RAINFOREST AREAS

Logging companies bulldoze one giant tree in 30 secs (average) and clear giant areas for timber, fuel and global paper industries

New roads, railways & airports use 0.5 million hectares per year

Over 2 million hectares per year are cleared by slash & burn for new farmland (most of which is infertile in 5 years)

Cattle ranches replace forest (over 2.5 million hectares)

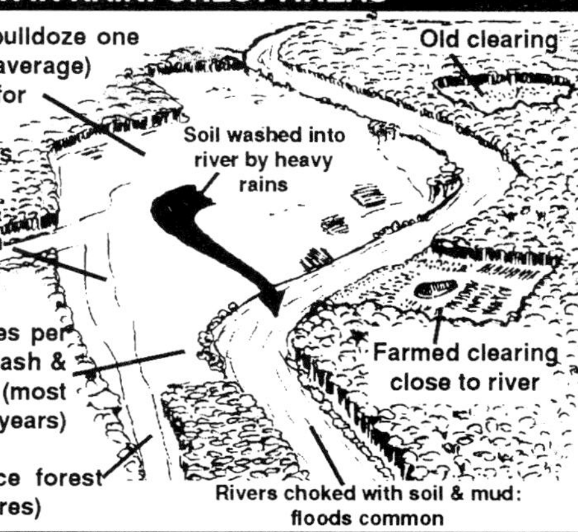

Traditional rainforest agriculture is known as "Shifting Cultivation"

Forest peoples such as the Warani clear a small patch of forest by chopping down trees and burning the trunks. Plants such as yams and cassava are grown whilst other foods are collected (berries & fruits) or hunted (monkey, fish). The soil is delicate and after 2-5 years becomes leached of its nutrient value. The group 'shift' to a new clearing and begin the farming process again. Small forest areas are affected but are 'rested' and regenerate slowly.

There is worldwide concern over the destruction of rainforests, their flora and fauna and the effect deforestation is having on the traditional inhabitants of these areas. Some of the major problems associated with deforestation on a massive scale are listed opposite. But agreeing solutions to both the deforestation and associated problems is proving almost impossible. Many developing countries view their rainforest areas as a national resource, the development of which is thought to be their best hope of alleviating many serious economic and social problems. Developed countries often blame the developing nations for the environmental and social problems associated with deforestation. Most environmentalists consider these problems so serious that they merit immediate international co-operation and understanding, worldwide agreement is required now to reduce the rate of forest destruction before they are lost.

PROBLEMS ASSOCIATED WITH DEFORESTATION OF EQUATORIAL RAINFORESTS

SOIL EROSION & FLOODING

Where the forest floor is exposed to sunlight & heavy rain, tropical storms cause severe erosion of topsoil. Much of the topsoil is washed into rivers and streams causing flooding and silting up of lakes & reservoirs. The Panama Canal is slowly silting due to deforestation.

DESERTIFICATION

Scientists believe that the deforestation of the rainforest areas is linked to worldwide problems of desertification. Removing rainforest would eventually make their climate hotter & drier, destroying the soil, making new desert.

LOSS OF WATER & OXYGEN

Over 25% of the world's fresh water is stored in rainforest areas and over 30% of the world's oxygen comes from rainforests. These would be lost through deforestation and destruction of major rainforest areas.

GLOBAL ATMOSPHERIC PROBLEMS

Deforestation would lead to a major change in the global climate. The '**greenhouse effect**' would steadily increase due to loss of the forest filter effect on CO_2. The result would be a worldwide rise in temperature (**Global Warming**), changes to climate (UK would become steadily milder and wetter, Europe drier and warmer), and the melting of the ice caps flooding crowded coastal areas across the world, e.g. E.China, Netherlands, Bangladesh, etc.

LOSS OF FLORA & FAUNA

Deforestation leading to the major loss of thousands of species of insect and animal. Perhaps the most serious loss would be that of the forest plants. Already they supply worldwide markets with coffee, nuts, fruits, hardwood timbers, rubber and chocolate. 40% of all medicines & drugs contain substances from rainforest plants. Some more recent discoveries include a drug for combatting leukemia (blood cancer).

EFFECT ON TRADITIONAL PEOPLES

Rainforest destruction directly affects the way of life of countless traditional peoples. They are often forced to move to other areas, infected by new diseases (such as influenza, HIV, etc) and lose their traditional knowledge & skills as they gain employment in logging camps or mines. Some are killed and young people often move to large settlements for a modern way of living.

Assignment Twenty-seven

1a Describe the main factors which influence the worldwide distribution of Equatorial Rainforest.

1b Describe a typical Equatorial Rainforest landscape. Illustrate your answer.

2 Write the meaning of each of the following terms:- emergent, canopy, humus, buttress root, leaching,

3a Compare the Equatorial Rainforest and Hot Desert climates

3b Why are Rainforests sometimes referred to as the "Lungs of the planet" ?

4 Describe the main plant adaptations to the rainforest climate.

5 Why are Rainforests considered delicate environments ?

6 What are the advantages and disadvantages of the Equatorial Rainforest for agriculture ?

7a Why are Rainforests considered very important ?

7b In which ways does the Rainforest protect
i. the soil ii. water supplies iii. wildlife ?

7c Describe the main reasons why Rainforest areas are being deforested.

7d What is the relationship between deforestation and climate change ?

8 "***The problems created by rainforest clearance can only be solved on an International scale.***"
To what extent do you agree with this statement ?

35. EXAM STYLE QUESTIONS

CLIMATE & PHYSICAL ENVIRONMENT

1 The diagram illustrates the impact of rapid exploitation of the Tropical Forests in the Amazon. Explain the differing views of the people who live in the Tropical forests, towards rapid exploitation and predict the possible consequences of developments continuing at this pace.

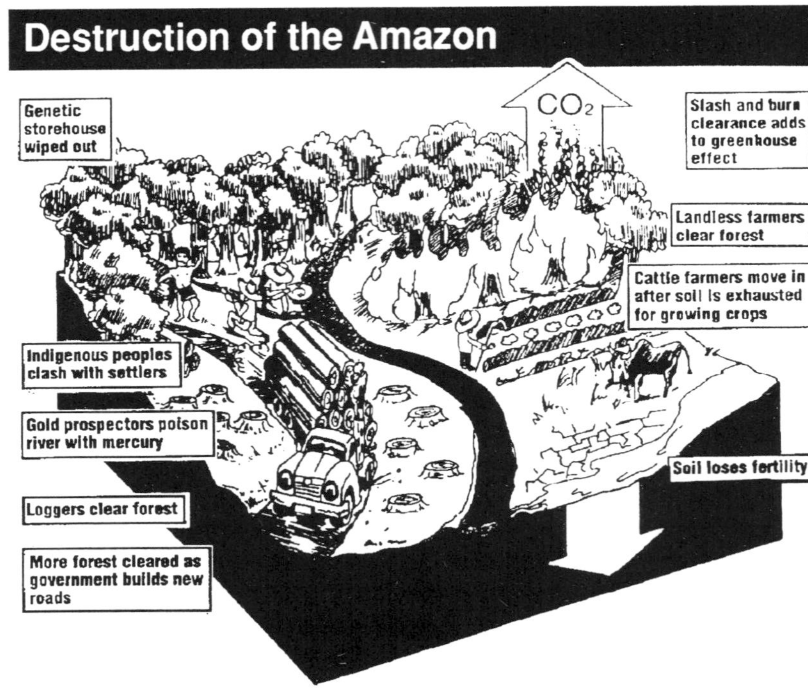

2 Explain why the world's Tropical Rainforests are disappearing so rapidly.

3 The spread of Tropical Deserts, for example the Sahara into the Sahel region, has caused suffering and misery to millions. Suggest some possible short-term and some long term measures to ease the problems that areas such as the Sahel have suffered.

4 Quoting examples you have studied describe how a national government has planned the development of a Tropical Forest.

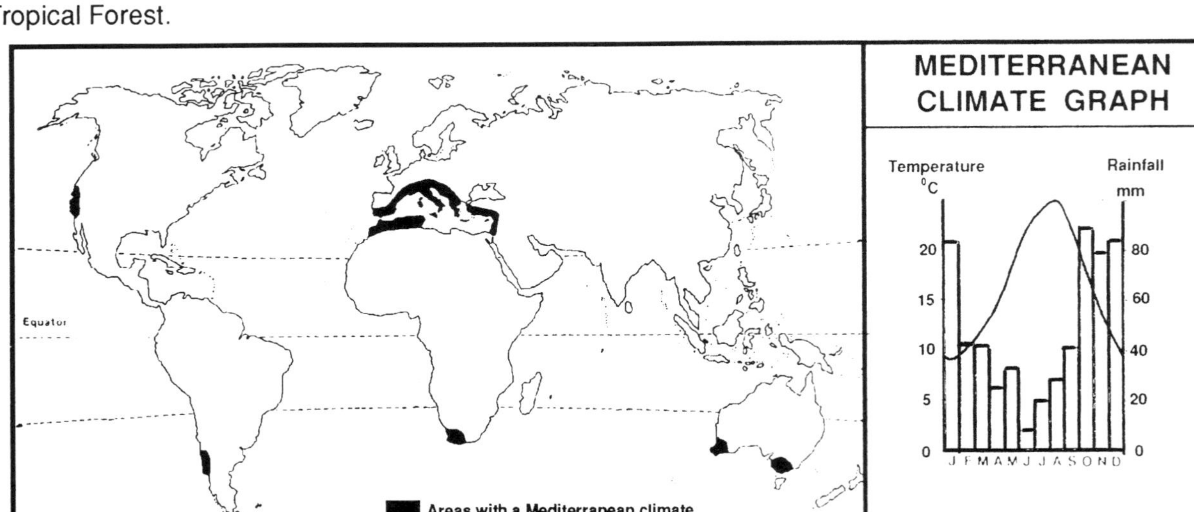

5a Describe the characteristic features of a Mediterranean Climate as shown in the climate graph.
5b Describe the world distribution of areas which experience a Mediterranean type climate.

6 The Mediterranean Climate offers a range of possibilities for and limitations on farming and tourism. Quoting examples you have studied discuss the advantages and disadvantages of a Mediterranean climate.

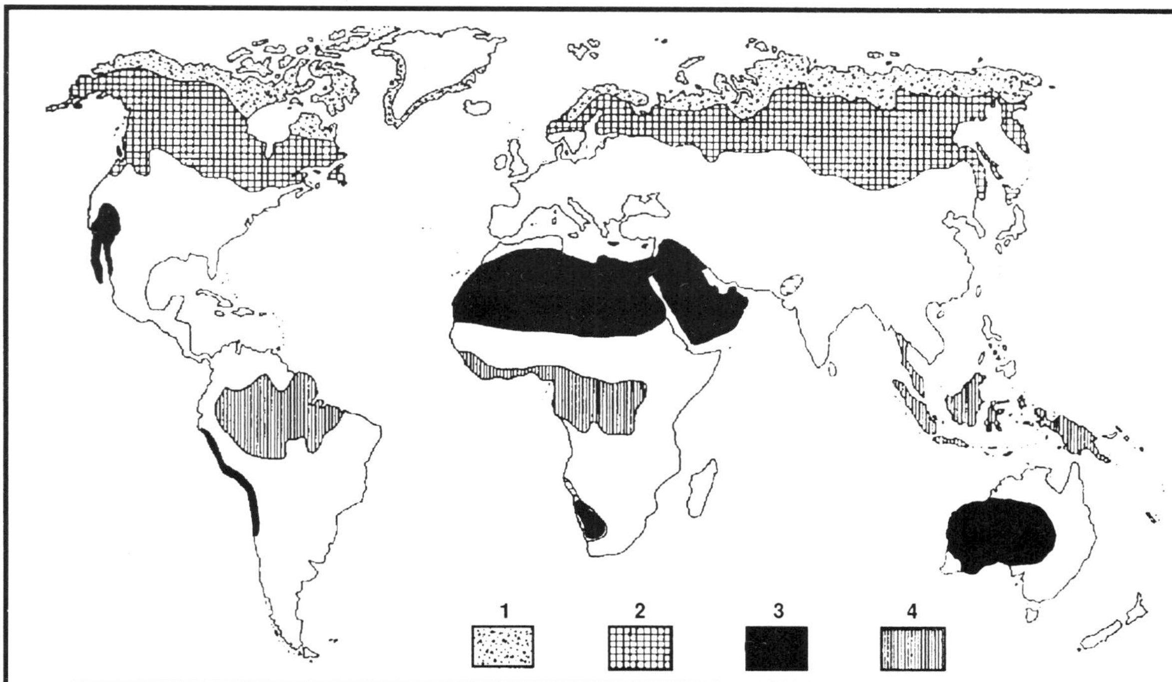

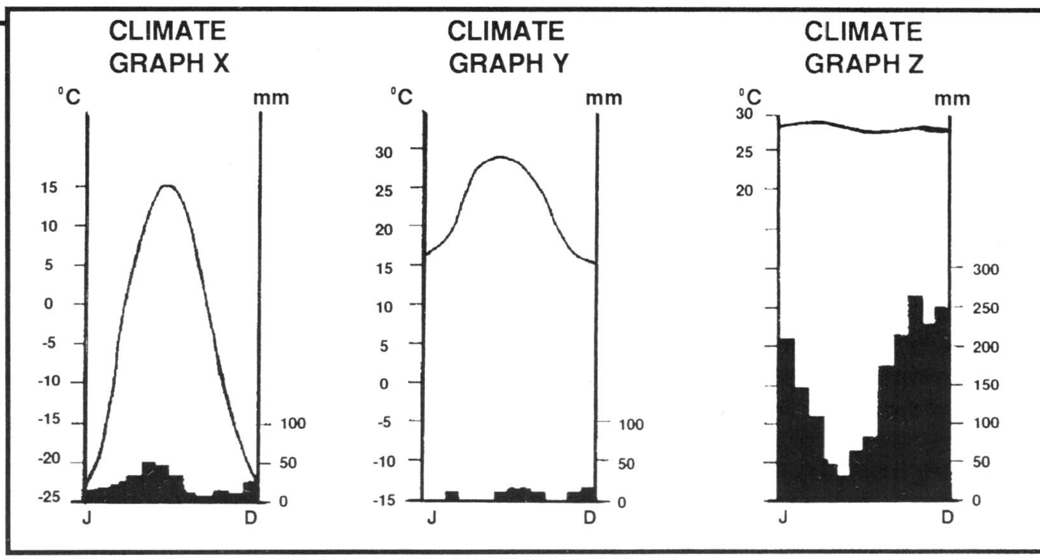

7 Match the three climate graphs **X, Y and Z** to three of the four climate zones **1, 2, 3 and 4** shown on the world map.
Name each of the three matches climates and state which climatic features enabled you to identify them.

8 Referring to any of the three identified climates describe how agriculture has attempted to overcome the problems posed by the climate.

9 Describe how increased exploitation of natural resources has endangered the natural environment, of any of the three climatic types.

10 Why is coastal pollution so damaging, when the oceans are so vast?

11 Describe 3 ways that the oceans can be misused and suggest ways in which the damage caused by these developments could be restricted.

OPULATION: *Measuring change*

Key Ideas: Populations have measurable social and economic characteristics. In any area, the size and structure of the population are subject to change.

Fig.129

Figure 129 illustrates what many geographers and population experts (demographers) consider to be the most serious problem facing the world today. The growth of the world's population - the number of people inhabiting our small planet - has been steadily increasing both in terms of numbers and the rate of growth (Fig.130).

Demographers have calculated that the world population increases by an average of over 8500 every hour; by 6 million more people each month and by 75 million each year. The world's population has been growing for many centuries. In 1750, the population was less than 1 billion. By 1930 it doubled to 2 billion. The next billion was added by 1950 (despite WW2) and the fourth billion by 1970. Currently, the planet houses over 5.5billion and it is estimated that the sixth billion will be reached by about 2008. In other words the **rate of natural increase** has increased rapidly. The natural increase of a population is the difference between the **birth** and **death rate** (Fig.131).

Demographers use various types of population information in studying population change. This information is collected by governments and international organisations such as the U.N.O. (United Nations Organisation) by a regular count or **census** in countries every ten years. The latest census of the U.K. population occurred in 1991; the next will take place in 2001. The census is a very expensive and time-consuming exercise, often fraught with problems, but very necessary for planning future developments, social welfare and government policy. Census information provides statistics about a country's population and the ways in which it is changing.

Fig.130

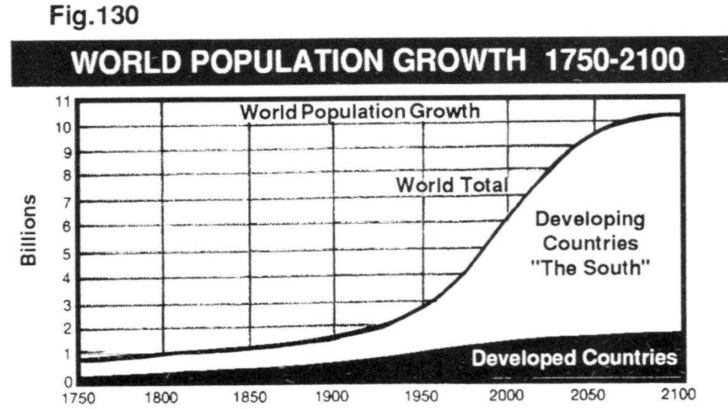

POPULATION INFORMATION

Fig.131

Population Census	A count of the total number of people living within a country's boundaries.
Birth Rate	The number of babies born in a year for every 1000 people in the population.
Death Rate	The number of deaths in a year for every 1000 people in the population.
Infant Mortality	The number of infants under 1 year old who die each year out of every 1000 babies born alive.
Life Expectancy	The average life span of the population of the country.
Dependency Ratio	The %age of the population not earning an income and are dependent on others. The Ratio is calculated thus: $\text{Dep.Ratio} = \left(\frac{\text{Children (0-14)} + \text{Aged (65+)}}{\text{Adults (15-64)}}\right) \times 100$

Fig.132

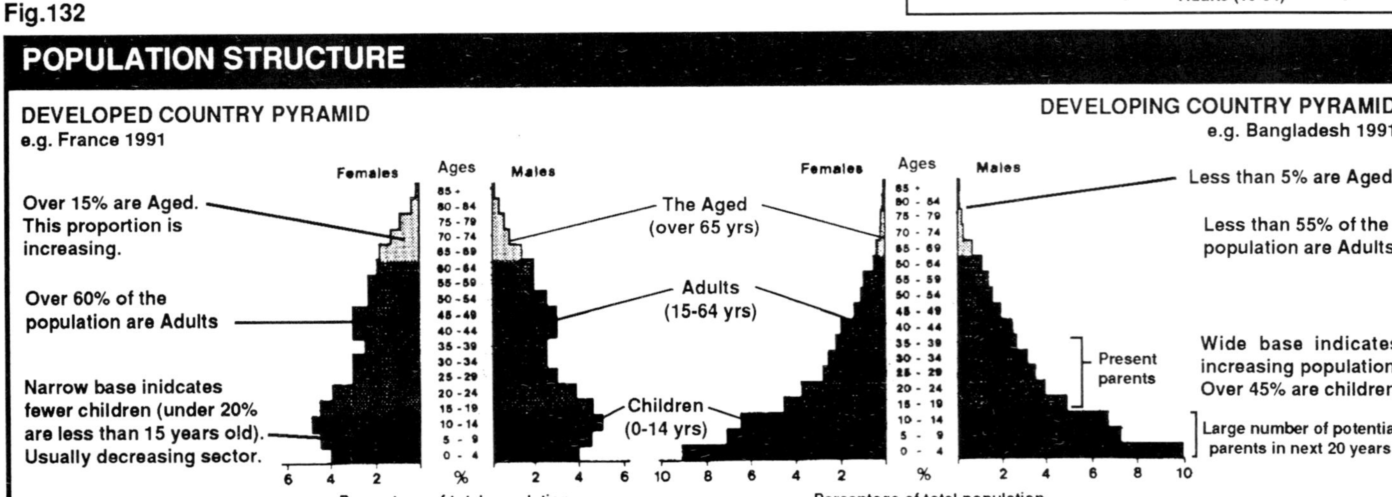

Fig.133 The Demographic Transition

THE DEMOGRAPHIC TRANSITION MODEL (or the Population Cycle)

The graph shown opposite details the **Population Cycle** or a model of **Demographic Transition**.
Demographers believe that all countries pass through the stages of this model over time. However, different countries are at different stages and may take different lengths of time to pass through each stage.

For example, before 1750, both birth and death rates were high in Scotland. The average family had 8 or more children but only half grew to become parents. Medical knowledge was limited and infant mortality was high. Few people lived to their 60's and famines, war and diseases reduced the population regularly. Scotland's population remained stable (**Stage 1**). Today, countries such as Ethiopia remain in Stage 1, for similar reasons.
Scotland's population increased rapidly between 1750 & 1875 (**Stage 2**). Advances in medical science (antiseptics, medicines, etc), improved diets, clean piped water and decent housing combined to reduce the death rate and increased life expectancy, whilst birth rates remained high. A similar, large natural increase is experienced today in countries such as India and Brazil.
Between 1875 & 1940 (**Stage 3**) Scotland's population growth rate decreased. Improvements in public health and better drugs further reduced the death rate and increased life expectancy. A rapid decrease in birth rates, due to greater awareness of and efficiency of methods of contraception and the emancipation of women (greater choice in marriage, the 'vote') combined to reduce the natural rate of population increase.

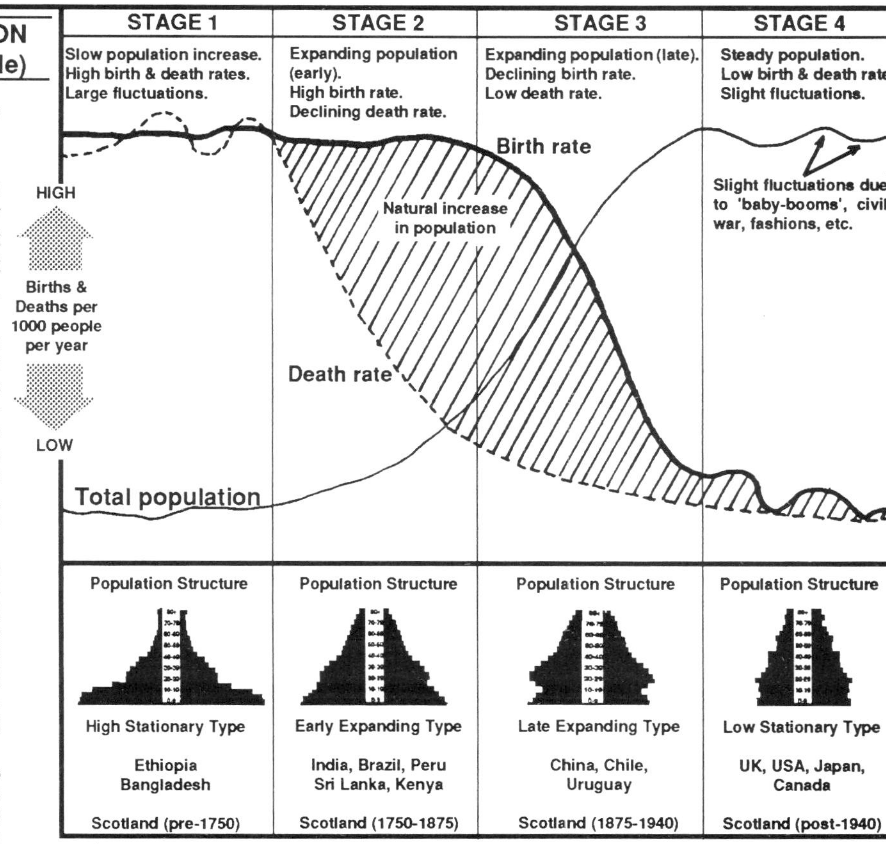

Countries such as China & Thailand are thought to be in Stage 3 today. Indeed both nations are currently attempting to improve public health and introduce public contraception programmes to reduce their birth & death rates.

Scotland since 1940 has had low birth & death rates; the population growth is very low. Other developed countries such as the USA and Japan also have stable or stationary population growth rates.

The census statistics once collected can be mapped to indicate variations between different areas (and countries) or collated as a **Population Pyramid** - a graph which illustrates the structure or age variations within a given population. Both figures 130 and 132 also illustrate differences between the developed countries (or "**The North**") and developing countries (or "**The South**"). Countries of the South, e.g. Angola and Brazil are experiencing population growth rates in excess of 2% whereas countries of the North, e.g. Austria, Denmark and the UK have very low growth rates of about 0.01%. The greatest increase in terms of world population will continue to take place in developing countries.
These differences are also illustrated in the structure of both developed and developing countries (Fig.132). Developed countries have population pyramids roughly rectangular in outline. A narrow base (low birth rate) and expanding top (increasing life expectancy rate) indicate a stable population. Population pyramids for developing countries are roughly triangular in outline. The wide base (high birth rate) and tapering top (lower life expectancy) indicate a much less stable population with higher growth. Differing population structures create differing problems for governments.
Demographers also use the census information to chart the progress or cycle of a country's population (Fig.133). The cycle is known as the **Demographic Transition Model** - the rate and change of natural increase in population studied against time. The stages recognised within the demographic transition model are also linked to the level of development of a country, where countries in Stage 2 are considered to be less 'developed' than those in Stage 3, etc. Other changes in population also take place, including **migration** - often classified as either **out-migration** (movement out of an area or country) or **in-migration** (movement into an area or country).

Assignment Twenty-eight

1 Describe the growth of the world's population since 1750.

2a Give the meaning of each of the following terms: birth rate, death rate, life expectancy, infant mortality rate, census, natural increase, The South, The North, dependency ratio.
2b Calculate the dependency ratio for both the countries shown in Fig.132.
2c What are the consequences for a country with a high dependency ratio ?

3 What are the main points the cartoonists are attempting to make in Fig.129 ? Do you agree ?

4a Describe the differences between the population pyramids shown in Fig.132.
4b Describe the effects on **population pyramids** of
i. Birth control programmes
ii. War (eg. the Gulf War)
iii. More rapid population growth

5 What problems will the structure of population of the countries in fig.132 cause for their governments ?

6a Describe the changes from Stages **1-4** of the Demographic Transition model in terms of birth, death and growth rates.
6b Compare Scotland's population cycle with that of any current stage 1 country.
6c What is meant by **population change** ?

37. POPULATION: *Factors affecting change*

Key Ideas: Populations have measurable social and economic characteristics. In any area, the size and structure of the population are subject to change

It is predicted that the world's population will exceed 6 billion by about 1998. Much of the growth in population will take place in Africa, Asia and South America with more than half the growth taking place in Africa and SE Asia. Some 83% of the next decade's population growth will take place in urban areas, e.g. Mexico City, Calcutta and Shanghai. According to projection studies of population by region (Fig.134), the world population will reach 8.5 billion by the year 2025, and beyond that, 10 billion by 2050. In contrast, population growth in developed countries, already low, will slow further as the population of the North ages. World population projections are made by various bodies including the World Bank and the UNO. They recognise current trends and cannot make assumptions about future factors which may change the population growth rate.

The population of any area depends upon the balance between annual losses and annual gains (Fig.134). Change should not solely be associated with population growth - population change also encompasses population decrease, slowing of the growth rate and migration (in- and out-migration). Population Change is the result of a *combination* of physical-environmental and human-social factors.

Physical-environmental factors which influence change include natural disasters such as earthquakes (eg. Los Angeles 1994), floods, cyclones and severe drought. Environmental factors include the desertification of formerly fertile areas, the deforestation of large areas of rainforest, the spread of new diseases and pollution of water, coastlines or farmland.

Human-social factors influencing population change are more complex and difficult to isolate. The quality of life within an area is a vital factor. The provision of medical care, education, food, housing and sanitation facilities together with Government policy, distribution of wealth and level of technology are all important influences on population change within any country or area.

It is important to note that change is usually influenced through the interaction of both physical and human factors. For example, the population of China is estimated (at the last census) to exceed 1.2 billion people. The government of China recognises that the population growth rate (>2%) will increase crowding in Eastern China, reduce the amount of food per citizen and further threaten soil fertility in various areas. In order to lower the population growth rate and maintain the drive to raise standards of living for all people, the government introduced a "**One-child Policy**' in 1984 (Fig.135). Couples are restricted to having one child by a stringent birth control and public education programme. The environmental and social threat of both a large population and high growth rate is, at present, curtailed by government policy. Attempts to change the population growth rate are also being made in other countries, with varying degrees of success. For example, there is a Transmigration policy in operation in Indonesia where people are forced to resettle outer islands in order

Fig.134 Projections of population for different regions

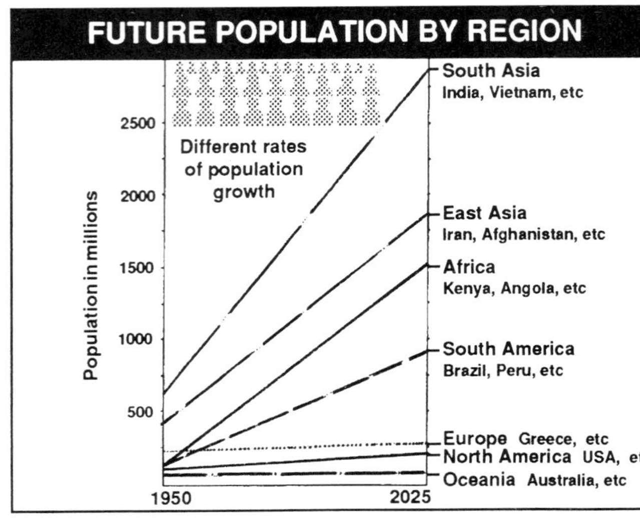

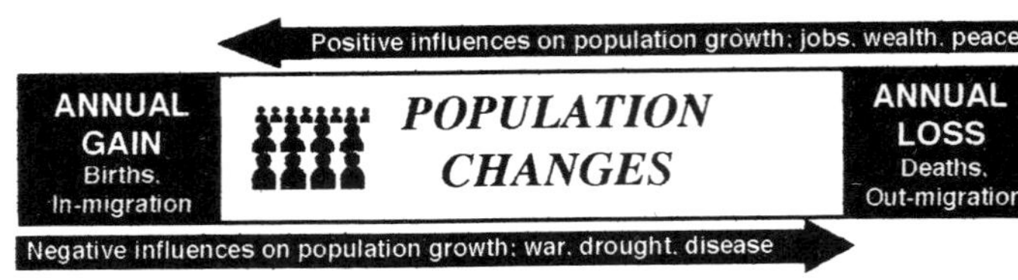

Fig.135 Giant posters in Beijing remind citizens of China's one-child per family policy

Total: 1992=12m, 2022=5m

to relieve overcrowding and pressure on the land in the main islands of Java, Bali and Madura. Since 1969 over 3 million people have been resettled. In this way, Indonesian government policy has directly influenced population change.

In developing countries, the main population change is that of rapid growth. The main reasons for high growth rates in excess of 3% (e.g. in Rwanda or Uganda) are a combination of physical and social factors. Whilst death rates are falling through government and international aid for medical care, education and food production, birth rates remain high for a variety of reasons. People in many developing countries have large families *not* through ignorance of birth control methods but for positive reasons. Children are not regarded as a financial burden but as a boon. Children help in the fields when young and later may get a job and contribute to the family income. There are few welfare schemes in developing countries. The only real way to safeguard old age is to have children who will provide for their parents. Many religions encourage the birth of children (e.g. Hindu, Muslim) and discourage many methods of birth control. People also have large families for negative reasons. The infant mortality rate remains high. When one child in four dies due to diseases caused by poverty (Fig.136), people have more children to ensure some survive. In many countries men exert power over women who, as a result, often have no control over the use of birth control methods. In some societies there is great social pressure on both men and women to have large families. Many people cannot afford effective methods of birth control (e.g. birth pill, sterilisation, etc) or live in rural areas with no access to health clinics. In many countries migration changes the population growth rate in various ways and for various reasons (Fig.137). Migration creates problems in both North and South. Common problems involve rural depopulation, overcrowding in urban areas, shortages of work, housing and discrimination of all types.

In **developed countries** such as Denmark and Norway, the main population changes involve very low growth rates and ageing. Death rates are low, life expectancy is high (often over 75yrs) and there is increased wealth. Birth rates remain low mainly because infant mortality is low and there is less need to have large families. Children are often viewed as a cost and the desire for a higher living standard with high cost of living tend to restrict family size. Women increasingly follow their own career often combining work with having children, in many cases limiting family size.

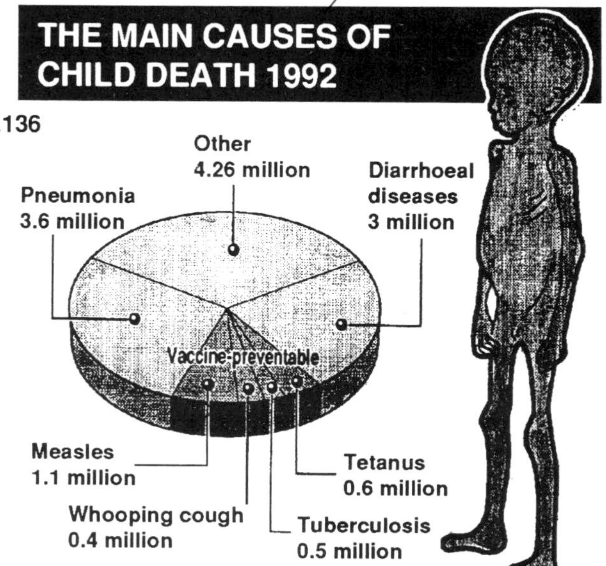

Fig.136

Over 70% of all child deaths are caused by vaccine-preventable diseases.

Fig.137 MIGRATION AND ITS CAUSES

Types of Migration

TEMPORARY MIGRATION
- Seasonal (eg. nomads)
- Daily (eg. Commuters)
- Long Term (eg. foreign workers)

PERMANENT MIGRATION
- Rural to Urban (eg. Deccan Plateau to Calcutta, India)
- Urban to Rural (eg. London to a Sussex commuter village)
- Urban to Urban (eg. Glasgow to London)
- Between Countries (eg. Hong Kong to UK)

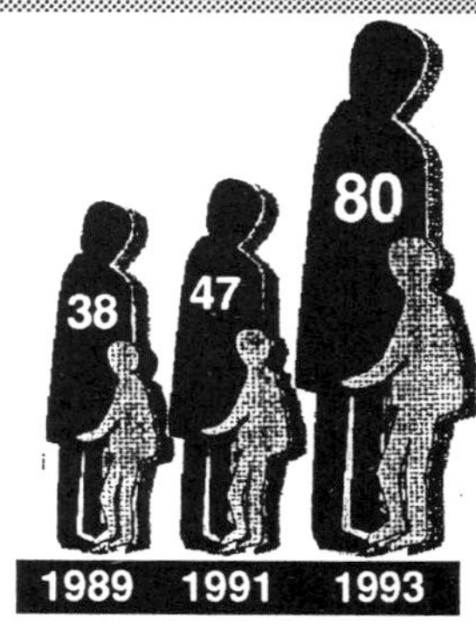

Out of the 80 million displaced people, nearly half are refugees in their own country.

Causes of Migration

Lack of basic amenities, overcrowding, civil war, shortage of labour, poverty, polluted environment, better life with paid work, high infant mortality rate, medical serves provided for all, lack of land, safer environment, radioactivity in environment, markets and food shops, desertification, poor health care, high population growth rate, entertainments, long-term drought, television & media, famine, better housing, earthquakes & floods, noise pollution, schools open to all, vandalism & crime, higher living standards, religious bigotry, ethnic cleansing, deforestation.

Assignment Twenty-nine

1a Describe the differences between the projected population growth for developing and developed regions of the world.

1b What factors influence change in population ?

2 Write the meaning of each of the following terms:- ageing, quality of life, transmigration, refugee, migration

3a Describe the main population changes in
 i. Developing countries
 ii. Developed countries

3b Explain why there are likely to be different rates of population growth in different parts of the world.

4 The reasons for migration may be a combination of **Push factors** (negative factors which encourage people to move out of an area) and **Pull factors** (positive factors which attract people to new areas).
 i. Classify the causes of migration (Fig.137) as Push or Pull factors.
 ii. Re-classify the causes of migration as Economic, Political, Natural or Environmental.

Fig.138

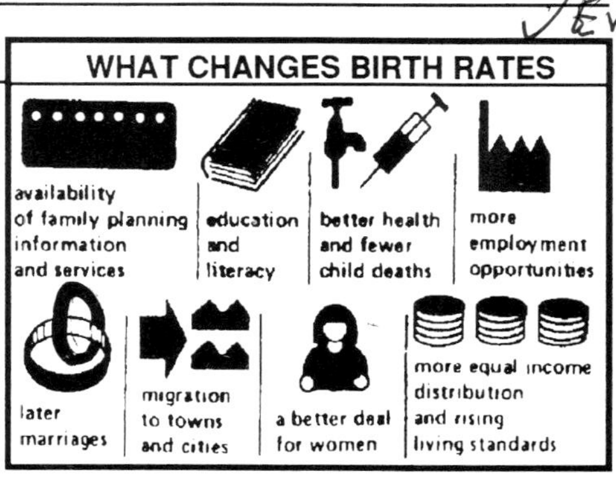

5a Why are child deaths (Fig.136) a result of poverty ?

5b For any **three** factors shown in Fig.138, describe and explain their effect on the population growth rates of developed and developing countries.

6 How would a population policy such as that of China (One-child policy) be received in a developed country such as the UK ? Explain your answer.

38. DEVELOPMENT: *Quality of life*

Key Ideas: Schemes of self-help, along with national and international aid, seek to encourage social and economic development.

Fig.139

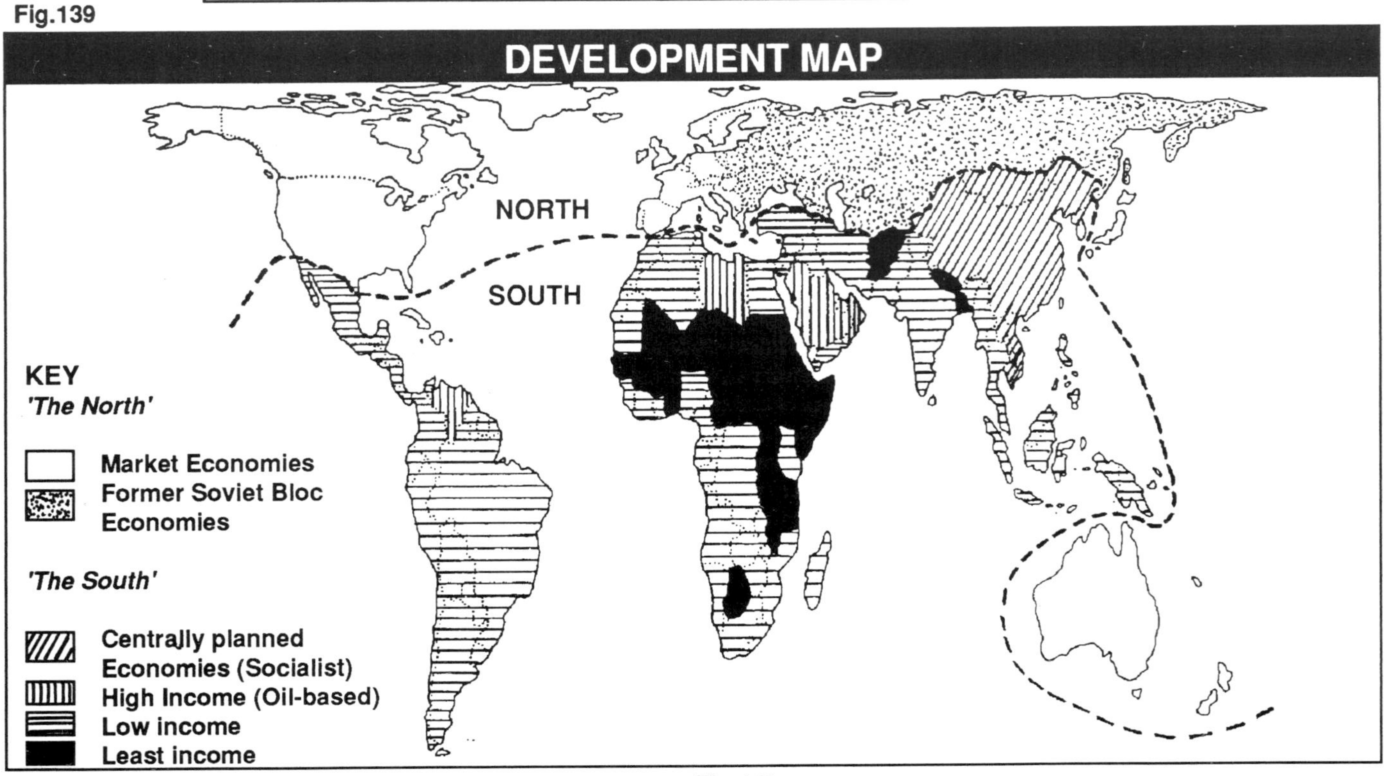

Census and other population information can also be used to compare different countries and areas of the world by studying social and economic factors (Fig.139). The world is divided by levels of wealth and poverty, with the richest 10% (the 'haves') controlling over 60% of the world's wealth and the remainder (the 'have-nots') linked to the economies of the rich countries. Countries may be classified according to their level of development.

Development involves progress in a number of different directions including:-

Economic development - leading towards a stronger economy and increasing wealth

Technological development - increasing the ability of machines to improve human life

Welfare development of the population - improving health, well-being, human rights, etc.

The **Modernisation** of society for 20th.Century living.

There are two main categories of indices (information) used to classify and measure development (Fig.140):-

Economic Wealth - based on Gross National Product (GNP - total wealth produced by a country, per head)

Cultural, Social and **Welfare** indices including the **PQLI** (the Physical Quality of Life Index) and **HDI** (Human Development Index).

Economic wealth is often the easiest to measure and obtain. Relevant economic statistics are accurate for countries with market or money economies. But there can be problems in countries with informal economies with few cash transactions as measurements can be inaccurate and give at best a crude average hiding hidden and uneven wealth distribution in poorer countries. GNP is measured in $US but exchange rates frequently fluctuate. Economic measurements often do not work in centrally-planned, socialist economies.

Fig.140

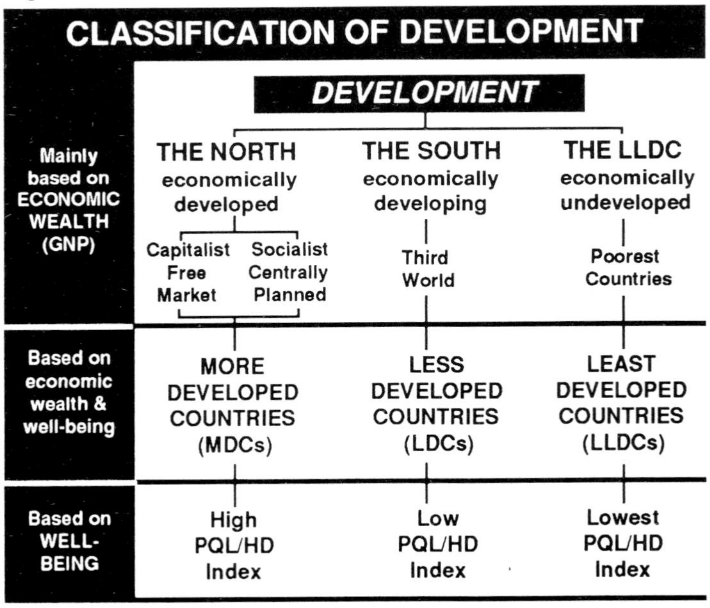

Fig.141 QUALITY OF LIFE ?

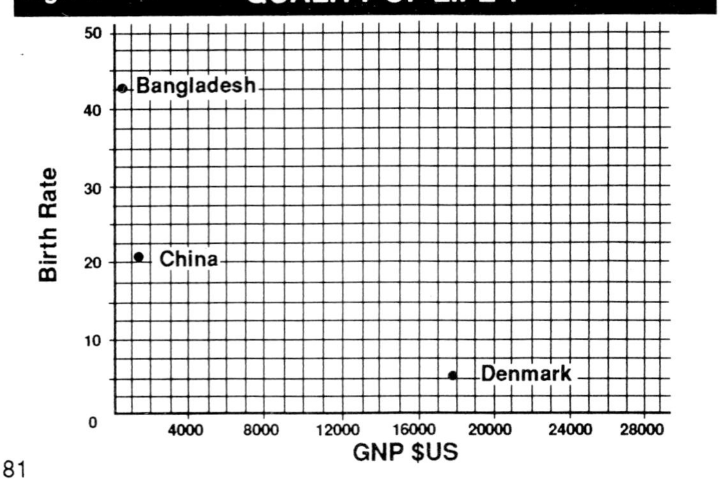

Cultural, Social and Welfare indices are often based upon information linked to the Physical Quality of Life Index where an average of 3 main indices (Life Expectancy, Infant Mortality and Literacy) is used. The United Nations Human Development Index also uses 3 indices (Adult Education, Life Expectancy and GNP) as measures of development. Other criteria are also employed to assess development including birth and death rates, population growth rate and daily calorie-intake compared to GNP (Fig.141). Other indicators of a country's development are very difficult to measure but are regarded as very important to their quality of life, e.g. personal happiness, peace, freedom of speech, emancipation of women, etc. The development of any country should be an accurate combination of both Economic and Social indicators.

Using these as a basis for study, countries may be grouped in terms of their development as Developed, Developing or Least Developed. The quality of life in many developing countries is often difficult to measure since the accuracy of census data can be questioned. In developing countries such as Nigeria, there are also big contrasts between urban and rural living conditions. For example, access to safe water in large modernised urban areas is much easier than that of remote poor rural areas where people and livestock share the same sources of water supply (Fig.142). Extreme differences between countries can be revealed by comparing development indices (Fig.143). In 1981 the United Nations drew up a list of 31 countries which it called LLDCs (Least Developed Countries). These poorest nations in which the quality of life is considered very low, are largely tropical. Most of the world's poor live in two **poverty belts**: one stretching from the Sahara to Malawi and the other from Ethiopia to East Asia (Fig.139).

In recent years attempts have been made to explain the lack of development in some areas of the world. **Physical environmental** problems (drought, isolation, extremes of heat and cold, earthquakes, soil infertility, tropical storms and diseases such as malaria & cholera, etc) are major influences. But **socio-economic** factors are also vitally important influences on development and include widespread poverty & wealth distribution, rapid population growth, infant mortality rates, religion, investment in medical care, shelter, education and national infrastructure.

Fig.142

Fig.143

DIFFERENCES IN DEVELOPMENT

Country A	*Indices of Development*	*Country B*
$345	**G.N.P.** (Gross national Product) per person (in $US)	$21,570
48	**Life Expectancy** at birth (years)	77
232	**Infant Mortality rate** (per 1,000 of population)	7
81	**Average daily Calorie intake** as % of healthy intake	113
5	**Televisions** per 1,000 people	471
86	**Percentage of population employed in agriculture**	3.9
52	**Percentage of population under 15**	21
3	**Percentage of population over 65**	14
8355	**Number of people per doctor**	355
67	**Percentage of population with access to safe water**	100
25	**Adult literacy rate (%)**	99
3.1	**Population growth rate (%)**	0.1
6.5	**Number of children** per woman	1.9
9	**Urban population** (% of total popn)	83
31	**Energy consumption per head** in kg of coal equivalent	17m. tonnes

Assignment Thirty

1a What is **development** ?
1b Explain how development may be measured.

2a For each **Key category** in Fig.139 list at least 3 named countries.
2b Give the meaning of each of the following terms:- GNP, Rich country, HDI, Developing country, LLDC.

3a Complete a larger copy of Fig.141 using the birth rate and GNP indices listed in Fig.144.
3b Describe the relationship between birth rate and GNP for the selected countries (above).
3c Carry out similar exercises for Life Expectancy and GNP and Adult Education rate and GNP.

4a Classify the indicators used in Fig.143 as either Economic or Cultural-Social.
4b Which level of development is indicated by Country A and Country B ? Justify your answer.

Fig.144 DEVELOPMENT INDICES

Country 1992	Birth Rate per 1,000	Life Expectancy	% Adult Education	GNP $US
USA	16	76	99	21790
HAITI	36	70	57	375
MEXICO	32	71	87	2490
BRAZIL	31	66	81	2680
AUSTRALIA	15	76	99	14500
JAPAN	13	79	99	25430
SAUDI ARABIA	42	65	61	10785
NEPAL	43	52	28	180
PERU	36	63	83	1012
UK	12	76	98	16100
SWITZERLAND	11	77	99	29880
ETHIOPIA	43	46	31	120
INDIA	34	57	49	350

5a What are some of the main influences on the development of a country ?
5b Why is measuring development fraught with difficulties ?
5c Draw your own map of development showing the two main poverty belts, the North-South divide, etc.

39. DEVELOPMENT: *Problems inhibiting progress*

Key Ideas: Schemes of self-help, along with national and international aid, seek to encourage social and economic development.

For over 40% of the population of developing countries, life at a subsistence level is a serious matter of survival. Many people live on a knife-edge between constant hunger and starvation, in poverty and hardship (Fig.145). The pattern of global poverty and development (pages 83-84) reveals great differences between the wealthy nations of the North and the poorer countries of the South, for example Ethiopia, Chad and Bangladesh. In countries such as these, whose average GNP per person is less than $200, the majority of inhabitants live below subsistence level without access to medical care, adequate food or safe water supplies. Trapped by poverty in a vicious circle of despair, they survive varying degrees of malnutrition, illness and high death rates. The poverty trap and associated ill health are perhaps the biggest factors inhibiting the further development of many developing nations.

The **World Health Organisation** (WHO) estimate that in 1993 over 21% of the world's population (est.1 billion people) are malnourished, in ill-health or diseased. The greatest problems are found in Sub-Saharan Africa where over 160 million people (or over 30% of the population) are ill and undernourished. The U.N.O. have recently reported that the process of further development in most developing countries must have a solid foundation of equal access to food, safe water and shelter, medical care and education for all.

Fig.145 The face of poverty

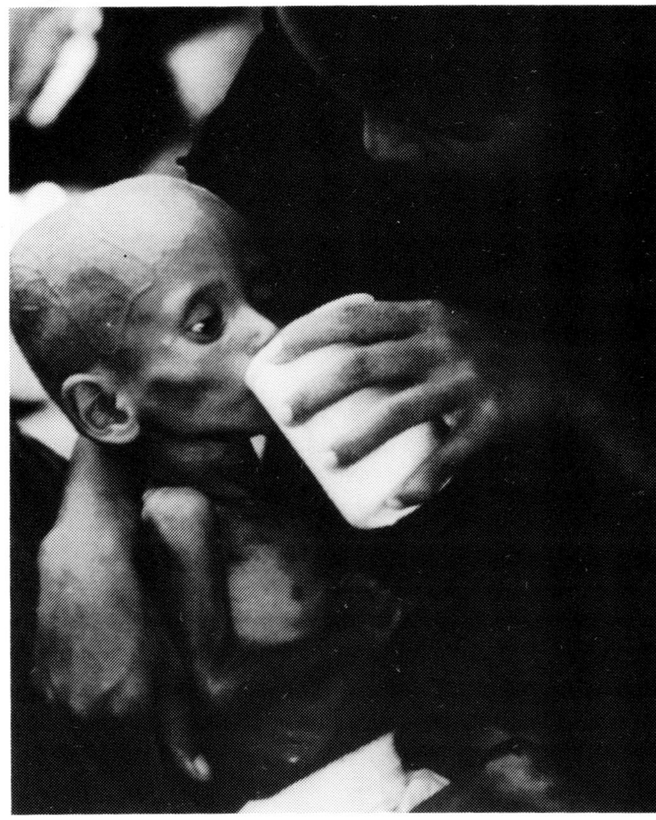

Fig.146

WORLD HUNGER & FOOD SUPPLY

Many developing countries exist today on the edge of crisis. Countries such as Angola and Bangladesh are not able to afford mass health and education programmes for all their citizens. Often there is little secondary industry. Farming is the main way in which people live and agriculture supplies most of what the countries need: raw materials, employment & money for trade.

In such **Primary Production Countries** any relatively small disturbance can trigger a crisis and the result can be a major shortage of food supply and famine.

The map of Calorie Intake (opposite) shows the areas of the world in which people have the **minimum calorie requirement** for healthy living (approx. 2400 calories per day). The population of many developing countries exist on diets below the minimum level of daily calorie intake and most of the least developed countries have diets below 80% of the minimum calorie intake.

The results of which are often lack of progress in development, diseases linked with a lack of a balanced diet (malnutrition) and lack of food to eat (undernourishment or starvation) and political instability.

Famine does not only occur because of a problem with food production. It is the most obvious sign that there are underlying problems of poverty within the country.

Poverty, problems of food supply, hunger and dietary diseases are problems inhibiting the development of countries in the South.

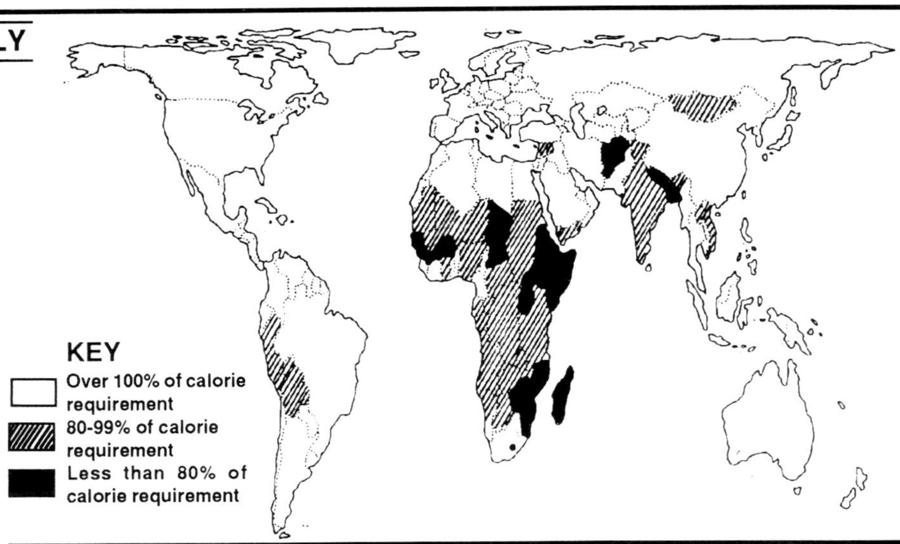

MAJOR DIET DEFICIENCY DISEASES COMMON IN DEVELOPING COUNTRIES

Type	Disease	Symptoms	Distribution	Treatment
Protein Deficiency	Kwashiokor	Retarded growth, swollen stomach skin rashes. Deadly if untreated.	Africa, SE Asia	Well-balanced diet, proteins
	Marasmus	Severe starvation & lack of proteins	Africa, SE Asia	Food - fats, oils & cereals
Vitamin Deficiency	Beri-beri	Severe Vit.B deficiency,wasted limbs skin sores, heart failure	S.America, West Africa, SE Asia	Vit.B rich foods balanced diet
	Pellagra	Lack of Vit.B, skin inflammation, diarrhoea, dementia	Maize eating areas, Italy South Africa	Meat & veg diet balanced diet
	Rickets	Vit.D deficiency, bone deformity of bones, legs and spine	SE Asia	Calcium-rich diet & Vit.D
	Scurvy	Vit.C deficiency, hair & teeth fall out internal bleeding, skin sores	Africa	Fresh fruit diet veg & fish
	Night Blindness	Severe Vit.A deficiency, dry skin, kidney infection, impaied vision	W.Africa, SE Asia,	Green veg, fruit, milk, eggs
	Anaemia	Iron deficiency, breathlessness, child killer	Africa, SE Asia S.America	Meat & iron-rich diet

Fig.147

Fig.148

from "New Internationalist" July 1983

HOW TO FEED THE WORLD ?

Food aid is very necessary in a crisis but it is not a long term solution to the problems created by lack of food, malnutrition and poverty. In a world with twice as many people as 35 years ago, there are still major problems with adequate food supply. The following are 5 ways to address the causes of world hunger:-

Land Reform Policies

Much of the fertile cultivable land is owned by relatively few rich land owners in developing countries. Land Reform (the distribution of land ownership) could help increase food production since smallholders can often farm more efficiently than large landowners. A UN study of land use in central America, for example, showed that farmers who owned up to 4 hectares cultivated 75% of their land, while farmers with over 35 hectares cultivated only 15%. The study also showed that 80% of the land was owned by less than 10% of the population.

Food for Locals

Developing countries are locked into a farming system created for the benefit of the North. Their best land d resources are often used to grow cash crops for export rather than for food. If developing countries move away from exporting foodstuffs and pay their farmers more for their harvests they will be able to improve the quality of food intake per person steadily.

Reduce Developing country Debt

Huge debts have been crippling developing countries for decades. Many countries now repay their debts to banks in the North with up to 50% of their export earnings thus reducing the amount of investment in the country's food, medical, educational and infrastructure systems.

Control Transnational Corporations

Large Transnational companies control prices paid for food and set contracts for export crops. At present large corporations control over 85% of world tea, coffee, cocoa, sugar & tobacco. International control over TNCs and the freeing of trade barriers for developing countries would be a good start.

Improve Social Justice

Hunger affects the poor and it is often the case that there are no truly hungry countries - just differing proportions of hungry people within countries. A commitment to equality and justice should be the highest priority within any nation since this is the real way to reduce poverty, inequality and hunger.

Assignment Thirty-one

1a Economic, social and environmental problems often result in a **vicious circle of poverty**. Rearrange the following factors to design and complete your own vicious circle of poverty:- Lack of money, no savings, low-level technology, ill-health, low production level, earning level reduced, lack of food

1b Describe the relationship between poverty and lack of development.

2 Give the meaning of each of the following terms: Subsistence, Primary Production country, malnutrition, starvation, calorie intake, famine, diet deficiency disease.

3 For each **Key category** in Fig.146 list at least 3 named countries.

4a What is the minimum calorie intake for healthy living ?

4b Describe the distribution of daily calorie intake across the world.

4c What is the difference between diseases of protein and those of vitamin deficiency ?

5a What is the main message of the cartoon strip (Fig.147) ?

5b If the world produced twice as much food as it required in 1993, why did people still starve ?

5c Design a poster to answer the question above.

6 What steps should be taken to solve the problems of food supply

i. in the short term

ii. in the long term ?

40. EXAM STYLE QUESTIONS

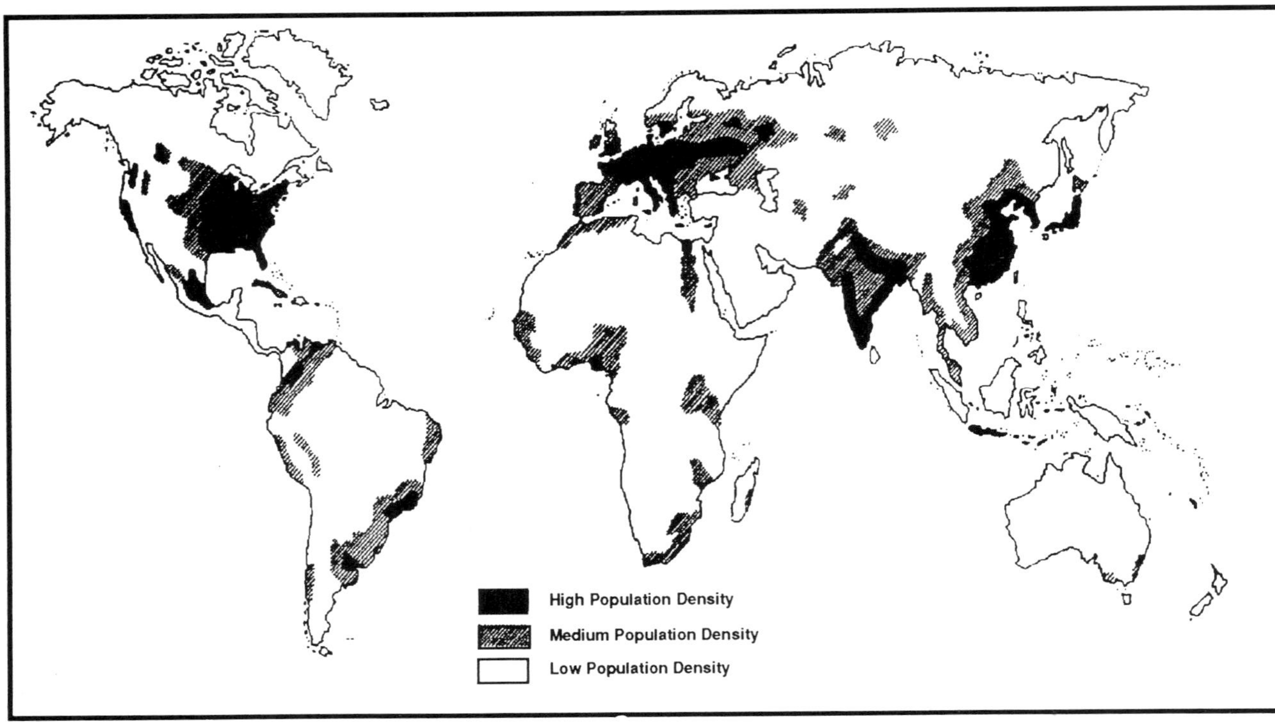

POPULATION

1 Describe the world distribution of areas of high population density, as shown on the world map above.

2 Quoting examples you have studied explain why some areas have a high population density.
You might refer to factors such as climate, relief, natural resources and historical factors.

3 Examine the diagram and tables which provide information on quality of life.
What is meant by the term "**Quality of Life** "?

HOW THEY MEASURE UP

*HDI : Human Development Index is a broad measure of the quality of life based on longevity, education and income.

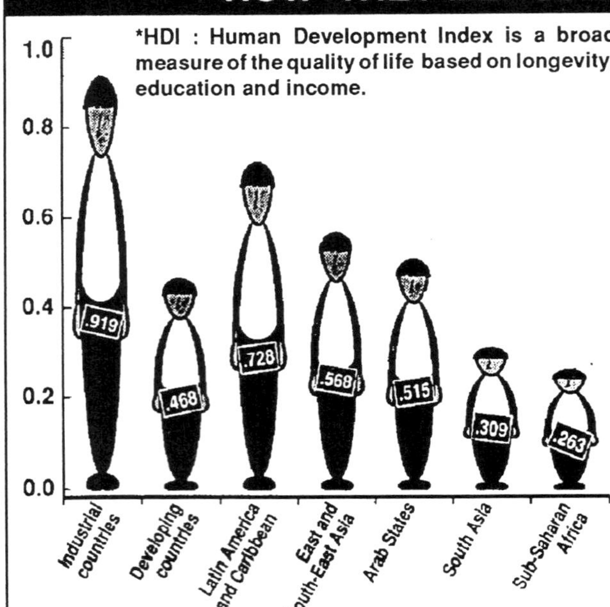

TOP 5 DEVELOPED COUNTRIES	HDI	Rank
Japan	0.983	1
Canada	0.982	2
Norway	0.978	3
Switzerland	0.978	4
Sweden	0.977	5

TOP 5 DEVELOPING COUNTRIES	HDI	Rank
Barbados	0.928	20
Hong Kong	0.913	24
Cyprus	0.890	27
Uruguay	0.881	30
Trinidad & Tobago	0.877	31

Source: UNDP, 1993

4 Justify the use of longevity (life expectancy), education and income as **indices of quality of life**. Explain why one index, such as income per capita, would be less reliable than three taken togeth[er].

5 Why are some developing countries able to offer a good quality of life even though they are classed as "**developing**"?

6 Suggest **two** ways in which developed countries can help the developing countries raise their quality of life.

7 Life Expectancy figures vary widely even within the developing countries. With reference to countries you have studied indicate what **physical and human factors** might influence life expectancy.

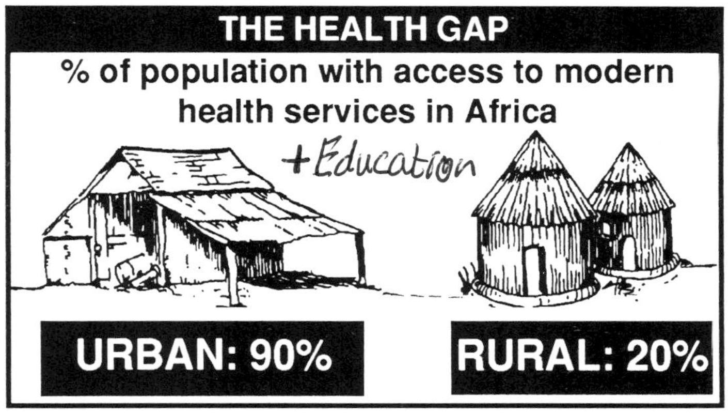

8 Why has life expectancy risen over the last thirty years in **developing** countries?

9 For both a developed and a developing country you have studied explain the factors which have influenced changes in birth and death rates **since 1900.**

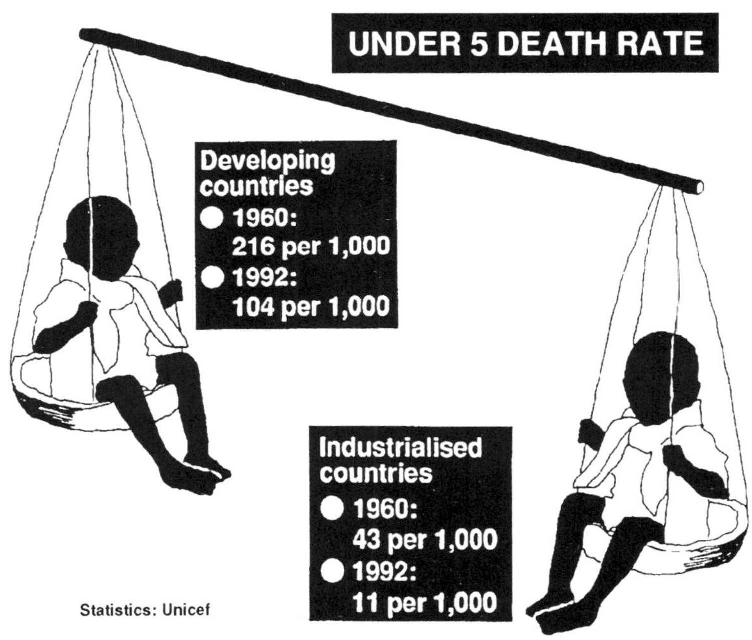

10 How have **changing birth and death rates** affected population growth in the countries you mentioned in you answer to question 9.

11 What problems can a **falling birth rate** cause for developed countries?

12 Account for the large scale **rural-urban migration** which is common in developing countries.

13 What possible approaches are open to governments that wish to relieve population pressure on **overpopulated** areas?

14 Examine figure 133 on page 79.
Explain why population **growth** is so different for the regions shown.

15 Five out of the world's ten largest cities are in Asia and population is rising fast in these cities.
Why is population rising so fast in the **cities** of developing countries?

41. AID: Towards development

Key Ideas: Schemes of self-help, along with national and international aid, seek to encourage social and economic development.

Fig.149

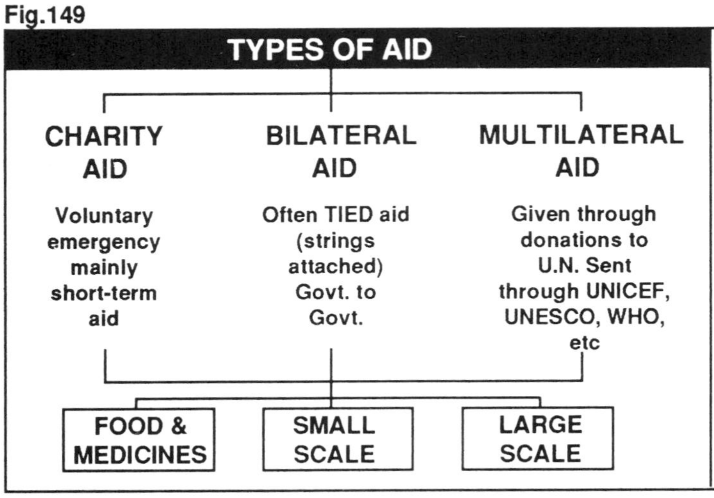

Fig.150

Aid is co-operation, support, emergency relief and help. On a global level, aid consists of countries helping one another to develop their economies and their standard of living. There are various types of aid (Fig.149). **Charity aid** is collected in many countries and used to finance small scale schemes such as improving water supply, education of farmers in new techniques, providing irrigation or building a local health centre. In times of emergency such as famine or war, voluntary agencies such as Oxfam, Save the Children, etc, make special appeals for blankets, toys and money for medicines and food to relieve the suffering of the victims. **Bilateral aid** is aid given from one country to another, e.g. when the UK gives aid directly to a country such as Kenya. Often bilateral aid is tied, in other words, given under certain conditions. **Multilateral aid** is aid given by international organisations such as the UN. Member countries donate money and resources which are then used by a variety of UN organisations such as the World Bank, UNESCO (United Nations Educational, Scientific & Cultural Organisation) and WHO.

Aid can, therefore, take many forms from the funding of multibillion dollar HEP and irrigation schemes to simply helping people help themselves and become self-reliant. Some would argue that the development of **self-reliance** should be the main aim of all aid and development schemes. There are many debates over the appropriateness of the types of aid given (Fig.150). The 1980 Brandt Report and the 1992 UNCED (UN Conference on Environment & Development) Reports call for the countries of the North to donate a minimum of 1% of their GNP to development aid by the year 2000 to avoid worldwide disaster. UNCED estimates that over $600 billion are required now to overcome the growing threats of environmental and development problems. $125 billion are urgently needed in the form of 'aid' but current donations fall short of this total (Fig.151). And there are further aid-related problems. Bilateral aid (which forms over 65% of global aid at present) is not always effective. For example, technological aid in the form of tractors can often be well-intentioned but inappropriate. Tractor cemeteries (Fig.152) reveal problems where lack of diesel, spare parts, trained mechanics and drivers combined to render technological aid redundant. Locals break up the tractors to make 'useful' things like spades, seats and water pumps.

Fig.151 AID IN FIGURES

Aid Givers	$US 1990	Aid as a % of GNP '90
OPEC		
Saudi Arabia	3692	3.90
United Arab Emirates	888	2.65
Nigeria	13	0.06
Algeria	7	0.03
Venezuela	15	0.03
Qatar	1	0.02
Libya	4	0.01
OEDC		
Norway	1205	1.17
Netherlands	2592	0.94
Sweden	2012	0.90
France	9380	0.79
Belgium	889	0.45
Germany	6320	0.42
Japan	9069	0.31
Switzerland	750	0.31
U.K.	2638	0.27
Aotearoa	95	0.23
US	11394	0.21

OPEC Organisation of Petroleum Exporting countries
OECD Organisation for Economic Co-operation & Development

Fig.152 A Tractor cemetery in West Africa

Fig.153

LARGE SCALE AID

Brazil's Government invested money borrowed from the World Bank in the 1970s in order to develop its poor, drought-stricken NE zone. A large scale water/HEP scheme, built along the River Sao Francisco involved the construction of 2 massive dams, the creation of the continent's largest lake and the extension of the electricity grid, leading south to Brazil's largest urban areas (Rio, Sao Paulo, etc).

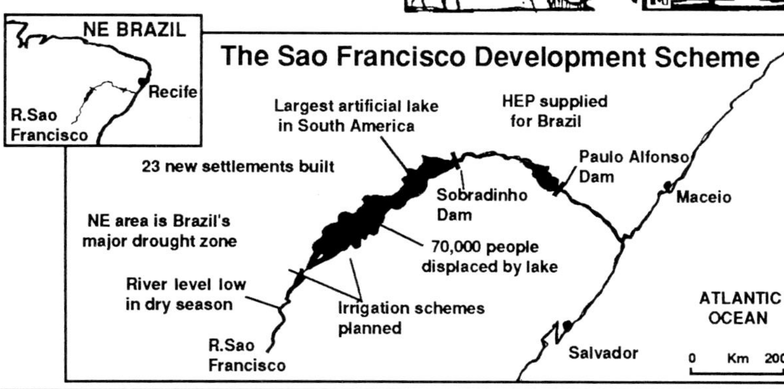

PROBLEMS ARISING FROM THE SCHEME

A very expensive aid project which created few local jobs.
Thousands of valley dwellers lost fertile land & homes as the lake was created.
The Sobradinho Dam flooded the region's most fertile farmland but no attempts were made to improve soil quality in the resettlement areas.
Resettled farmers had to borrow money to restart farming and received little training in new irrigation schemes.
Social unrest was caused by lack of compensation for farmers who lost their land & homes. Rural depopulation occurred to Brazil's already overcrowded large cities.
The scheme benefited rich landlords who claimed and received compensation. Surplus farms products were exported. The cheap electricity benefited large urban industries not locals.

Much of foreign aid is spent on large-scale development schemes (Fig.153). But loans for these types of development maintain large debts for the countries of the South while creating wealth in the North. Development loans generate poverty since much aid ultimately benefits the rich - the poor are forced to destroy their environment not through ignorance but in order to survive.

Aid, in the opinion of UNCED must be 'targeted' so that it reaches the people it is intended to help in the most effective way. Local people should be consulted wherever possible and encouraged to 'own' the development projects designed to help them. All aid projects should never endanger the environment and should enable the recipients to become self-reliant and free of the need for aid in the long term. Small scale aid schemes carry with them the benefits of local short term help and long term development that can be sustained (Fig.154).

UNCED insist that aid must be viewed as improving the quality of life for people in developing countries in the long term. Until then, relief agencies will need to continue to provide emergency aid (Fig.155).

Fig.154

THE BARBED-WIRE MAKER

Small-scale aid can be most effective where basic training and local ingenuity combine. The Barbed-Wire Maker is made from recycled bike parts. Plain wire is fed into the maker and twisted into barbs. Designed for hand-use, using cheap plain wire, this simple machine will provide useful local employment and directly benefit the local area. A very useful tool in desertified areas where dead ground can be surrounded by barbed-wire and then reseeded. The barbed-wire keeps goats and cattle out, giving the piosphere time to regrow and soils to be stabilised.

Fig.155

Assignment Thirty-two

Fig.156

1a What is meant by **aid** ?

1b Describe the main types of aid. Support your answer with a simple diagram.

2a Study Fig.151.
Describe the trends indicated for both OPEC and OECD countries in terms of aid given.

2b Why should the rich countries heed the call of the UNCED report and donate more aid ?

3 Complete a larger copy of the following table after studying the information given in Figs. 149, 151-155.

TYPE OF AID	ADVANTAGES	DISADVANTAGES
Emergency		
Large Scale		
Small Scale		

4a What message is the cartoonist attempting to send in Figs.150,155 & 156 ?

4b To what extent do you agree with each message ?

5a An Asian proverb states, "Give a person a fish and you provide a meal. Teach a person how to fish and they are able to feed themselves" Describe the link between the proverb and effective aid.

5b Many rich countries have started to reduce the amount of aid donated to the UN. Write a letter to your MP explaining your views and outlining what you regard as good, effective aid.

TRADE: *Interdependence*

Key Ideas: Regions of the world are linked through trade

There are over 150 countries involved in world trade. Each nation sells goods (**exports**) to other countries and buys (**imports**) goods from other countries. The difference in value between imports and exports is called the **Balance of Trade**. Not all countries can sell more than they produce and some have a trading **deficit** (loss) while others operate on a trading **surplus** (or profit). Where countries regularly trade with each other they develop a trading relationship. The greater the volume of trade the more the countries involved become interdependent.

It is clear that the North, especially Western Europe, Japan and North America dominate world trade (Fig.158) and have grown stronger in the last 40 years. The countries of the South are involved in less than one-quarter of world trade. Most export raw materials, such as coffee, oil, cotton, cereals and timber, to the North where secondary industries produce manufactured goods for large wealthy markets. Prices paid for raw materials to countries of the South are low. In return, developing countries purchase manufactured goods from the North at high prices. The result is an increasing struggle against **foreign debt**. At present the pattern of world trade favours the North, industrialised nations. Many raw materials are manufactured by giant corporations such as Exxon or Nestle. Most of these huge companies are located in the North but operate in many parts of the world and are therefore called **Transnational** or **Multinational Corporations** (Fig.159). Over one-third of all world trade is between Transnationals and some such as Ford or GM are far more wealthy than many developing nations.

Transnationals form their own trading groups. Other groups can also have a impact on world trade. For example the **OPEC** (Organisation of Petroleum Exporting countries) group set the world trading price for oil. In 1973 they increased the oil price by 400% which had a major impact on world trade. Groups which set prices are called **cartels**. The **European Community** (E.C.) currently consists of 12 trading nations and exists to promote, develop and protect the economic and social well-being of all its members.

Fig.157 CHANGING WORLD EXPORTS

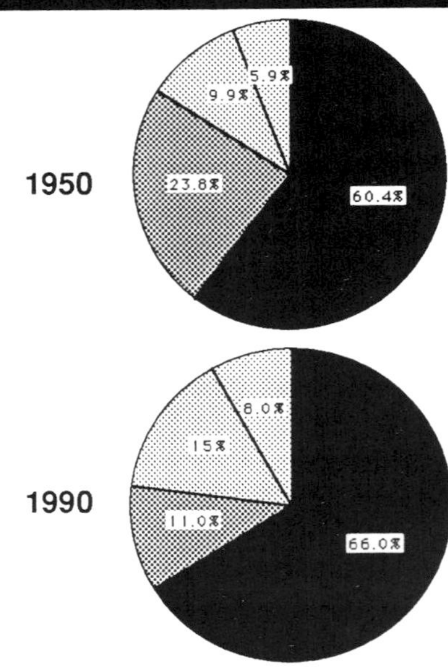

Fig.158

Top 10 Transnational Corporations

Royal Dutch Shell	(Oil - UK/Netherlands)	**$175.70bn**
Ford	(Vehicles - US)	**$152.90bn**
General Motors	(Vehicles - US)	**$151.80bn**
Exxon	(Oil - US)	**$150.76bn**
IBM	(Computers - US)	**$114.75bn**
British Petroleum	(Oil - UK)	**$90.67bn**
Asea Brown	(Industrial - Switz)	**$53.65bn**
Nestle	(Food - Switz)	**$50.15bn**
Philips	(Electronics - Neth)	**$49.18bn**
Mobil	(Oil - US)	**$49.00bn**

UNCTAD 1991

Fig.159 FREE TRADE GROUPINGS

Fig.160

TIMBER TRADE

Each year timber from rainforests, worth over US$8 billion is shipped from poor countries to rich, destroying 12 million hectares of rainforest.

Uncontrolled logging has left many rainforests in critical condition. Deforestation has already become a major problem in intensively logged areas such as Thailand and Indonesia. Some former exporters of timber are now net importers, having long since run out of their own timber. Of 56 timber-exporting countries, 23 are now net importers. Major logging continues unabated today.....

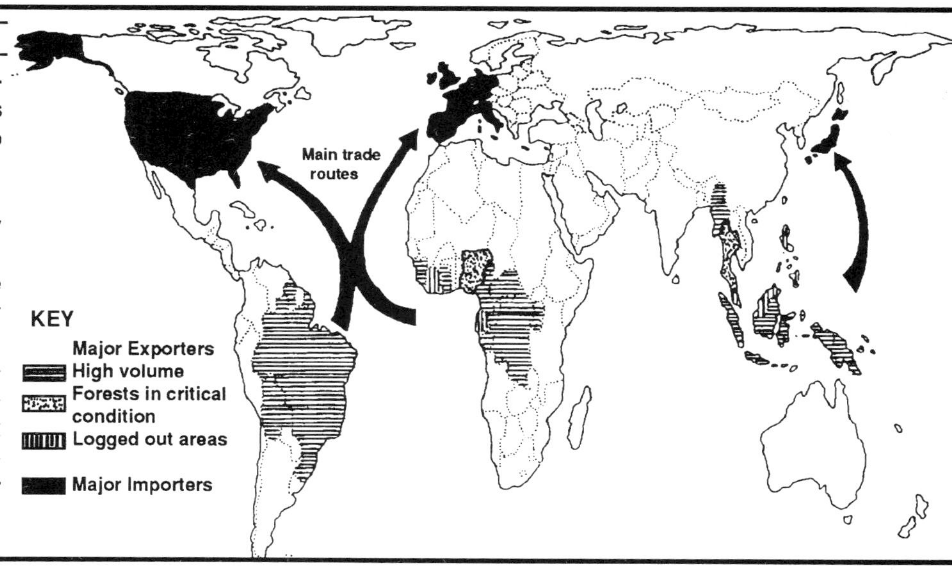

Many trading groups set **trade barriers** (restrictions or taxes on imports from countries outside the group). Others impose pricing policies on raw materials imported from developing nations such as the world price for timber (Fig. 160). In an attempt to trade more freely some trading groups are relaxing their trade barriers in order to increase trade during world recessions (Fig.159).

It is often stated that the wealthy North and the poor but developing South are interdependent. The South imports manufactured goods from the North, who import mainly raw materials and foodstuffs from the South. But because over 75% of exports from the South are unprocessed, primary products there are major trading problems. Prices fluctuate frequently and where countries are dependent upon one raw material for export (such as Copper from Zambia) there are related problems. The cost of world manufacturing and goods has increased much more rapidly than the prices paid for raw materials. There exists a **trade gap** in which many developing nations are caught. In attempts to develop their economies and social systems developing nations borrow money from the North building up significant debts as they do so (Fig.161). The introduction of **countertrade** agreements (e.g. where manufactured goods are traded for raw materials) are one way of breaking the debt cycle (Fig.162). The **GATT** (General Agreement on Tariffs & Trade) talks held in 1993 involved 117 countries in an attempt to free more trade across the world. However economists believe the talks may well increase the trade gap and not close it.

Fig.161 **The Debt Mountain**

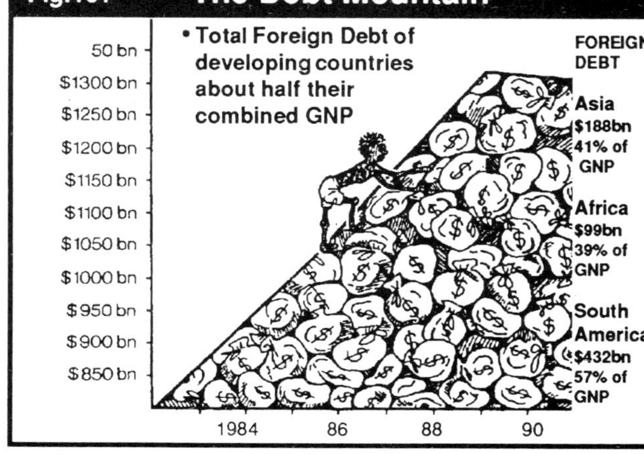

Fig.162

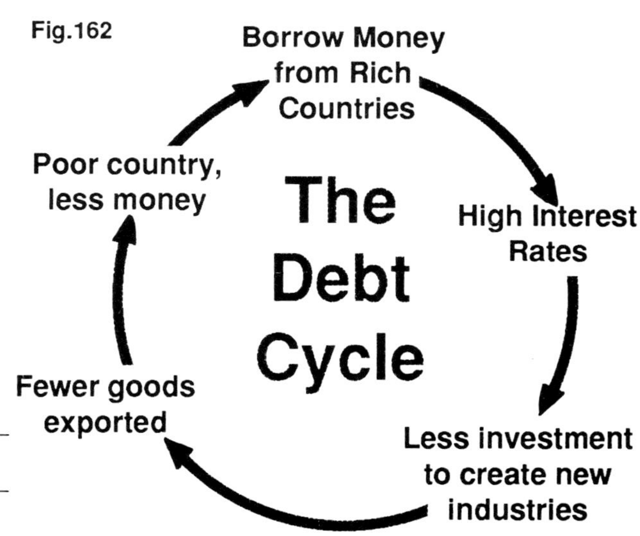

Assignment Thirty-three

1a What is meant by **trade** ?
1b Draw a simple diagram to illustrate Balance of Trade.

2a Describe the changes in world trading relationships shown in Fig.157 between 1950 and 1990.
2b What is a Transnational Corporation (TNC) ?
2c Using Fig.158, describe the role of TNCs in world trade.

3 Write a definition of each of the following terms:- exports, imports, cartel, trade gap, countertrade.

4a Study Fig.160. Name at least 3 countries for each key category.
4b Describe the relationship between the timber trade and deforestation.

5a What is meant by **interdependence** in trade ?
5b Give some examples of trade interdependence.

6a What is meant by the term **Trading Group** ?
6b Give some examples of such groups.
6c Why has OPEC increased wealth in some countries of the South ?

7 Why do many countries of the South claim that much of world trade benefits the North ?

8 Explain why it is very difficult for a developing country to break out of the **Debt Cycle** (Fig.162) ?

9 What are the likely effects of a fluctuating world price on a developing country dependent upon **one** raw material for export ? (Hint: economic, social, environmental effects ?)

43. INTERNATIONAL RELATIONS: *Alliances*

Key Ideas: International relations are dominated by a limited number of countries acting in conjunction with others.

The **United Nations** was set up after World War 2 in 1945. Most countries are members but not all have equal influence within the UN. The real politik (reality of modern politics) is that the most powerful nations exert the most influence. These powerful nations are the world's **superpowers**.
The status of superpower is one that has changed with time. The 19th century dominant world powers were Britain, France, Russia and later Germany. Today there are three main superpowers all of which have characteristics which make them outstanding when compared with other world nations. Superpowers have a large land area, a large population, great military strength and large and diverse reserves of natural resources. Figure 163 shows the main superpowers - USA, China and the C.I.S.. Since 1945 the superpowers have been involved in a **cold war** - where each nation has attempted to prove themselves superior without the need for war with the others. Dislike and distrust have characterised their dealings over the last 50 years and centred over their different political systems with an escalation of the nuclear arms race. The USA is a **capitalist** system where most of the wealth of the country is held by individuals and not the state. The former USSR and China were **communist** systems with most of the wealth of the nation in the hands of the state. Each superpower viewed the others as a threat to their nation, its way of life and influence. Stockpiles of nuclear armoury, the deployment of huge military forces and propaganda were utilised to maintain the cold war. Each superpower developed **alliances** - partnerships of associated and like-minded nations. The **Eastern Bloc** were countries closely linked with the former USSR. The USA developed strong links with other **NATO** (North Atlantic Treaty Organisation fig.165) countries. Each alliance was mainly created as protection against the other.

Fig.163

SUPERPOWERS

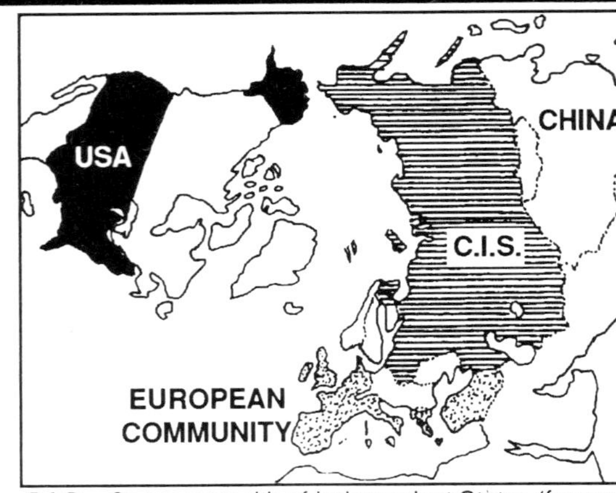

C.I.S. - Commonwealth of Independent States (former USSR states)

Indicators	USA	CHINA
Government	Capitalist democracy	Communist
Size	9,363,000 sq.km	10,000,000 sq.km
Population	249.2 million	1100 million
Regions	50 states	27 Provinces
Languages	English (+ 11 others)	Han (+ 99 others)
Military Strength (% world total)	32%	21%
GNP per person	$21790	$ 370
No. of Nuclear Missiles	10,011	638
Food Supplies	>$1bn surplus	$387million deficit
Life Expectancy	76 years	70 years
%Employed in Agriculture	2%	71.7%
Daily Calorie Intake	139% of minimum 3577	112% of minimum 2453
No. of People per doctor	419	1191

Fig.164 **THE WORLD: NUCLEAR NATIONS & FLASHPOINTS**

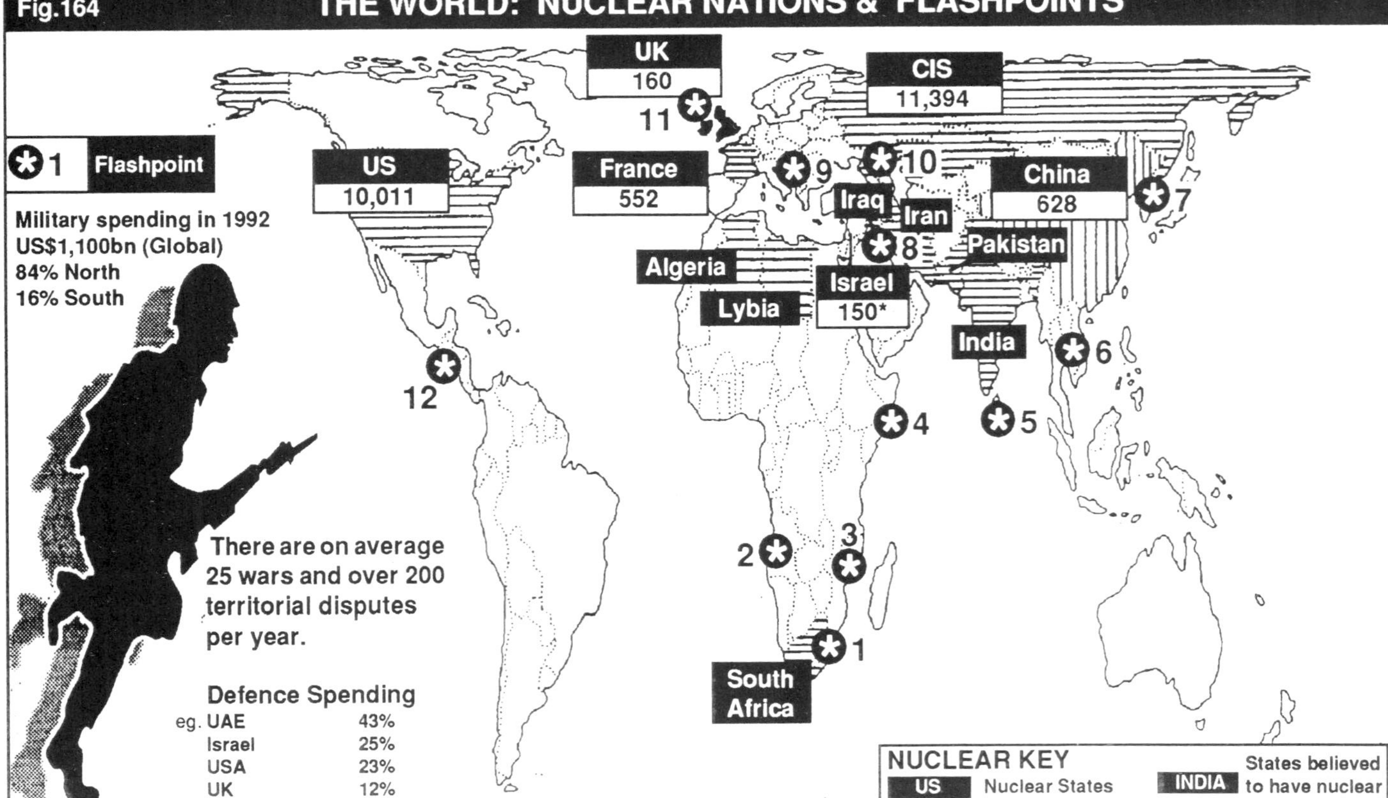

However the superpower situation has altered in the last 5 years. With the development of the **C.I.S.** and the break up of the former USSR, the alliance of Eastern Bloc nations has weakened. The C.I.S. however remains a powerful alliance holding a stockpile of over 11,000 nuclear missiles (Fig.164). While the C.I.S. and China are very powerful, the USA is much more wealthy and modernised. There are many economic difficulties within the C.I.S. as it attempts to develop into a freer, market-oriented economy and political system. China remains a developing nation with many economic and social problems. Japan is an emerging industrial and economic superpower, more wealthy than its near neighbour China.

An alliance exists and develops where a group of nations form an official organisation to help all their members. Alliances may be trade organisations such as the **E.C.** (European Community) (Fig.166) and **OPEC**. Other important alliances have been created for military reasons such as NATO. These alliances may be dominated by a superpower or may not contain a recognised superpower. Many countries do not wish to become part of a military alliance. Countries such as Switzerland, Eire and Sweden remain neutral countries. Other nations attempt to join existing alliances. For example, Turkey, Lithuania and Sweden are currently interested in becoming members of the E.C.

Although it is stated that the cold war is over the world is not a safe and peaceful place. Each year there are at least 25 on-going wars and over 200 border disputes. In various worldwide locations, tensions between groups of people can erupt into conflict. Most **flashpoints or** areas of conflict take place within one country although some develop into international conflicts, such as the Gulf War 1992.

The United Nations' role in world geopolitics is evolving. In the last decade the UN has become a **peace-keeping** organisation in addition to its roles in combating hunger, disease, repression and ignorance and in furthering self-reliance, education, human freedom and human rights. The UN is now involved in keeping the peace in a variety of flashpoints (Fig.167) and helps observe fairness in elections or the transition of power. The superpowers remain important influences within the UN and supply many resources and military, educational and medical personnel where required.

Fig.165

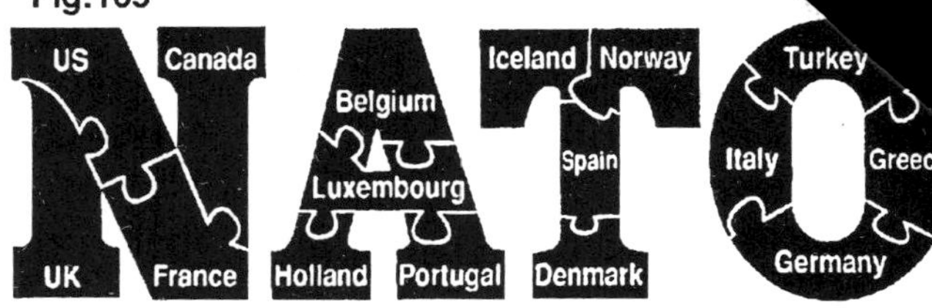

THE EUROPEAN COMMUNITY Fig.166

Member Countries 1994

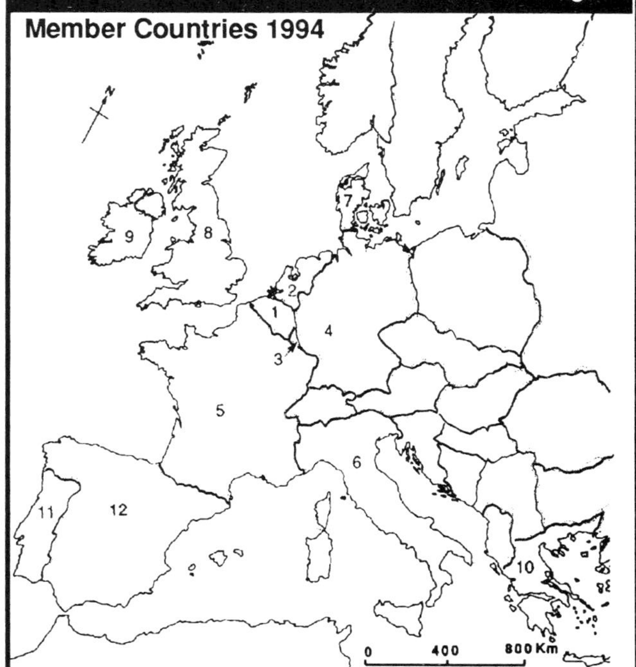

Fig.167

UNITED NATIONS
Keepers of the Peace
UN Forces around the world 1994

UNPROFOR	UN Protection Force Croatia & Bosnia 1994	23,000 troops
UNTAC	UN Transitional Authority Cambodia	22,000 troops
UNOSOM	UN Operation in Somalia	3,550 troops
ONUMOZ	UN Operation in in Mozambique	8,000 troops
UNIKOM	UN Iraq-Kuwait Observation MIssion	500 observers
ONUSAL	UN Observer Mission in El Salvador	1,000 troops
UNAVEMII	UN Angola Verification MIssion II	476 observers
UNDOF	UN Disengagement Force in Syria	1130 troops
UNTSO	UN Truce Mission in Jerusalem. Israel	250 observers
UNIFIL	UN Interim Force in Lebabnon	5,000 troops
MINURSO	UN Referendum Mission in W.Sahara	400 observers
UNIFICYP	UN Peace-keeping Force in Cyprus	1,500 troops
UNMOGIP	UN Military Observer Force in Pakistan	50 observers

Assignment Thirty-four

1a Study the information below carefully

Nation	Area sq.km	Popn Millions	GNP per head	Life expect	%Employed in agriculture
UK	0.25m	57	$16,100	76	3%
JAPAN	0.40m	123	$25,430	79	8%
CANADA	25.75m	26.25	$21,570	77	5%

1b Explain why each nation listed above is **not** a superpower. Which of the nations above have similar characteristics to those of a superpower ? Justify your answer.

2a What is a **superpower** ?
2b Why are superpowers important in today's world ?

3a Name the member countries of the E.C (Fig.166).
3b Should the E.C. be classified as a superpower ? Why ?

4a What is an **alliance** and why are alliances created ?
4b Draw a simple world map to give listed examples of various alliances and their member nations.
4c What effect did the **cold war** have
i. on world politics ii. on developing countries ?

5a Define the term **flashpoint**. Give some examples.
5b Name flashpoints **1-12** on Fig.164.

6 Describe the relationship between the UN, superpowers and peace-keeping across the world.

AM STYLE QUESTIONS

AID, TRADE AND RNATIONAL RELATIONS

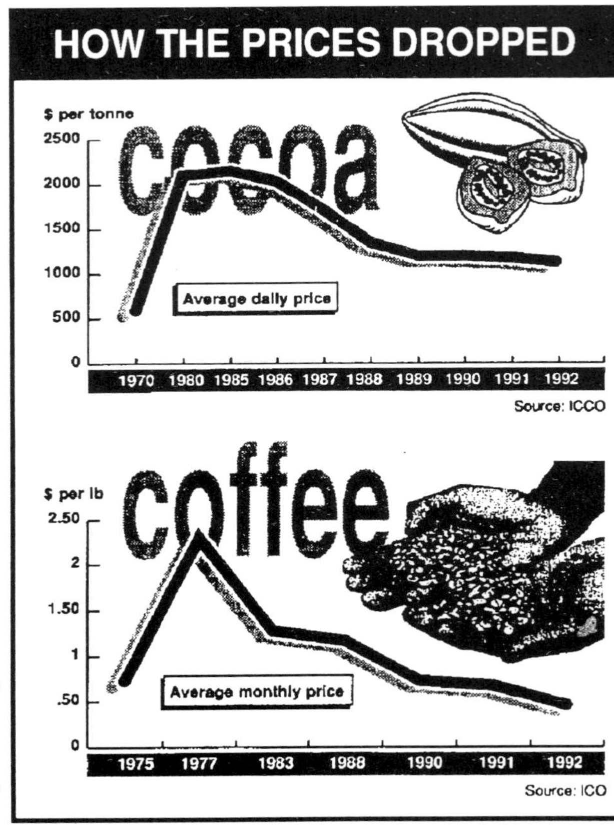

1 Study the **graphs** which show how the prices of cocoa and coffee have changed since the 1970's.
What impact will the reduction in prices for these commodities, throughout the 1980's, have had on the producing countries ?

2 What can **developing countries** do to protect themselves from falling world prices and why are these measures so difficult to implement?

3 Describe a typical **pattern of trade** (imports and exports) for a developing country.

4 **One third of the world's private assests are held by Transnational Corporations (TNC's) and they control 70% of world trade**
"Developing countries can be held to ransom by the TNC's"
Do you think this statement is true?
Explain your answer.

5 Explain the advantages and disadvantages (to the developing country) of TNC's expanding their operations in a **developing** country.

6 The collapse of communist governments in Eastern Europe has been followed by many of these countries getting ready to apply for membership of the European Community. What are the advantages of membership of **trade alliances** such as the European Community?

7 What does the **cartoon** say about attitudes of industries in the developed countries toward the developing countries (Third World)?

8 Describe the **trade imbalance** between developed and developing countries.

9 Describe how **international aid** can play an important role in helping people hit by natural disasters.

10 What does the **cartoon** suggest about the effectiveness of aid?

11 Describe the **advantages** of small-scale self-help aid schemes over the large multi-purpose projects.

12 What are the benefits of giving aid from the **donor** country's point of view?

13 In what ways is aid from **voluntary** organisations such as Oxfam different from the aid given by a national government?

14 World trade and aid should be narrowing the gap between rich and poor countries but the gulf between North and South does not appear to be closing.
Explain why the differences between **North and South** are so dramatic.

A DIVIDED EARTH

NORTH

25% of world population.
80% consumption of world energy
86% of world industry.
350 - 1000 litres daily water use
Pays 4% interest on foreign debt

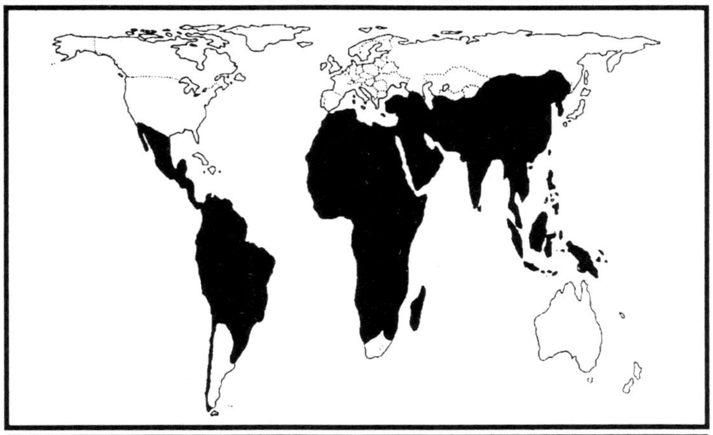

75% of world population.
20% consumption of world energy
14% of world industry.
20 -40 litres daily water use
Pays 17% interest on foreign debt

SOUTH

Index